THE ARCHITECTURAL HISTORY OF SCOTLAND

General Editors
CHARLES MCKEAN
and
DEBORAH HOWARD

SCOTTISH ARCHITECTURE

Reformation to Restoration 1560–1660

DEBORAH HOWARD

EDINBURGH UNIVERSITY PRESS

This book is for Malcolm Longair

© Deborah Howard, 1995

Edinburgh University Press Ltd
22 George Square, Edinburgh

Typeset in Perpetua
by BPC Digital Data Ltd, and
printed and bound in Great Britain

A CIP record for this book is available from the British Library

ISBN 0 7486 0530 4

The Publisher acknowledges subsidy from
the Scottish Arts Council towards
the publication of this volume.

Contents

List of Illustrations

Note: The country houses have been described in the captions under their modern names as 'castles' for ease of recognition, although this was not Renaissance usage. In the period of this book, country seats were described either simply by the name of the estate, or as 'the House of ...'. The largest houses, usually those with courtyard plans, were called 'Place' or 'Palace'. As far as possible these conventions have been preserved in the text.

The dates of the photographs have only been given when these record significantly earlier views.

Acknowledgements

The research for this book has been facilitated by the kind co-operation and encouragement of so many people that it is impossible to list them all individually. I am much indebted to all the owners of houses of the period who have been generous with both information and hospitality. Of these, I wish to thank, in particular, Kathleen Dalyell, Marc Ellington and Bruce Urquhart. Of the many institutions whose staff have shown me around their buildings and provided information, I am grateful especially to the Headmaster and Trustees of George Heriot's School. Ministers and caretakers of churches have been equally welcoming. To all these generous and knowledgeable supporters, I owe a great debt.

I have benefited greatly from the willingness of colleagues and friends to share information and offer expertise. Among these, I mention the following for their help on various occasions: Christy Anderson, Elizabeth Beaton, Howard Colvin, Kitty Cruft, John Dunbar, Caroline Elam, Claire Gapper, Simon Green, Harry Gordon Slade, Gillian Haggart, Neil Hynd, Maurice Howard, Wouter Kuyper, Helen Leng, John Lowrey, Deborah Mays, James Simpson, Christopher Smout, Ross Sweetland, Ben Tindall, David Walker and Jean Wilson. The encouragement I received from colleagues at the Department of Architecture at Edinburgh University, and subsequently at the Faculty of Architecture and History of Art at Cambridge University, sustained me even through the worst periods of pressure. Madeleine Brown has been especially supportive and helpful. Warm thanks are due to Margaret Gilfillan and Debbie Mays for their hospitality on many occasions.

The staff of the RCAHMS have supported me throughout the period of preparation of the book with their time and expert advice. In the Commission, Geoffrey Stell, Neil Cameron and Ian Fisher kindly read drafts of my passage on tolbooths. At the NMRS I have received unfailing support from Graham Ritchie, Ian Gow, Jane Thomas, Ruth Wimberley, Victoria Collison Owen and Veronica Steele. Roger Mercer kindly authorised the publication of a large number of illustrations from the National Monuments Record.

My travels within Scotland were assisted by a generous grant from the Paul Mellon Centre for British Art, to whom I wish to express deep gratitude. Olive Duncan kindly drove me around Perthshire and shared her knowledge and enthusiasm. My son, Mark Longair, acted as my research assistant in Ayrshire and in Shetland, and my daughter, Sarah Longair, provided me with skilful sketches of belfries in the North-East.

The manuscript was read by Charles McKean, whose boundless enthusiasm for the period has been highly stimulating. Ever since we worked together on the RIAS

Edinburgh Festival exhibition on the Scottish Renaissance in 1990, Charles has eagerly passed on his knowledge and discoveries to me, and I am most grateful for this. Aonghus MacKechnie, too, has shared his erudite researches with great generosity. Rosalind Marshall kindly read the whole text, and offered numerous expert suggestions as well as much-needed encouragement. Conversations with Christy Anderson over the same years have been unfailingly inspiring. Paul Joannides kindly read much of the text in proof. At Edinburgh University Press, Vivian Bone has been continually positive and patient; this series could never have come to fruition without her help and initiative. I have much appreciated Penny Clarke's good-humoured care at the production stage.

Finally, I wish to thank, above all, my husband Malcolm Longair, whose contributions have been not only fundamental, but also so miscellaneous as to be unlistable. I could not have finished the book without his caring and supportive presence in the background. This book is dedicated to him with gratitude and affection.

DEBORAH HOWARD
Cambridge

CHAPTER ONE

Introduction

Through wisdom is an house builded;
and by understanding it is established;
and by knowledge shall the chambers be filled
with all precious and pleasant riches.
Proverbs 24, 3–4 'King James' Bible

On his journey to the Hebrides in 1775, Dr Johnson met some of the greatest minds of the Scottish Enlightenment, but he was even more impressed by the force of Scotland's *earlier* intellectual tradition. Boswell recalled that Johnson had 'owned that they [the Scots] had been a very learned nation for a hundred years, from about 1550 to 1650.'[1] This book is about the architecture of that 'very learned nation' during the century following the Reformation.

Scottish architecture of this era has too rarely been seen as a topic worthy of special investigation on its own merits. For some, this was the final flowering of the Middle Ages, an age of blood and thunder, where plotting, feud and murder were common events.[2] Others have seen the gradual introduction of Renaissance forms as the first tentative traces of Scottish eighteenth-century classicism. Some historians have been puzzled by the insistent Scottishness of the architecture, as if it ought to have looked more Italian, more French or more English. Sir John Summerson wrote of Scotland's 'somewhat delayed development and a vigorous tendency to convert old forms to new purposes'.[3] Even John Dunbar, one of the pioneer scholars in this field, once described Scottish buildings of the period as 'obstinately Scottish'.[4] The strong national identity in the buildings has often been regarded as a state of sleepy ignorance, rather than as a sign of creative energy and self-assurance. In 1910, A. N. Paterson was perplexed that 'the Scots love for the old ways was not to be won over so easily'.[5] Stewart Cruden wrote of the post-Reformation 'castle': 'It is not great art; it achieves no sublimity, it forms no laws and conforms to none.'[6] Meanwhile, those who have recognised the vigour of this Scottishness have often failed to appreciate the importance of the pan-European dimension – the cross-cultural fertilisation that allowed Scotland's native architectural traditions to evolve and flourish. Perhaps only MacGibbon and Ross, a century ago, though aware of European influences, sensed the inherent vitality of Scotland's Renaissance:

When we examine the Scottish buildings carefully and in detail, we discover that the design is of native growth, that it has a national and distinctive

character, and forms a style quite as independent as, if not more so than, any
of the Renaissance styles of the other countries of Europe.[7]

To adopt a negative attitude towards local tradition seems to misinterpret the
European spectrum of Renaissance culture.[8] Brunelleschi's architecture in Florence
had a close affinity to Tuscan medieval tradition. Bramante in Rome borrowed
extensively from local early Christian sources. The French Renaissance hôtel
as well as the château evolved from Gothic predecessors. German Renaissance
architecture, with its steep-pitched roofs and enormous gables, looked recognisably – even ostentatiously – German. In Denmark, Gothic and Renaissance
forms were intricately blended. In other words, Renaissance architecture was not
just a classical system which would sweep older practices aside. Its classicism was,
indeed, international, just as Latin had been the medium of cultural exchange across
Europe since the Middle Ages. But unlike the twentieth-century International Style,
it did not displace local technology and materials; and regional and national loyalties
were deeply felt.[9]

The term 'Renaissance' is a convenient style label which, in architecture, is
usually assumed to indicate a self-conscious revival of classical – and specifically
ancient Roman – forms. It is associated with, and generally preceded by, humanist
scholarship, that is to say, the study of Greek and Roman texts.[10] Humanism in the
Renaissance, however, was not an irreligious movement, but one that viewed
classical writings within the framework of the Christian tradition, a trend that had
long been anticipated by medieval philosophers. In Scotland, the Renaissance in
architecture blossomed in the early sixteenth century, under the artistic leadership
of James V,[11] but even by 1560 this was not an Italianate style, and with a few
exceptions did not even aspire to appear either Italian or antique Roman.[12] To
assess our period in Vasarian, that is Tuscan, or even Vitruvian terms would be
insensitive to the richness and vitality of the architecture that we shall observe.[13]
The term 'Renaissance' will be used in this book loosely, and without strictly
defined limits of style or period, to refer to buildings in a broadly classical idiom
erected in Scotland between about 1500 and 1660. The limitations of the
Vasarian model to the study of the Northern Renaissance were aptly described by
Benesch:

> Humanism tries to revive the classical personality and its proper diction. *Thus
> it established a new human ideal, based on intellectual culture*, an ideal of spiritual
> freedom and autonomy of personality. This is the deeper meaning of that
> renascence which the Italians call *rinascita*. It is independent of superficial
> imitation of ancient forms.[14]

Styles do not start and end suddenly, but are transformed gradually by the
interaction between continuity and change.[15] They can only be seen retrospectively,
by overlooking those dead-end experiments that did not take root, and giving
prominence to those traits that became dominant and inspired further invention.
Tradition is a stronger force than innovation; it is understood by the spectator and

technically mastered by the builder. In the dialogue between tradition and innovation, tradition itself does not remain static, but absorbs outside influences, at
first knowingly but later less self-consciously as these foreign elements become
integrated.[16] And the influences are not only one way – Scottish elements in their
turn were exported to other countries.[17]

The disruption caused by the Reformation at the outset of the period had far-
reaching cultural consequences, although there was much less physical destruction
of religious works of art and buildings than in England.[18] Its main impact was in
the removal of the institutional framework of the church and the dissolving of
certainties of faith and doctrine.[19] The Catholic church had become recognised as
an organisation infused with corruption, but no institutional structure was at hand
to replace it, and the society that emerged, especially in the towns, was one which
offered scope to individual initiative and self-expression. Many individuals – nobles,
lairds and burgesses – profited from the Reformation through the redistribution of
wealth and power. Burckhardt's definition of the pre-conditions necessary for the
Renaissance seems particularly apt in this context: 'It was needful that noble and
burgher should first learn to dwell together on equal terms, and that a social world
should arise which felt the want of culture, and had the leisure and the means to
achieve it'.[20]

The Renaissance architectural culture which we shall be investigating in this
book is not one focused primarily on the study of antiquity, although it is true to
say that Gothic arches and vaulting became rare, being supplanted by classical forms
learned from treatises and foreign travel. Antiquity was absorbed only through the
mediation of other national styles – the French, the Dutch, the Italian, the Danish
or, especially after 1603, the English. Respect for antiquity itself was tempered by
a link that was perceived between ancient Rome and the Papacy. John Napier, for
example, was delighted by the destruction of a Roman monument discovered in
Musselburgh.[21] More impressive than any superficial imitation of antique or foreign
precedent, however, was the dynamic display of virtuosity, both technical and
rhetorical, within the framework of what one might call tradition. In other words,
familiar local models were subtly transformed, without the destabilising destruction
of historical roots.

This period was one in which Scottish history was written and rewritten,
reinventing the nation's origins whenever a different cultural orientation was
needed.[22] As Lowenthal observed, 'the diffusion of all manner of history, whether
fact or fable, fosters the feeling of belonging to coherent, stable and durable
institutions'.[23] Myth-making – both re-creating the past and reformulating the
present – was a crucial element in both verbal and architectural expression.
Sensitive to the need for history, even the most avant-garde patrons retained a
respect for ancient buildings. In 1577, Regent Morton, for instance, was depicted
in Bronckhorst's portrait with the fourteenth-century Tantallon Castle in the
background, rather than with one of the houses which he himself had transformed,
such as Drochil, Aberdour or his 'Newhous' on Loch Leven (see Figure 1.1).[24]
(Morton himself did not even own Tantallon, which belonged to his nephew, the

FIGURE 1.1   Portrait of James Douglas, 4th Earl of Morton (c.1516–81), Regent 1572–8, attributed to Arnold Bronckhorst.

Earl of Angus.[25]) And as we shall see, the ancient abbey churches of Dunfermline and Holyrood were reverendly restored by the Stewart court.[26]

The transfer of the court to London in 1603 only intensified this creative tension between tradition and experiment. Scottish courtiers in London, seeking acceptance among the English aristocracy, could read the English equivalent of Castiglione's *Cortegiano* – that is to say, Henry Peacham's *The Compleat Gentleman* – published in 1622. On its frontispiece, two figures frame the title: on the left, Nobility, dressed in an old-fashioned long robe and coronet, accompanied by armour and a hunting horn; and on the right, Scientia (or knowledge), a classical nymph with a sunburst and laurel branch (emblems associated with James VI himself), and shown with books, artists' tools, a globe and a wind instrument (see Figure 1.2).[27] The dialogue between tradition and the new learning could hardly be more directly expressed, and its capacity for image-making is clear from the title itself: *The Compleat Gentleman*

FIGURE 1.2   Frontispiece of Peacham's *The Compleat Gentleman*.

Fashioning him absolute in the most necessary and commendable Qualities concerning Minde or Bodie that may be required of a Noble Gentleman.

The potential of architecture to express deeper values than its purely decorative qualities depends on a knowledgeable audience, able to grasp the allusions and aspirations to be conveyed. The role of the spectator in the creation of a visual culture should not be forgotten. The audience, as well as the patron, needed to be well informed, and any recondite allusion assumed an educated public. In Renaissance Scotland, written sources and the evidence of the buildings themselves show a remarkable awareness of other national styles, and an ability to differentiate between them.

As we shall see, different social groups felt affinities with different European cultures, and developed a distinctive architectural identity (though the boundaries

between them are not tidy and clean-cut because of the social and artistic com-
plexities involved). This book will therefore be arranged typologically, considering
first the court, and then each of the Three Estates of the Scottish Parliament in
turn: the nobility, the burgesses and the church. Finally, the overall development
will be considered, defining artistic trends shared by every social group, and
showing how the architectural profession evolved and matured during the period.

The century between 1560 and 1660 was a time of rapid social and political
change, which facilitated and even encouraged architectural transformation, but
did not cause it directly.[28] It must be emphasised that this was not a monolithic,
steady-state society. Within each type of building there was a radical transformation
from the earliest to the latest examples. In architectural terms, the first twenty
years and the last twenty years will receive relatively little attention in this book,
for both were too unsettled to allow as much ambitious architectural patronage as
the middle years. The start of our period saw the reign of Mary Queen of Scots
and the minority of James VI; and its close coincided with the disruptions caused
by the Civil War. It is because of these 'slack' periods that the chosen dates have
been adopted, for they act like book-ends in defining and supporting the central
decades. The long reign of James VI forms the core of this book. Although his
departure for London in 1603 had far-reaching consequences in Scotland itself, this
remained a fertile period for architectural initiative, as the courtiers and the burghs
took over the artistic leadership at home. James VI's reign was also a time of peace
and stability, allowing prosperity to grow and releasing capital for building.[29]

This book comprises a great variety of buildings, from the smallest salmon house to
the most splendid royal palace. These cannot be isolated from their use, whether
practical or ceremonial. The research has therefore involved wide-ranging investigation
into the broader historical context, which has, of necessity, been derived mainly from
secondary sources. Even for the history of the buildings themselves, though I have tried
to study as many of them as possible at first hand, I have had to rely on published
documentation to make this book a realisable proposition. The number of surviving
buildings of the period is so enormous that it will not be possible to include more than
a limited selection here. It will not even be feasible to illustrate all those mentioned in
the text. I have attempted to make the choice as representative as possible, both
geographically and typologically. If the North-West Highlands and the Hebrides seem
poorly represented, this is because the number of buildings in these more rugged areas
was much smaller than elsewhere.[30]

It would not have been possible to write this book without the pioneering
researches of other enthusiasts and scholars. If Billings first recognised the quality
of the buildings,[31] MacGibbon and Ross, travelling by train and on foot, laid the
foundations for all future work in the field.[32] More recent pathfinders include W.
Douglas Simpson, Stewart Cruden, Harry Gordon Slade, John Dunbar and George
Hay, all of whose work is indispensable.[33] Among younger scholars, the work of
Aonghus MacKechnie is rich in new discoveries and insights. Finally, the energetic
efforts of Charles McKean to reinstate the Scottish Renaissance have been constantly
stimulating.[34]

THE SCOTTISH CONTEXT: COMMERCE AND CULTURE

To a large extent, the failure to integrate Scotland in our view of the art and architecture of the European Renaissance as a whole results from the country's marginal geographical position. It is important to remember, however, that in a period when the sea was the normal means of long-distance travel, Shetland was hardly more inaccessible from mainland Europe than London. Norway was only a four-day voyage from the east coast of Scotland in good weather, whereas to sail to London took five or six days. Communication between Rome and Scotland might take a month or more, but this does not mean that the Scots were unaware of Italian artistic innovation. Diplomats from the Scottish court frequently travelled to Rome as well as the other courts of Europe.[35] Meanwhile, friendly relations with France were the legacy of the Auld Alliance, cemented by the marriage of Mary Queen of Scots to the Dauphin in 1558. Although anti-French sentiment was felt in Protestant circles immediately after 1560, the antipathy was rapidly forgotten.[36] French and Scots merchants were welcomed in each other's ports, and Scottish trade with France continued unabated until the Anglo-French War after the death of James VI.[37] Even in 1630, the Edinburgh merchant William Dick had a factor in Paris.[38] In the 1640s, John Clerk of Penicuik was active as a merchant and dealer in Paris as well as the Low Countries, his range of merchandise including Old Master paintings.[39] Scotland still enjoyed trading privileges in France as late as 1659.[40]

Trading voyages to Italy were rarer, but not exceptional – in 1627 Dick himself chartered a ship to transport fish, grain and wax to Italy.[41] Some Scots penetrated yet further into the Mediterranean: in 1605 an English traveller was amazed to discover a Scotswoman in Palestine singing Scots nursery songs to her baby.[42] Travellers from the Mediterranean were often to be found in Scotland, from Giovanni Ferrerio, the Italian tutor at Kinloss Abbey in the 1530s, to the Venetian craftsman brought to Fife to advise on glass manufacture by George Hay, later Earl of Kinnoull.[43] Scotland found its place in Italian culture, too, if in a somewhat exotic form: Pope Pius II's visit to the court of James I, before his election to the Papacy, is depicted by Pinturricchio in the Piccolomini Library in Siena; and the court of James V makes its appearance in Ariosto's *Orlando Furioso*, where James is named Zerbino, a prince 'of unexampled virtue and beauty rare'.[44]

By far the strongest overseas connections (Ulster excepted) were with the Low Countries and Scandinavia. Close links with Denmark, established long before, when James II married Margaret of Denmark in 1469, were reinforced by the wedding of James VI to Christian IV's sister, Anne of Denmark, in 1588.[45] As well as the sea-borne merchant visitors, there were Scots living in Denmark. Richard Wedderburne, for instance, was able to lodge the Scottish Ambassador in his Danish home in 1587. The Danish Lutheran Bishop and hymn-writer Thomas Kingo was the grandson of a tapestry-worker from Crail who had settled in Elsinore.[46]

There were sizeable Scots colonies in Holland, Germany, Poland and Sweden – an unreliable estimate by William Lithgow claimed that there were 30,000 Scots families in Poland alone in the early seventeenth century.[47] Sweden was an important

source of iron, while Norway supplied the bulk of Scotland's timber.[48] The
'Eastland boards' mentioned in documents of the time probably came from
Estonia.[49] Shetlanders had close trading links with the Hanseatic league, and German
merchants lived on the islands.[50] And Holland, then one of the greatest trading
nations of the world, could supply almost anything through its role as an entrepôt.[51]

Merchants might live abroad for months or years, and many settled permanently,
together with their families. In the Baltic, there were Scottish kirks in both Königs-
berg and Danzig – a suburb of Danzig is known as Little Scotland to this day.[52]
The Scottish staple in Holland was based in Veere, but there were other Scots
colonies in Rotterdam and Middleburg.[53] In Sweden, many Scotsmen settled
permanently and were absorbed into local communities.[54] Some were small itin-
erant pedlars (the use of the word *skotter* for a hawker in Swedish may be significant),
but others rose to greater prominence. Scotsmen were even represented on
the town council of Gothenburg from 1621.[55] Scottish factors, or local trade
representatives were to be found in Veere, Rotterdam, Danzig, Elsinore, Hamburg,
Stockholm and Trondhjem, as well as Bordeaux, Dieppe and London.[56] In addition
to those who lived abroad, there were many Scots merchants who made two or
three trips to the Continent every year.[57] Flexibility was the key to their success –
a form of insurance against risk: each individual merchant dealt in a wide variety
of goods and travelled to a range of ports from the Bay of Biscay to the Baltic.[58]

The thirst for education provided a further incentive to embark on foreign
travel. Scotsmen were to be found in all the major European centres of learning,
from Louvain to Vienna and from Orleans to Wittenberg.[59] Writing in 1628,
William Lithgow drew attention to the common Scottish practice of educating
landowners' sons abroad: 'Now as for the nobility and gentry of the kingdom,
certainly, as they are generous, manly, and full of courage; so are they courteous,
discreet, learned scholars well read in the best histories, delicate linguists, the most
part of them being brought up in France or Italy.'[60] This was such a prevalent
custom that the church feared they were being exposed to unhealthy 'papist'
propaganda. An Act of Parliament of 1609 required that the tutors of young men
studying abroad be first approved by the bishop of the diocese as 'godly and of
good religion, learned and instructed in the same.'[61] Wealthy merchants preferred
to send their sons to Holland rather than France or Italy, to be schooled in
arithmetic, book-keeping and Dutch. During the seventeenth century, the nobility,
too, made increasing use of Holland as an intellectual resource by sending their
sons to Dutch universities.[62]

By European standards, Scotland's volume of trade was small, especially in
comparison to Holland or England, though not inconsiderable for so modest a
population. Its natural resources, after all, were limited by both climate and terrain.
The climatologist H. H. Lamb showed that the period between 1550–60 and 1700
was exceptionally cold, Scotland being affected by cold northern and easterly winds
in winter, and by wet and stormy summers.[63] The fertility of the Lowlands and
the plains of the Moray Firth impressed visitors, but the Highlands were bleak and
barren by comparison.[64] The living conditions of the labouring classes in both

Highland and Lowland were austere. Poor communications hampered progress in the countryside, where wheeled transport was still little used.[65] In a land generously pierced by firths and sea lochs, heavy loads were carried by boat, but there were few navigable rivers.

Overland, both goods and passengers travelled on horseback; over limited distances, heavy loads could be borne on rollers or horse-drawn sledges. Carts were used in the larger towns in the Renaissance period, but one report (surely exaggerated) claimed that there were no wheeled vehicles in the whole of Ayrshire before the eighteenth century![66] When a carriage was imported from France for Mary Queen of Scots in 1561, this was considered a remarkable event.[67] Not to be outdone, Regent Morton was using one by 1577, but coaches were not widely owned in Scotland, except by the wealthy, until the later eighteenth century. Before 1600, the exceptions were conspicuously rare: Anne of Denmark brought her own royal carriage from Denmark in 1590, just as both Mary of Guise and Mary Queen of Scots before her had used French coaches.[68] By 1603, Queen Anne was even able to order a new carriage from an Edinburgh coach builder, George Hendry, for her journey south.[69] But many country roads, churned by hoofs and squelching in the rain, were still unsuitable for wheeled traffic in the seventeenth century.

Renaissance Scotland, therefore, was a land where many overland tracks were merely rough rides, and the rural poor lived under the same roof as their animals, in conditions little different from those of prehistoric times. To be fair, one should not forget that peasant housing throughout Europe was similarly simple at this time. More important in the present context is that urban Scotland was developing apace, both economically and culturally, and living standards of both city burgesses and country landowners rose sharply during the Renaissance. Population, too, increased rapidly, especially in the capital where it tripled between 1550 and 1650.[70] Glasgow, like Edinburgh, grew dramatically, rising from fifth to second place among Scottish royal burghs between 1594 and 1670.[71]

Admittedly cash, in the sense of coinage, was said to be in short supply, but since most goods were exchanged in kind this does not indicate a general state of national poverty.[72] As the Frenchman Estienne Perlin wrote in the 1550s: 'Nothing is scarce here but money ... the Scots do not pay for the wine they buy from the people of Bordeaux, but in lieu thereof give them other merchandise.'[73] Notable exceptions suggest that such reports were exaggerated: the courtier-architect Sir James Hamilton of Finnart had £1,500 in gold coins in chests at his execution in 1540,[74] and Shetlanders were said to have plenty of ready silver.[75] Of course, cash alone does not ensure civilised living, as the biblical inscription on a sixteenth-century drinking cup made for the Lord Provost of Edinburgh piously asserted:

> Ane good mane
> is to be chosen
> Above great riches
> And loving favour

Is above silver
And above
Most fyne
Golde
1569[76]

Certainly the vast number of new buildings of all kinds erected in Scotland in the century following the Reformation does not suggest an all-pervasive state of poverty.

The temptation to regard Renaissance Scotland as a backward, impoverished nation is reinforced by the fact that most of its main exports were primary products. In modern economic terms, this suggests a third-world status, but in the period we are considering things were otherwise. Indeed, manufactured goods *were* exported, especially woven woollen cloth and hosiery. The linen industry, too, grew rapidly during the seventeenth century.[77] Moreover, Scotland's chief exports – hides and skins, fish, wool and linens, salt, grain and coal – were valuable commodities which enjoyed a steady European demand.[78] Coal-mining and salt-panning in particular involved considerable technological skill, while improved farming methods allowed increasing yields of grain, especially after about 1620. The country which saw such major advances as the invention of logarithms, or whose monarch was the dedicatee of Kepler's *De Harmoniae Mundi*, hardly lacked scientific ingenuity.[79]

It is instructive to look at the title-page of Napier's *Mirifici Logarithmorum*, first published in Edinburgh in 1614 (see Figure 1.3). The engraving is skilful, the design complex and sophisticated, the strapwork ornament in the mainstream of European book design, the typography proficient. A fluency in Latin and a European readership are both assumed. The invention of printing had proved an invaluable stimulus to Scotland's intellectual development, for buying a book was cheaper and simpler than travel or study abroad; books were easily portable, even on packhorses.[80] The range of titles in the inventories of Scottish Renaissance libraries is impressive: Adam Bothwell, Bishop of Orkney, for example, had works in Latin, Greek, Hebrew, French, Spanish, Italian and English, on subjects ranging from religion to medicine, and even including titles on cookery and duelling.[81] The books owned by the minister of Cranston, Sir John Greenlaw, valued at £26 13s. 4d., were worth almost twice as much as all his other household goods put together.[82]

The first Scottish printing press was established in Edinburgh by Royal Charter in 1507–8 by the merchant Walter Chepman and the printer and bookseller Andrew Myllar, who brought French typesetters and a Gothic typeface from Rouen.[83] James V's royal printer, Thomas Davidson, began to set Latin texts in Roman typefaces, emulating French and Italian models, a trend followed by James VI's printer, Alexander Arbuthnot.[84] Court patronage of printing both stimulated literary effort and extended the reading public by reducing the price of books. Just as Roman typefaces began to supplant Gothic print, so, too, Italic handwriting begins to appear in documents of the time.[85]

FIGURE 1.3   Frontispiece of Napier's *Mirifici Logarithmorum* (1619 edition).

It would be difficult to underestimate the importance of the Stewart court in fostering literary culture and humanist scholarship in Scotland. James I had established the tradition of the poet-king with his masterly work, *The Kingis Quair*. The courts of James III, IV and V had been lively centres of artistic, literary and musical activity. The poet William Dunbar gives an engaging picture of the rich cultural mix at the court of James IV:

> Schir, ye have mony servitouris
> And officiaris of dyvers curis,
> Kirkmen, courtmen and craftismen fyne,
> Doctouris in jure and medicyne
> Divinouris, rethoris and philosophouris,
> Astrologis, artists and oratouris,

> Men of armes and vailyeant knychtis,
> And mony uther gudlie wichtis:
> Musicianis, menstralis and mirrie singeris,
> Chevalouris, cawanderis and flingaris:
> Cunyouris, carvouris and carpentaris,
> Beildaris of barkis and ballingaris:
> Masounis lyand upoun the land
> And shipwrichtis hewand upone the strand:
> Glasing wrichtis, goldsmithis and lapidaris,
> Pryntouris, payntouris and potingaris.[86]

At the court of James VI, the circle of court poets was given the recondite name 'the Castalian Band', after the Fountain of the Muses on Mount Parnassus. James himself received a rigorous academic education from his scholarly humanist tutor George Buchanan, as well as from the more genial Peter Young. James was later ruefully to lament that 'They gar me speik Latin ar I could speik Scottis.'[87]

With the growth in the literacy of the layman came the refinement and flowering of both poetry and prose in written Scots. But the Scottish grammar-school education gave a solid grounding in Latin language and literature and even offered the rudiments of Greek. Not only royalty and the scholarly bishops such as Adam Bothwell owned classical texts. In his *Compt Buik* around 1600, the Dundee merchant David Wedderburne proudly referred to his copy of 'Metamorphosis Ovidii in Laten with the pictouris bund in ane swynis skyn of werry braw binding sumtyme apertening to Robert Wedderburn my uncle'.[88] Wedderburne came from a scholarly family – his kinsman John was a zealous supporter of Galileo and friend of Kepler[89] – but a fondness for the classics was not unusual among the more cosmopolitan Scots of the time. Latin was the international language of the European Renaissance in both science and the humanities.

It has been observed that the Gothic style lasted longest in those countries that were split from the Catholic world by the Reformation.[90] On a purely practical level, the Reformation made travel to Catholic countries more difficult, but communications by no means ceased. Even after 1560, merchants sailed to Spain and south-west France to procure cargoes of wine, salt and dried fruits.[91] Protestant disapproval was no deterrent: John MacMorran of Edinburgh 'the richest merchant of his tyme', for example, 'was not gracious to the common people because he carried victuall to Spaine, not withstanding he was often admonished by the ministers to refraine'.[92]

While the Scottish Presbyterian Kirk attempted to restrict interaction with Catholic Europe, we should not underestimate the positive intellectual results of the Reformation.[93] The English Bible and services in the vernacular not only encouraged literacy, but also – unintentionally – fostered the Anglicisation of the Scots language.[94] As we shall see in Chapters Four and Five, the whole education system was reformed and expanded, to include, in principle, children from all classes of society. So many of the historical records dwell on the Kirk's measures against fornication and adultery that it is easy to overlook their less repressive role in encouraging individual enterprise. The revival of the parish structure improved administration and poor-relief, as well as education. Although there is no real evidence that the Reformation consciously favoured incipient capitalism, the passage of church lands into lay ownership – a process already underway in the fifteenth century – greatly increased the economic potential of the land-owning classes, allowing holdings to become rationalised and consolidated. The high profile of the Kirk in burgh affairs led to a new relationship between merchant and minister, and it is surely no coincidence that the century following the Reformation marked a high point in the political and economic power of the Royal Burghs.[95]

The Scottish court's move to London in 1603 had far-reaching political and economic consequences, not least of which was the new prominence of upper-class women, left behind to manage the estates when their husbands followed the King to London. Some noblewomen became successful entrepreneurs in both coal-mining and salt-panning, and supervised the construction of estate buildings, schools and almshouses.[96] Great households, as in England, had few resident female servants apart from nurses and washerwomen. In the towns, widows were in charge of many households, and some women burgesses set up their own businesses as laundresses or caterers. At the opposite end of the scale, we should remember the large number of women doing heavy work on the land.

It is important to consider architecture in its overall cultural context, as a means of expression as well as a practical necessity. The century 1560–1660 saw marked changes in both dress and language in Scotland. In the second half of the sixteenth century, French taste still permeated Scottish society. The influence of James V's queen, Mary of Guise, as a fashion-leader had left its mark. 'Les bourgeois de villes d'Écosse, comme les nobles,' wrote Boissonnade, 'se flattent de suivre le goût de nos tailleurs.'[97] After 1603, little difference could be observed between fashionable dress in England, Scotland or France, French influence in costume predominating both north and south of the border.

Conscious of the patronising English attitude to the Scots at court as coarse, impoverished spongers, James VI himself even tried to encourage a degree of Anglicisation in the dress of his homeland. In 1608, planning a return visit to Scotland (a trip which did not materialise until 1617), the King asked the Convention of Royal Burghs to ensure not only that the towns were respectably clean, but also that 'ane decent, handsome and comlie sorte of habile, apparrell, and heid attyre' be worn. Most Scottish burghs had already tried to ban merchants and their wives from wearing plaids and cloaks in public: in 1580, for example, women in Aberdeen were forbidden to wear plaid 'except thai be harlottis and suspect personis'.[98] The implication that to be respected on the European stage the Scots had to wear an internationally acceptable form of dress, even in their own streets, shows a new concern for image and modernity. It would be surprising, indeed, if we did not find this preoccupation making its mark on architecture as well.

Buildings, like clothing and verbal expression, communicate the ideas and ambitions of their users, but the relationship between language and architecture is not always a direct one.[99] Although the Gothic style never died out completely in church architecture, secular patronage was more adventurous. While Latin ceased to be the language of the church, the lay classes increased their familiarity with the classical tradition as the education system was broadened and improved. Of course, there is no simple equation to link humanist learning with the adoption of classical forms in architecture. The relationship is complicated by the fact that the vernacular also developed as a literary language during the Renaissance, in Scotland as in such influential European artistic centres as Florence and Venice. Before 1600, there was a pride in the distinctiveness of the Scottish tongue and its syntax, that finds its parallel in the architectural culture of the time. James VI himself declared, 'we differ from thame [the English] in sindrie reulis of Poesie, as ze will find be experience'.[100]

The Scots tongue underwent considerable modification during our period. By 1500, 'Middle' Scots had become the language of government as well as the main vehicle of expression in both prose and poetry, and the Reformation was to bring the vernacular into the Kirk. Although many of the aristocracy could still speak French in the later sixteenth century, just as they enjoyed French fashions, this was no longer the language of the court. The result was that except in the Gaelic-speaking Highlands all classes of society now spoke the same tongue, a factor which must have eased both social mobility and the spread of education. Gaelic was still a largely unwritten language, although educated Highlanders were fluent in both Latin and Scots.[101]

After 1603, James VI tried to draw Scotland and England closer together in his passionate but unsuccessful ambition to see the two countries united. The insecurity felt by the Scots in England promoted the modification of manners and language as well as costume, and again we shall see evidence of this trend in their buildings.[102] English became the language of courtly literature, even from Scots pens such as that of William Drummond of Hawthornden.[103] The effects of this metamorphosis may be reflected in the observation, made at the Port of London in 1617, that it was no longer necessary to provide Scottish interpreters, as the two languages had become so similar.[104]

Was this transformation a state of paranoid uncertainty, a crisis of national confidence; or was it a new openness of mentality, an eagerness to embrace progress and innovation? The pages of this book will try to answer this question as we observe the rapid changes in Scottish architecture between 1560 and 1660. Shaken to the foundations by the Reformation and the combining of the two monarchies, Scotland's deep-rooted assumptions were challenged and undermined. Society underwent such rapid transformations that experiment and cultural renewal must have seemed the only possible reactions.

The fascinating dialogue, even tension, between the long-established national (and local) traditions of the late Middle Ages and the widening horizons of the European Renaissance provides the setting for this book. Initiative and resource, display and ostentation, uncertainty and conservatism – all these responses can be seen in the buildings of the time. The architectural solutions, like the intellectual developments, cannot be classified simplistically, nor can every building – or even every surviving building – be incorporated into so brief a survey. But if this book stimulates others to explore this rich and exciting theme, the task will have been worthwhile.

CHAPTER TWO

The Court

INTRODUCTION

Renaissance princes across Europe used architecture and visual display to express their dynastic right to rule, their virtue and authority, their wealth and power, and their learning and civilisation.[1] Often the display was ephemeral – court masques, state entries into towns, coronations, the reception of ambassadors, all these were ceremonies performed with lavish scenery and spectacle, ranging from temporary triumphal arches to dance and music. The iconography was complex, erudite, and often deliberately, teasingly obscure.[2] The learned courtiers flattered themselves on recognising recondite allusion and symbolism, while the less educated public enjoyed the glitter and entertainment on a more direct level. Some of these spectacles have come down to us in the form of descriptions or engraved views, but many others have faded into historical obscurity. Some were even financed by loyal subjects or patriotic towns: Lindesay of Pitscottie described the 'curious palace' built to welcome James V and his court by the Earl of Atholl in 1531, costing the staggering sum of £1,000 a day:

> Which was builded in the midst of a fair meadow, a fair palace of green timber, wind and green birkes ... fashioned in four quarters, and in every quarter and nuik thereof a great round ... which was lofted and gested the space of three house height ... And also this palace within was hung with fine tapestries and arrasses of silk and lighted with fine glass windows ...[3]

THE LEGACY OF JAMES IV AND V

King James V (1513–42) and, before him, his father James IV (1488–1513) had endowed the Scottish court with a series of fine palaces across the Central Lowlands.[4] At Linlithgow, the town was now dominated by an imposing quadrangular courtyard palace with corner towers, the royal theme later evoked by the Earl of Atholl's temporary castle. In the centre of the courtyard stood James V's elaborate stone fountain, richly carved with a mixture of Gothic and Renaissance elements and topped by a dome in the form of a crown resting on four colonnettes (see Figure 2.1). At Falkland Palace, the royal hunting lodge, three sides of the courtyard were now enclosed. The north wing has since disappeared, but the rest was in a francophile Renaissance style with large cross-mullioned windows between buttresses (see Figure 2.3).[5] The gatehouse was flanked by a pair of machicolated towers with conical slate roofs, strongly reminiscent of the Renaissance châteaux of the Loire, seen by James V on his visit to France to wed his first French bride, Madeleine, the daughter of King François Ier, in Paris (see Figure 2.2).[6] The courtyard façades were decorated with classical medallion heads, another Renaissance motif borrowed from the Loire (see Figure 2.3).[7] The sickly Madeleine did not long survive the Scottish climate, and within a year, in 1538, James had married his second French wife, the daughter of the Duc de Guise. Mary of Guise was an enthusiastic partner in improving the royal buildings; through her parents, she soon helped to acquire French masons for the royal works, and her architectural interests continued through her own period as regent until her death in 1560.[8]

Each of the early sixteenth-century Scottish royal palaces had its own distinctive character. The royal masters of works involved were Sir James Hamilton of Finnart at Linlithgow and Stirling, and John Scrymgeour at Falkland and Holyrood. The former has only recently been rescued from obscurity by Charles McKean,[9] the latter remaining a shadowy figure. While Falkland emulated the erudite classicism of François Ier and his courtiers, Linlithgow preserved a sense of Scotland's Gothic heritage, just as the royal palaces of Denmark proudly presented a Gothic image.

At Holyrood, meanwhile, James V began by erecting a stout tower block in 1528–32 in the style of the Falkland gatehouse, but then unexpectedly burst out of this French idiom with the new west front, built in 1535–6 (see Figure 2.4).[10] What can have inspired this Tudor-style, horizontal façade, with its great double-height state rooms lit by huge, glittering windows and its central turreted entrance? Henry VIII's magnificent palace of Nonsuch was not yet begun, but perhaps word had spread of his temporary castle erected near Calais for the celebrations of the Field of the Cloth of Gold in 1520. The French writer's description of this ephemeral palace, 'La moitié de la maison estoit toute de verrine', might almost have applied to the new west wing at Holyrood.[11]

But James V's zest for experimentation went further still. The new palace block which he afterwards built at Stirling Castle in 1540–2 was even less disciplined in its teasing Mannerism (see Figure 2.5). Whereas its solid buttressing walls are pierced by large windows, its restless, twisting columns are perversely recessed within cusped niches, standing impotently on animate corbels and topped by contorted statues. In their Northern grotesqueness the statues and gargoyles recall German sculpture of the period, while the baluster-like columns, ringed around the waist, can be seen in both German and Spanish architecture of this period.[12] The cusped arches recall the Moorish legacy in Andalusia, revived in the same years in buildings such as the Alcazar in Seville.[13]

This building seems to be James V's artistic challenge to the Emperor Charles V, who was François Ier's greatest rival, and since the Battle of Pavia in 1525 had presented a real danger to the French king. France and the Holy Roman Empire had resumed their hostilities, and François Ier was sinking into a state of melancholy. Meanwhile, James V, too, was becoming increasingly despondent. This is not a confident, serene building like Falkland, but an attempt to make a bold statement in an idiom that was unfamiliar and alien. Spanish and German models were faintly remembered by returning travellers and imperfectly understood, but they were

FIGURE 2.1 (*above*)   Linlithgow
Palace, West Lothian, view to the
south-west angle of the courtyard in
the nineteenth century, before the
restoration of the fountain.
FIGURE 2.2 (*right*)   Falkland Palace,
Fife, the gatehouse, water-colour by
David Roberts, signed and dated 1846.

FIGURE 2.3   Falkland Palace, Fife, the courtyard, from the site of the demolished north wing.

probably distinctive enough to be recognisable to the Scottish audience. From the letters written by James V to Charles V on behalf of his subjects abroad, we can be sure that numerous Scotsmen visited the territories of the Holy Roman Empire.[14] The relevance of the emulation of a Catholic emperor and powerful European ruler could hardly have escaped notice.

THE REIGN OF MARY QUEEN OF SCOTS

In less than six years between her return from France in 1561 and her detention in Loch Leven Castle, Mary roamed the length and breadth of her land. Apart from the North-West Highlands, the Hebrides and the Northern Isles, the Queen visited every region of Scotland, travelling mainly on horseback and sometimes in small boats. (Nothing more was heard of her French carriage, after it was under repair in St Andrews in 1562!) She made state entries into towns, visited her noble subjects, and stayed in royal castles and bishops' palaces. In all she is known to have visited eighty-two different hosts, most of them loyal supporters, but also others whose allegiance she no doubt hoped to win.[15]

Apart from Linlithgow, Stirling, Falkland, Holyrood and Edinburgh Castle, Mary stayed in the lesser royal castles of Dunbar, Dumbarton, Carrick, Dunoon, Inverness, Lochmaben and Peebles, as well as in the royal Benedictine abbey of Dunfermline. The minor royal houses were, in effect, the seats of their hereditary keepers, the prominent nobles who were responsible for their maintenance. The only court palaces where architectural evidence of Queen Mary's time survives are

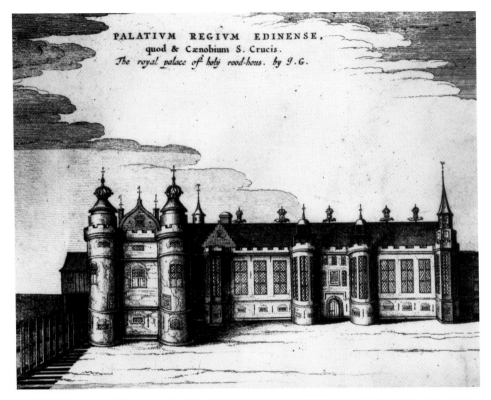

FIGURE 2.4 (*upper*)   Holyrood Palace, Edinburgh (Canongate), the west front, by James Gordon of Rothiemay, 1647.

FIGURE 2.5 (*lower*)   Stirling Castle, the palace block, from the north, 1539–41.

Holyrood Abbey and Edinburgh Castle. At Holyrood, the Queen's private apartment on the second-floor of the north-west tower still preserves some of the original interior decoration, in the form of panelled ceilings and painted friezes.[16] At Edinburgh Castle, the birthplace of her only son, the southernmost doorway of the courtyard façade of the palace block, rusticated in the Florentine manner, is dated 1566. Though bearing the initials of Mary (Queen of Scots) and Henry (Lord Darnley), this entrance seems to date from the later remodelling of 1615–16 which will be considered later in this chapter.[17] It leads to a straight staircase, an innovatory feature at the earlier date (see Figure 2.6). Most of the work on the castle in Mary's reign was aimed at improving the defences.

It is perhaps an indication of her precarious political and financial situation that the most extravagant project of her reign was an ephemeral one. This was the festivity held at Stirling in December 1566 to celebrate the baptism of her son and heir, six months after his birth at Edinburgh Castle. This was the one great occasion when the Queen could return the hospitality enjoyed on her royal progresses. The ceremony was described in contemporary sources – even by John Knox – as a 'triumph', the word used across Europe to describe Renaissance court spectacles.[18] Michael Lynch has shown how the ceremony adopted features of Valois court festivities, especially those staged at Bayonne in honour of Charles IX in 1564–5.[19] Indeed, the master of ceremonies was a Frenchman, one of the Queen's *valets de chambre*, named Bastien Pagez. Ambassadors were sent from the courts of France, England and Savoy.

The three-day festivities cost the exorbitant sum of £12,000, raised by national taxation. The climax was a firework display – a mock battle enacted on the Esplanade of Stirling Castle, in which a timber fort was attacked by 'hieland wyld men' clad in goatskins and moors in lambskin wigs. The theme of barbarism versus civilisation is a familiar one, which pervaded European art from the Parthenon marbles onwards. In this case, the victory of the fortress symbolised the triumph of the Queen, reconciliation with her Protestant nobles, and hence the endurance of the Stewart dynasty.

JAMES VI AS A PATRON OF ARCHITECTURE

James VI's reign in Scotland before 1603 has earned a range of responses from historians: for some, he was the most successful of all the Stewart kings;[20] for others, he was uncouth and interfering.[21] His literary enthusiasms are well known, but he has been generally dismissed as a king with little interest in the visual arts.[22] He was a zealous promoter of initiative and enterprise,[23] but how far this extended to royal building and architectural design remains enigmatic. His humanist education gave him an awareness of European culture and events – he even wrote an epic poem on the Battle of Lepanto, a recent Venetian naval victory over the Turks in 1571. It is illuminating to reflect on his choice of this subject. His views on kingship, seeing the monarch as God's representative, independent of church hierarchy, would have made him sympathetic to the Venetian Republic's role as defender of the Christian faith without subordination to the Papacy. He must also have shared

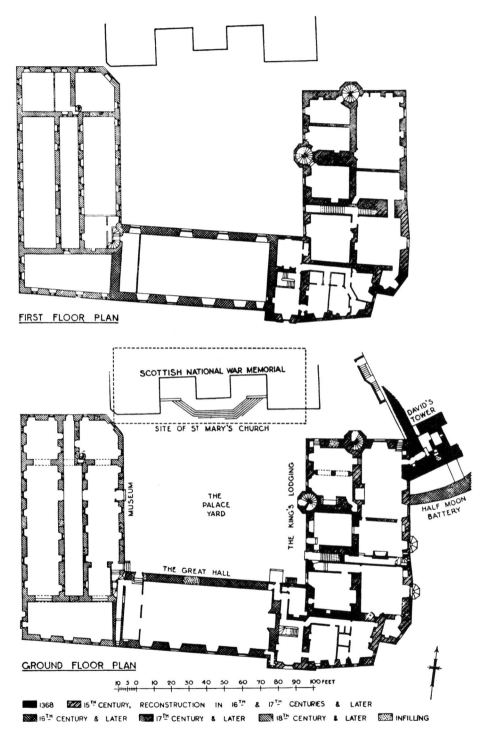

FIGURE 2.6   Edinburgh Castle, plan of the ground floor (below) and first floor (above).

the respect for chivalry and honour which pervaded Renaissance princely courts all over Europe; he belonged to the same international culture which produced Tasso's beautiful crusader epic, *Gerusalemme liberata* (1593). Like *Lepanto*, Tasso's poem glorified traditional knightly virtue struggling against the barbarian infidel.

James's clear-sighted sense of the monarch's place in society was eloquently expressed in the *Basilikon Doron* (1599), his book of advice to his young son and heir, Prince Henry, a work that was to become a best-seller when it was translated from Scots into English in 1603.[24] James himself, christened with the names of Charlemagne – Charles James, James Charles' (these were also the names of Charles IX of France) – was likened to Caesar in the 1603 translation of the *Basilikon Doron*, and throughout his reign he was regaled with imperial imagery.[25] Coins, for instance, show him between two columns, a familiar emblem of imperial power.[26] As early as 1590, he was depicted in Roman dress on his marriage medal, and he entered London in 1604 in the style of a Roman emperor.[27] During his reign he was also compared, more patriotically, with the historical figures of King Arthur and Brutus (as the Roman founder of Britain), as well as with the biblical Kings David and Solomon, to give a Christian dimension to the imperial pose.[28] Finally, like his mother before him, he adopted a mythological guise: as leader of the circle of court poets known as the Castalian Band, named after the sacred spring on Mount Parnassus, he was represented as Apollo 'brother of the muses'. A poem written in his honour on his return to Scotland in 1617 shows that the sun-king imagery of his youth had not yet been forgotten:

> Since our much lov'd Apollo doth appeare
> In pompe and pow'r, busked with golden rayes …[29]

One cannot divorce the court's visual culture from the literary scene. As early as 1584 James published his *Essayes of a Prentise in the Divine Art of Poesy*, in effect a public manifesto of his role as leader of the Castalian Band.[30] The young King wanted to portray his court to the European audience as a fountain of civilisation and artistic creativity. From his youth he seems to have cherished a belief in the value of poetry and learning to overcome discord in his society.[31] As Goldberg aptly remarked, 'The root of authority is author.'[32] But the setting for poetry was a visual one, for song and dance were an integral part of the performance, and these dimensions implied the existence of a visible setting.[33]

With his awareness of his role on the European stage and his conviction of his own right to rule, James VI must have been acutely aware of the need to keep up a dignified public image, both at home and abroad. The problem was money. His forebears, James IV and V, those enthusiastic palace builders, had swelled their treasuries by feuing crown lands, and James V had diverted wealth due to the church for his own needs as the price for his loyalty to the Pope.[34] In post-Reformation Scotland, papal allegiance was not an issue, and feued royal lands no longer provided a major source of revenue. Nor was there any regular system of taxation.[35] A modest subsidy was paid annually to James VI by Queen Elizabeth, but this could be reduced if she were displeased with any of his actions. The cumulative amount paid by 1603 amounted to only £58,000.[36] The German nobleman Lupold von Wedel, who visited Scotland in 1584–5, described the King as 'nicely dressed after Italian fashion in a red coat', but added disparagingly, 'The court does not show much royal splendour.'[37] In 1594, James VI wrote wearily to the Earl of Mar, lamenting 'the straitis I ame castin in'.[38] Taxes were raised every few years whenever special circumstances required this, and both the frequency and the amounts raised tended to increase during the 1580s and 1590s. But at the parsimonious Scottish court, nobles were still asked to contribute food from their own estates for major festivities such as baptisms or coronations.[39] Rather pathetically James VI even had to borrow 'the pair of silken hose' belonging to the Earl of Mar, in order to receive the Spanish Ambassador.[40]

It was not until 1611 that James sought to regularise court finances, setting up a special committee of eight known as the 'New Octavians'.[41] Meanwhile, however, the Convention of Royal Burghs, with its power to raise customs dues, enjoyed unprecedented prosperity during the peaceful years of his reign. James was able to profit indirectly from this civic wealth by investing funds from his queen's dowry with the Royal Burghs to yield regular interest, as well as by requesting funds from the burgh coffers for building projects. Large sums were raised from Edinburgh, for example, both for building work at Holyrood and to finance the construction of Parliament House.[42]

James VI's Scottish court was tightly enmeshed in the whole web of Scottish society – it did not stand at the apex of a pyramidal hierarchy like European princely autocracies such as Piedmont, Bavaria, Saxony or Spain.[43] The King's lifestyle was hardly more lavish than that of the richest of his nobles, and his treasury was dependent on subsidies from the Royal Burghs, in effect the country's *bourgeoisie*. His authority depended on preserving a delicate equilibrium between the 'Thrie Estates' of his Parliament: the nobility, the church and the burghs.[44] The court could provide artistic leadership – it could even mobilise all the available craftsmen for a special royal project[45] – but it could neither spend extravagantly nor dictate fashion.

The architectural history of the five main Scottish royal palaces – Edinburgh Castle, Holyrood Palace, Linlithgow Palace, Falkland Palace and Stirling Castle – is complicated and elusive. Every Stewart king made additions or alterations in at least one palace, while at Edinburgh and Stirling later military occupation further embroidered the picture. The only surviving portions that were entirely constructed for James VI are the Chapel Royal at Stirling, rebuilt for the baptism of Prince Henry in 1594, and the north wing of Linlithgow Palace, erected after the King's return to Scotland in 1617 and completed in 1620. Neither of these has aroused as much attention as the earlier efforts of James IV and V: the Chapel Royal's severe exterior can hardly compete with James V's flamboyant palace block on the opposite side of the courtyard at Stirling, while Linlithgow's ruined state hardly does justice to its architectural splendour. As we shall see later, both these buildings need to be seen in their historical context to be properly understood.

COURT ARCHITECTURE IN JAMES VI'S REIGN BEFORE 1603 UNDER SIR
ROBERT DRUMMOND OF CARNOCK AND WILLIAM SCHAW

The first evidence of architectural concern in the reign of James VI dates from
1570, during the regency of the Earl of Lennox. In that year, the royal master of
works, Sir Robert Drummond of Carnock was asked to organise essential repairs
to the church of the royal abbey of Dunfermline.[46] This ancient Benedictine church,
with its strong royal connections, one of the masterpieces of Scottish romanesque
architecture, had been dedicated in 1150. The interest in the preservation of
historic medieval buildings is at first glance one of the most surprising and far-
sighted aspects of architectural activity in the reign of James VI. Evidence suggests
that conservation work was carried out not only to satisfy the needs of the reformed
church, but also because of genuine historical interest and respect for the traditions
and roots of the monarchy.

In 1583, Drummond again recommended works to be carried out in royal
buildings – the Chapel Royal at Stirling was so derelict that 'the kingis hienis may
nocht weill remain within the same in tyme off weit or rain', and Drummond
proposed that it should be rebuilt.[47] He also recommended adding a new apartment
over the Portcullis Gate of Edinburgh Castle. Drummond's stitch-in-time phil-
osophy was admirably sensible: 'ane hunder pund vill do mair presently to the said
work no ane thousand pundis will do quhen it is fallin downe'.[48] Within the year,
however, he was displaced from his (life) office as master of works, to be succeeded
by William Schaw who, ironically, would eventually carry out both these suggestions. On 21 December 1583, Schaw was appointed as 'grit maister of all and
sindrie his hines palaceis, biggingis and reparationis, and grit oversear, directour
and commandar' of Scotland's royal works.[49]

William Schaw was a major figure in the Scottish architectural profession, as we
shall see in Chapter Six. Not only was he one of the first to whom the term 'architect'
was directly associated (his epitaph describes him as 'architecturae peretissimus' –
most expert in architecture), but he was also a pioneer of the system of Masonic
lodges in Scotland and a founder Freemason.[50] Like royal masters of works before
him, such as John Scrymgeour and Sir James Hamilton of Finnart, he was not a
master craftsman, but rather, a designer and clerk of works, and like them he was
from the land-owning class. He was one of the Schaws of Sauchie, who enjoyed
close court connections as keepers of the royal wine cellar. In 1584, the year after
his appointment as royal master of works, William Schaw accompanied his patron,
Lord Seton, on a diplomatic mission to France, where no doubt his direct encounter
with French architecture contributed to his architectural education: in his epitaph
we learn that 'In his eagerness to improve his mind he travelled through France
and many other kingdoms.' Certainly his diplomatic gifts were noticed, for in the
following year, 1585, he was one of three men chosen by the King to entertain
Danish ambassadors at Linlithgow Palace. No architectural work is associated with
this visit, but it marks the beginning of Schaw's Danish association that was to
prove so important in the next decade.

The Danish court was one of Europe's most splendid in the late sixteenth

century. Denmark's lands extended to Norway and still had claims to Orkney and
Shetland. Its strategic geographical position allowed it to control shipping to and
from the Baltic, and its own merchants were successful traders and skilled seamen.
We have already mentioned the close mercantile links between Scotland and
Denmark, an affinity which was underlined by the Protestant religion now shared
by the two countries. It is thus no surprise that James VI eventually decided to
pursue a marriage alliance with Anne, the daughter of King Frederick II of Denmark.
Anne's brother, Christian IV, succeeded to the throne of Denmark in 1588, to
preside over one of the most artistically ambitious courts of Europe during his
long, prosperous reign.[51]

In 1589, the marriage took place by proxy in Copenhagen, but the ship bearing the
14-year-old Queen to her new home was delayed by bad weather in Oslo. Blaming
witchcraft for the storms, James impatiently set sail for Norway to claim his bride in
person, and Schaw was one of the courtiers who accompanied him. After a winter's
entertainment at the Danish court, Schaw returned ahead of the King's party to Scotland
to prepare for the royal couple's arrival. He had two principal tasks: to prepare
Holyrood Palace for the wedding celebrations, and to carry out improvements to
Dunfermline Abbey, part of the Queen's jointure settlement.

HOLYROOD PALACE BEFORE 1603

The early history of Holyrood Palace is still shrouded in mystery. We know that
after the extensive building programmes of James IV and V, it was damaged in the
English invasion of 1544; presumably this was the reason for the various works
carried out between 1554 and 1566.[52] In 1590, the Royal Burgh of Edinburgh was
persuaded to contribute £1,000 towards the wedding preparations, but both time
and money were short.[53] The main priority was the provision of a gallery wing of
additional lodgings for the royal retinue. Neither the form of the gallery nor its
location is known with any certainty.[54] For the entry of the royal couple, the
palace's great hall and state rooms 'were richly hung with claith of gold and silver,
and tapestry of silk'.[55] But it was the burgh of Edinburgh itself which provided
the most elaborate ceremonial for the Queen's royal procession through the
capital.[56]

DUNFERMLINE ABBEY BEFORE 1603

At Dunfermline, however, operations were more extensive. In 1590, Schaw was
paid £400 'by his Majestie's precept, for reparation of the House at Dunfermling,
befoir the Queene's Majesties passing thereto'.[57] Modernisation of the south-facing
palace block, dramatically clinging to a steep slope with the help of hefty buttresses,
was carried out. New fireplaces were installed, and the big cross-mullioned windows may date from this time. Aonghus MacKechnie has suggested that the three
bays at the west end of this southern range, with their symmetrical design centred
on a turreted oriel above a tall arched pend, may be entirely Schaw's work (see
Figure 2.7).[58] Admittedly, the arch is old-fashionedly Gothic, but this was an abbey
with strong historical roots. Schaw must have been struck on his recent foreign

FIGURE 2.7 (*upper*)   Dunfermline Abbey, Fife, view from the south-west.

FIGURE 2.8 (*lower*)   Dunfermline Abbey, Fife, view from the west, from Slezer's *Theatrum Scotiae*.

trip by the Danish court's willingness to blend Gothic and Renaissance elements in its royal buildings, such as Kronborg and Frederiksborg, to express the continuity as well as the modernity of the monarchy.[59]

Equally intriguing in the present context is the long-vanished palace block, apparently on the west side of the cloister, which appears in one of Slezer's views of Dunfermline dating from 1693 (see Figure 2.8). This, too, is a symmetrically planned range with a centrally placed projecting turret – perhaps a stair tower. Like the south guest range, the roofline is crenellated, while the large cross-mullioned windows again render the castellation purely symbolic. A somewhat French air, not unlike that of Falkland Palace, is conveyed by the tall buttresses between each bay and the conical roof of the turret, but there is no record of extensive work at Dunfermline in the francophile reign of James V. Moreover, the abbey was not formally annexed to the crown until 1587.[60] Was this part of the Queen's residence or jointure-house which, according to Mylne, was rebuilt by Schaw in 1600?[61] Schaw had visited France as well as Denmark, and the symmetry and central projecting bay of this wing are elements that recur repeatedly in works for James VI in Scotland, as we shall see. The west side of a medieval abbey cloister was often the position of guest accommodation, and its comparative privacy at Dunfermline may have encouraged its updating or rebuilding for the new Danish queen.

A structure believed to be the Queen's palace survived to be fully described in the *Statistical Account* at the end of the eighteenth century:

> The Queen's house continued in good repair long after the palace was in ruins ... Within these 15 years, part of it was inhabited, but no attention being paid to keep it in repair, it gradually became ruinous, and was lately sold, and made a quarry for stones, and is to be entirely removed.[62]

This description records the Latin inscription on the building, which used the Greek term 'propylaeum', or gatehouse:

> Propylaeum et superstructas, aedes
> vetustate et injuriis temporum
> collapsa, dirutasque a fundamentis
> in hanc ampliorem formam, restituit
> et instauravit Anna Regina Frederici
> Donorum Regis Augustissime Filia, Anno
> Salutis 1600.[63]

It seems likely that the 'propylaeum' was not the west cloister range just described, but rather, the wing projecting westward from the west end of the church, visible as a bold gable in Slezer's view. This building also appears in a drawing made from the north (see Figure 2.9), showing that, like the south range, it had a projecting oriel over a pend. The archway led into the palace precinct from the town, the perfect site for a 'propylaeum'. When Inigo Jones came to design a house for Anne of Denmark at Greenwich in 1616, he, too, conceived a residence that stood over a road between the main palace and the park, as if in recollection of her much-loved palace at Dunfermline.

The palace evidently pleased her, for by 1601 it was referred to as 'the ordinar

FIGURE 2.9   Dunfermline Abbey, Fife, Queen Anne of Denmark's building, demolished late
eighteenth century. Drawing of 1929 from a painting of unknown whereabouts.

residence of the Queen'.[64] Her walnut nuptial bed 'of curious workmanship, and
ornamented with several very antique figures neatly carved' was preserved in a
local inn until the mid-eighteenth century.[65] The English court poet, John Taylor
'the Water Poet', who visited Linlithgow in 1618, mentioned 'the Queenes palace,
(a delicate and princely mansion), withall I saw the ruines of an ancient and stately
built abbey, with faire gardens, orchards, medows belonging to the palace'.[66]

Schaw's personal loyalty to Queen Anne earned him a favoured place as
Chamberlain at her court. Perhaps her respect helped him to tolerate the unfor-
tunate fact that, whether out of negligence or shortage of cash, his salary of 500
merks a year from the King was only erratically paid. An investigation ten years
after his death revealed that, although 'in his lyfetyme, and during the tyme of his
service [Schaw] was a most painfulle, trustye, and well affectit servand to your
maiestie', his full salary had only been paid in five of his eighteen years of service![67]

In the abbey itself, Schaw carried out the repairs that had been urgently requested
by the General Assembly of the Kirk of Scotland in 1588.[68] Mylne tells us that 'To
the nave, the aisles, the steeple and the north porch he gave special attention.'[69]
The upper part of the north tower is usually regarded as his work (see Figure 2.7),
and it is fitting that his burial monument — ordered by the Queen, and erected by

Schaw's patron Alexander Seton, first Earl of Dunfermline — should lie beneath this tower (see Figure 5.22).[70] John Gifford has recently doubted Schaw's authorship of the spire, on the grounds of its resemblance to the early fifteenth-century west towers of St Machar's Cathedral in Old Aberdeen.[71] As we shall see, however, Schaw almost certainly visited Deeside with Seton, for whom he possibly designed Fyvie Castle, and may well have admired these Aberdonian spires. Did he perhaps recognise them as Dutch-style steeples and therefore consider them appropriate for a newly Protestant church under the patronage of a Protestant Queen (despite the fact that he was himself a Catholic)? A similar octagonal spire, tapering more steeply in the upper part, can be seen, for instance, in the church of Winterswijk in Holland, completed in 1507.

STIRLING CASTLE BEFORE 1603: THE NEW CHAPEL ROYAL

Most of the story of Stirling Castle in the reign of James VI is equally elusive. Drummond had recommended the rebuilding of the north-west wing, now known as the King's Old Building, 'in the maist plesand maner that can be dewyssit' as well as the addition of 'ane fair gallery ... and tarras'. This western block has been much altered, and little from our period appears to survive, leaving more questions than answers.[72]

The only well-documented building is the Chapel Royal, rebuilt in preparation for the baptism of Prince Henry on 30 August 1594. The account by the Queen's secretary, the poet William Fowler, records that, because it was 'ruinous, and too little', the old chapel was to be 'utterly rased and a new one erected in the same place, that shuld be more large, long and glorious ... to entertaine the great number of strangers expected'.[73] The festivity was conceived as a Renaissance triumph — significantly, Fowler himself had translated Petrarch's *Trionfi* in 1587.[74] The guests invited to the christening included ambassadors from France, England, Denmark, Holland and Zeeland — not to mention James's brother-in-law the Duke of Brunswick, and the Queen's grandfather the Duke of Magdeburg.

We know very little of the appearance of the old chapel, but during the reign of James V it had set the scene for the remarkable Renaissance music of Scotland's greatest court composer Robert Carver (c.1490–after 1546).[75] The complex polyphonies of Carver's choral writing, at the vanguard of European music, must have needed a spacious setting, but we have already heard Drummond of Carnock's complaints that by 1583 this old chapel was no longer weatherproof. It is thought to have occupied a site just to the south of the present chapel, now indicated by studs in the paving.

The necessary funds to pay for the rebuilding and the baptismal festivities, amounting to no less than £100,000 Scots (almost ten times the sum needed for James's own baptism), were raised by a special tax in 1593.[76] Preparations at Stirling were elaborate — the English Ambassador's late arrival must have been almost a relief to the court, although visitors from the Continent were more impatient, fearing they might be marooned by the onset of winter storms. Fowler relates that the King 'had the supply of the greatest number of Artificers in the

FIGURE 2.10   Stirling Castle, Chapel Royal, designed by William Schaw, 1593.

whol Cuntrie, convened there, of all craftes for that service, and his Maiesties owne person daily overseer, with large and liberal payment'.[77] The reference to 'his Maiesties owne person' attests to the King's personal involvement in the project, although his master of works, William Schaw, was officially responsible for the execution of the building.

The new Chapel Royal took the form of a long, low, single-storey building, with crow-stepped gables at each end and smooth ashlar masonry (see Figure 2.10). The two-light, round-arched windows, almost Florentine in appearance, broke new ground in Scottish religious architecture. The sacred role of the Royal Chapel at Linlithgow Palace had been differentiated by its slim, Gothic, lancet windows. But the religion had changed since then. James VI was Scotland's first Protestant monarch, confident of his right to be the head of the reformed church. Carefully balancing the pressures from episcopalian and presbyterian factions, while trying not to antagonise his most powerful Catholic subjects, he must have favoured a chapel with no obvious religious bias. Its simple, barn-like form was to inspire the design of new Protestant churches and private chapels over the next half-century, as we shall see in Chapter Five.

The Stirling entrance portal, the focal point in an otherwise plain and dignified exterior, takes the form of a classical triumphal arch, surmounted by a heraldic panel. The coat-of-arms itself, as well as royal ciphers, painted and gilded, over

FIGURE 2.11   Arch of the Sergii, Pula, Dalmatia, from book III of Serlio's *Tutte l'opere*. Book
III was first published in Venice in 1540.

the windows, are said to have been removed in Cromwell's time.[78] The arch has
paired Corinthian columns on either side, sharing single tall plinths, with the
entablature projecting over each pair, like the Roman Arch of the Sergii at Pula on
the Dalmatian coast. This type of arch had already been used on the Continent for
celebratory triumphal or royal entrances such as the gateway to the Venetian
Arsenal of 1460.[79] The Arsenal portal had recently been transformed into a
monument to the Republic's triumph at Lepanto in 1571, and James's interest in
this victory (his epic poem has already been mentioned) may have led him to
emulate the Venetian model. But the Scottish court was more likely to have had
direct knowledge of the similar arch erected for Philip II's triumphal entry into
Antwerp in 1549.[80] This was an ostentatious monument to Habsburg Imperial
power, surmounted by statues of Philip II and Charles V carrying a huge globe.
Engravings of the arches designed for the Antwerp entry were published in 1550.
More conveniently, though, the Dalmatian arch itself could be found in book III of
Serlio's treatise on architecture (see Figure 2.11). [81] Finally, as Alistair Rowan has
remarked, the doorway recalls the design of book frontispieces at this period.[82]
This is not a casual likeness – after all, the word 'frontispiece' also means a
pedimented entrance to a building, and books, like buildings, have columns and
capitals/chapters.[83] The frontispiece was the introduction to the narrative which
would be recounted inside – by the decoration and spectacle in the chapel.
    We should not, of course, forget that James IV had, literally, paved the way for

a classical triumphal arch at Stirling, when he built the inner gateway to the castle in about 1505–10. Aonghus MacKechnie has recently drawn attention to this triple arched forework, which similarly recalled antique models that were then being used as city gates in Renaissance Italy.[84] But with its Gothic-style hood mouldings the earlier version had been much less erudite in its architectural language.[85]

By contrast, the Chapel Royal's ostentatiously antique, demurely classical gateway must have made a deep impression. Modest though it now appears, it became the theme for Scottish royal gateways for a century to come, from the portal of the school endowed by the royal jeweller George Heriot in Edinburgh, begun in 1628 (see Figure 4.27), to Bruce's entrance to the new Holyrood Palace dated 1680.

Inside the chapel, all suggestions of architectural purity and seriousness would have vanished amid a festive profusion of painted decoration and expensive hangings. The surviving paintwork runs around the whole chapel at frieze level and fills the polygonal lunettes over the windows at either end (see Figure 2.12). Royal arms and crowns alternate with colourful bunches of fruit, suspended (as if weightless) from swirling, richly tasselled ropes. The whole frieze is framed by exuberant painted strapwork ornament and topped with an illusionistic cornice with egg-and-dart and dentilled mouldings. The walls were 'richelie hung, with costly tapestries', while the roof timbers were once painted blue and decorated with flower patterns.[86] The King's throne was in the north-east corner in a special royal enclosure, flanked by seats for the foreign ambassadors. In the midst of this partition, 'there was a newe pulpite erected: The same was richly hung with cloth of gold: All the pavement within this partition, was Prince-like laide with fine tapestrie'.[87] 'Prince-like' fittingly describes the whole tone of the festivities. After the sermon (on the appropriately filial story of Abraham and Isaac) and the explanation of the Sacrament of Baptism in both Latin and Scots, the 21st Psalm of David was sung by the Provost and Prebends of the Chapel Royal, 'to the great delectation of the noble auditory'.[88] One can easily imagine the powerful effect of its words:

> The king rejoices in thy might, O Lord:
> …
> the king puts his trust in the Lord;
> The loving care of the Most High holds him unshaken.
> Your hand shall reach all your enemies
> …
> They have plotted mischief but could not prevail;
> … &c[89]

The biblical King David was one of the historical figures with whom King James liked to identify, and the jubilant mood of this Psalm must have moved the audience just as much as the music delighted them.[90]

The same evening, a splendid banquet was held in the great hall at Stirling. The first dishes 'of patisserye, frutages, and confections' were brought in on a tabernacle accompanied by six women personifying Ceres, Fecundity, Faith, Concord, Liberality and Perseverance.

FIGURE 2.12   Stirling Castle, Chapel Royal, painted decoration on the west gable of the interior.

The original idea was that the tabernacle should be drawn by a lion (for lions were indeed kept in the 'Lion's Den' in the courtyard of the palace block), but in the end he was replaced by a Moor 'because his presence might have brought some feare to the neerest'.[91] In the open-air tournament that had preceded the baptism itself, the King himself had worn 'a Lyons heade with open eyes, which signifieth after a mistique and Hierogliphique sence Fortitude and Vigilance'.[92] The King's own participation served to emphasise that the allusion was fact rather than fiction.[93]

The next courses of the banquet were delivered on a 'most sumptuous, artificiall, and wel proportioned ship … Her motion was so artificially devised within herself, that none could perceive what brought her in. The Sea under her was lively counterfeit, with al coulours.' Neptune stood on the deck, symbolising the King's North Sea voyage to collect his Danish bride.[94] The painted, gilded vessel with white taffeta sails caused a sensation, 'the invention being the king's' according to Fowler. Its success must have dulled the memory of the banquet in the same hall for the King's own baptism in 1566, when the stage drawn by twelve satyrs and bearing the food collapsed.[95] The galley was still to be seen at Stirling Castle after the Restoration; it was mentioned by the English visitor John Ray in 1662.[96]

A series of musical performances, both vocal and instrumental, accompanied the banquet in the great hall, and William Schaw himself was the Master of Ceremonies.[97] After the feasting was over, 'at the sound of Triton's Wilde trumpet and the pilotte's whistle, she [the galley] weighed anchor, made sail, and with the noise of oboes and trumpets, retired'.[98] The eminent guests must have admired the virtuosity of the technical effects which allowed a moving ship to leave the stage, just as they relished the skill of the musical counterpoint and the polyphonic harmonies. This was a truly polymathic Renaissance spectacle.

EDINBURGH CASTLE BEFORE 1603

Whereas Stirling was traditionally the home of the royal children, Edinburgh's role as the capital of Scotland was taken for granted by the late sixteenth century. At Edinburgh Castle during his regency (1572–81), the Earl of Morton, an enthusiastic patron of architecture in private as well as public life, had commissioned the gateway now known as the Portcullis Gate, framed by spindly colonnettes and erratic stringcourses (see Figure 2.13).[99] The pedimented aedicule over the gateway, framing the royal arms, represents a later stage in the work, when in 1584 the young James VI ordered Chancellor Arran to have an upper storey added to the gate.[100] Its correctly detailed Ionic order, and its design recalling the Pantheon altars (and many later variations), suggests that William Schaw was the architect.

After the siege of 1573, Regent Morton was also responsible for the encircling of the ruins of David's Tower to make the semi-circular gun-terrace known as the Half-Moon Battery – rendering the ancient tower obsolete, invisible and inaccessible (see Figure 2.14).[101] This gesture was a significant one: courtly living was now no longer set in dark, lofty strongholds, but in well-lit suites of apartments ranged horizontally and reached by spacious staircases. (The new sense of security was not always justified: in 1594, for example, James VI had to stay at Robert Gourlay's lodgings in Edinburgh to avoid the Earl of Bothwell who had twice broken into Holyrood Palace.[102])

LINLITHGOW PALACE BEFORE 1603

On his visit to Scotland in 1600, the French visitor Henri, Duc de Rohan, reported that, while the young Prince Henry was to be found at Stirling and the Queen herself at Dunfermline, the King's daughter, Princess Elizabeth (later to become Queen of Bohemia, the 'Winter Queen') was living at Linlithgow.[103] Queen Anne herself hated to be separated from her children, but it was her husband's wish that in the traditional way the royal princes and princesses should each be entrusted to noble foster parents.[104] James himself, having hardly known his own mother, seems to have had little sense of the need for parental involvement. This fragmented family life meant the retention of several households, among which he himself travelled constantly as his royal duties – and the hunting season – dictated. Linlithgow was apparently considered the least important, for almost no expenditure is recorded on the palace in the late sixteenth century, despite the warning of Sir Robert Drummond in 1583 that 'the westquarter of the Paleys of Lythquow is altogidder lyk to fall downe'.[105]

SCOTTISH COURT ARCHITECTURE AFTER 1603: THE ROLE OF SIR JAMES MURRAY OF KILBABERTON

When James VI and his court moved to London in 1603, royal finances were so low that the King had to borrow 10,000 merks from the Royal Burgh of Edinburgh

FIGURE 2.13 (*left*)
Edinburgh Castle,
Portcullis Gate, completed
1584 (top part of upper
storey 1880s).
FIGURE 2.14 (*below*)
Edinburgh Castle from
the south, by James
Gordon of Rothiemay,
1647. Detail.

to pay for his journey south.[106] His entry into London in 1603 (1604 in the modern calendar) was celebrated with a series of remarkable triumphal arches, each one acting as a stage for entertainments by the leading dramatists of the day. The arches were commissioned by the City of London and designed by the joiner Stephen Harrison. Their designs were engraved for posterity (together with two further arches erected by the Italian and Dutch communities respectively) in Harrison's *The Arch's of Triumph* published in 1604, 'so that now they are to stand as perpetuall monuments, not to be shaken in peeces, or to be broken downe'.[107] In England, after 1603, James's court was richer and thus architecturally more ambitious. He was, after all, soon to employ Inigo Jones, both as masque designer and architect. Although he himself may not have been as discerning artistically as his gifted son, Prince Henry – who sadly died of typhoid at the age of 18 in 1612 – James was certainly aware of the international propaganda value of architectural distinction at court.[108] We should not forget Ben Jonson's remark about:

> Those Obelisks and Colunnes ...
> That shook the starres, and rais'd the British crowne
> To be a constellation.[109]

With the court's move south, one would have expected the royal purse strings to loosen in Scotland. Indeed, much larger sums were spent on the maintenance of the royal palaces, and on Holyrood in particular, during the early seventeenth century, but much of the funding still had to be raised from within Scotland. The first major programme of works involved the expense of over £100,000 on buildings alone, to prepare for James VI's return in 1617.[110] The King had promised to come back every three years with 'salmonlyke instinct' to his native land, but this was to be his only visit after 1603.[111]

William Schaw's death in 1602 almost coincided with the court's departure. He was succeeded as royal master of works in 1607 by James Murray, later to be the architect of Scotland's Parliament House.[112] Although Murray was described as the King's architect as early as 1612, his role as a designer has been doubted. John Dunbar believes that most of the design work was entrusted to the royal master masons, although Murray's day-to-day involvement with the royal buildings cannot be disputed. The recent researches of Aonghus MacKechnie suggest that his role was similar to that of Inigo Jones in London, as royal architect and clerk of works, like his predecessors William Schaw and Sir James Hamilton of Finnart.[113] In 1628, Murray was joined by a second master of works, Anthony Alexander; both of them were eventually knighted for their services by Charles I.[114]

James VI did not allow regular maintenance to be neglected, even after his departure. In 1619, for instance, he wrote of Inverness Castle, knowing he would probably never see it again, 'our respecte to our owne honour and the credite of that our kingdome, might be sufficient motives to perswade us to maynteyne it in reparation'.[115] Between 1614 and 1629, under James Murray's direction, the sum of £1,000 was provided annually for routine repairs to the Scottish royal palaces.[116]

EDINBURGH CASTLE AFTER 1603

James VI's return visit to Scotland in 1617 was the excuse for substantial alterations to the palace block of Edinburgh Castle, which involved as many as twenty-four stone masons.[117] The smooth ashlar masonry of the north section of the palace dates from this phase of building, executed in 1615–16 under the royal master mason William Wallace and the royal master of works James Murray.[118] One of the east-facing windows is dated 1616, while the ogee-domed polygonal tower in the centre of the north end is dated 1615. This block has been much altered, but early views allow us to reconstruct its original character.[119]

The returning monarch must have been struck by the careful symmetry of each façade and the fine quality of the stonework; but the palace was not all discipline and restraint. On the east side, facing the town, were three great oriel windows, each three storeys high, separated by heraldic panels (see Figure 2.14). Although the Half-Moon Battery gave some protection, the huge oriels on the accessible east side of the castle glorified the new confidence of James's position. They were prominently visible from the town below, and offered panoramic views from the royal apartments. At either end of the roofline were little corbelled square turrets topped by domes, decorative rather than functional, flanking a crenellated parapet. As at Dunfermline Palace, castellation now conveyed courtly chivalry and the historical roots of the monarchy, instead of military strength. The north façade has remained almost unaltered, with its central, ogee-domed, polygonal staircase tower. The stairtower in the centre of the west side, facing the courtyard, was also once roofed by an ogival dome (see Figure 2.6). Several of the window pediments are ornately carved, like those that Wallace was later to provide at Linlithgow.

Unfortunately, the arrangement of the state apartments inside is much altered, but the plan was in the form of a double pile with a spine wall along its length (see Figure 2.6). The King's own suite was probably along the east side, behind the splendid oriels overlooking his Scottish capital. The Queen's apartment was on the upper floor, although she did not in fact accompany her husband on his return to Scotland. The little cabinet room in which James himself had been born was decorated with commemorative inscriptions to form what Iain MacIvor has described as a 'secular shrine'.[120]

HOLYROOD PALACE AFTER 1603

A major refurbishment of Holyrood Palace was also carried out in 1616–17, costing as much as £40,000. The King himself was most preoccupied by the decoration of the Chapel Royal, a private chapel in the south wing of the main palace courtyard. (The abbey church was now used by the parishioners of the Canongate.) The English sculptor Nicholas Stone carved the choirstalls and pews in London, and they were sent up to Edinburgh to be installed, painted and gilded, together with an organ and paintings of the Apostles and Faith, Hope and Charity.[121] The whole scheme was carried out under the direction of Inigo Jones in London, although Jones himself never saw Holyrood Palace. James had probably not anticipated the

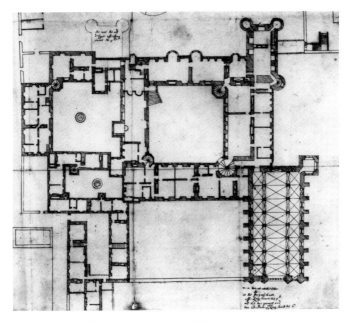

FIGURE 2.15   Holyrood Palace, Edinburgh, plan by John Mylne, 1663 (West front at top).

local opposition to this flamboyant religious interior: an English visitor claimed that 'For the graven images in the new beautified chapel, they threaten to pull them down after his departure, and make of them a burnt offering to appease ... the Almighty.'[122]

At Holyrood Palace the problems and opportunities were not unlike those at Dunfermline. Here, too, a monastery founded by King David I had bequeathed a church that was now a historical monument in itself, near-ruinous and costly to maintain. Here, too, the monastery cloister had generated the form of the courtyard plan, with extra courts added as more accommodation became necessary. And here, too, a magnificent Renaissance palace block, now lost, occupied the western flank. Luckily, the appearance of the Holyrood frontage is well known, thanks to the detailed engraving made by Gordon of Rothiemay in 1647 (see Figure 2.4), before the palace was damaged during the Civil War in 1650 and subsequently rebuilt by Sir William Bruce in the 1670s. A plan by John Mylne, made in 1663 and now in the Bodleian Library in Oxford, preserves the interior layout (see Figure 2.15), and its success is clear from the way in which so many of its characteristics – and possibly more of the structure than is realised – were retained in Bruce's rebuilding.[123] As we have seen, the west wing can be dated to the 1530s on the basis of the surviving accounts, but the size of the windows, if we are to believe Rothiemay, would have looked impressive even in late Elizabethan England, let alone in Scotland. It seems that in James VI's time, the King's own apartments occupied this west range – as at Edinburgh Castle facing the city (or rather, here, its elegant suburb, the Canongate). Here was the King's 'laigh (low) hall', elevated only above the entrance pend and stretching right up to the cornice.[124]

LINLITHGOW PALACE AFTER 1603

As we have seen, Linlithgow had long been the most neglected of the Scottish royal palaces. In 1607, the roof of the north wing collapsed, and the Earl of Linlithgow afterwards reported that its inner wall had begun to lean inwards so that it 'lukis everie moment when the inner wall sall fall, and brek you Majesties fontan'.[125] No action was taken, however, and by the time that preparations had to be made for the King's return in 1617, many of the palace contents had even been dispersed. The Privy Council humiliatingly had to request the return of 'tapestrie, bedding and household stuff' removed by 'diverse persons', including the Earl of Linlithgow himself.[126] The King's entry into the town must have been more comical than dignified, for he was welcomed by a poem specially composed by Sir William Drummond, recited by the burgh school master from inside a huge plaster lion.[127] The King stayed one night only, but this was long enough to persuade him of the urgency of rebuilding the roofless north wing.

The new north range was begun in 1618 and roofed two years later; the date 1620 is inscribed on the central turret (see Figure 2.16). This was a lodgings wing, a double pile with four upper storeys of bedrooms, each with its own fireplace, and served by garderobes on the outer wall (see Figure 2.17). A row of massive chimneys were lined up like soldiers behind a roofline crested with rhythmic, crisply cusped crenellations. Lodgings for courtiers were one of the most pressing needs in the Scottish royal palaces in the late sixteenth and early seventeenth centuries, for the upper members of the King's household were no longer expected to bed down in halls or closets, but were afforded some privacy.

The master of works was once more Sir James Murray of Kilbaberton, and the master mason was William Wallace, who had worked with Murray at Edinburgh Castle.[128] Indeed, there are many similarities between the two new blocks, with their centrally placed, polygonal stair towers, double-pile plans, smooth ashlar masonry and ornate window pediments. Another similar pediment, also bearing the arms of James VI, on the west courtyard façade at Linlithgow, may date from the time of the royal visit, together with the unusual horizontal 'ladder' window which must have been inserted to throw light on a newly painted ceiling in the King's hall (see Figure 2.1). Even more intriguing is the contract of 1629 for 'painting and laying over with oil colour and for gilting with gold the whole fore face of the new work with the timber windows and window boards, stone windows and crownells [pediments], with a board for the king's arms'.[129] The 'fore face' is presumably the courtyard front, for the plain outer façade, facing north on to the loch, was only only visible from a great distance. The chilly dourness of Linlithgow's present ruined state makes it difficult to imagine this vision of dazzling polychromy which would have faced the visitor as he entered the courtyard.

FALKLAND PALACE AFTER 1603

Falkland, like Linlithgow, was little altered under James VI, although it remained a popular hunting retreat. In 1598, the English traveller Fynes Moryson visited

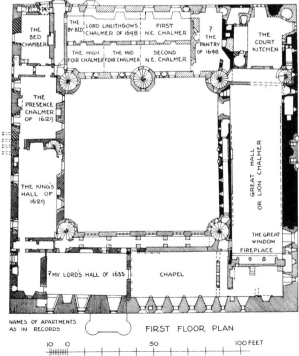

FIGURE 2.16 (*above*)   Linlithgow
Palace, West Lothian, the north
wing, rebuilt 1618–20, master
mason William Wallace.

FIGURE 2.17 (*left*)   Linlithgow
Palace, plan of the first floor.

Falkeland then the Kings House for hunting ... where I did gladly see James the sixth King of the Scots, at that time lying there to follow the pastimes of hunting and hawking, for which this ground is much commended; but the Pallace was of old building and almost ready to fall, having nothing in it remarkable.[130]

Despite this dismissive comment, however, royal pride still demanded embellishments to Falkland. Tantalisingly, the glorious, intricately carved oriel window, shown in a water-colour of 1846 by David Roberts, has almost disappeared (see Figure 2.2). Was this oriel, together with the flamboyant, gabled dormer rising confidently between the two towers, an addition from the reign of James VI? This was after all the age of showy oriels in Scotland – whether at the Earl's Palace in Kirkwall, at the Earl of Huntly's palace in Strathbogie, or at James's own at Edinburgh Castle. Oriels had been popular centre-pieces to English tudor gate-houses, but they also decorated the Renaissance palaces and town halls of Germany and France, from Paris to Altenburg, both to embellish buildings and to frame an impressive royal or civic appearance.[131]

THE REIGN OF CHARLES I

Charles I's reign showed an almost immediate concern for display. In the late 1620s, contracts were issued for the repainting of stonework and heraldic panels at Falkland, Stirling, Linlithgow and Holyrood. For instance, in 1629 a horse was hired to carry from Stirling to Falkland 'a case with three boards in it whereon the king's arms is', and the English painter Valentine Jenkin was paid £60 'for the painting of the foresaid three great boards and furnishing colours, gold, oil and the whole stuff theirto and for overlaying and marbling the three housings above the great gate where they stand'.[132]

Charles I's visit to Scotland in 1633 was a spectacular affair, although its memory has been overshadowed by the religious upheavals that succeeded it. Again, the preparatory building works probably cost over £100,000, although not all the accounts have survived.[133] One of the main problems was the size of the King's retinue, and in particular the extensive stabling needed. More than £17,000 was spent on Holyrood Palace alone, with work proceeding with such urgency that once again craftsmen were taken from other employment in various parts of Scotland. As in the case of his father's visit of 1617 and his own later trip in 1641, large amounts of money were borrowed from the wealthy Edinburgh merchant William Dick to finance the preparations for Charles I's return. The richest burgesses were the only source of large sums of ready capital in Scotland at this time.

The royal building accounts are not easy to interpret, and it is therefore hard to know which external alterations to Holyrood date from 1617 and which from 1633. From whichever royal visit, however, some of the embellishments on the west front seem to have been Murray's responsibility (see Figure 2.4).[134] All the fun was concentrated on the skyline: the ogee-arched gable over James V's tower, the slender little spire over the right-hand turret (as well as the spirelets peeping over the rooftops behind), the open, two-storeyed, domed turrets over the central gateway, the outsized finials along the ridge, and most ostentatious of all the huge crowns over the two north-west towers, replacing the miniature turrets and lions mentioned in the earlier accounts. The effect was rich and theatrical, a busy silhouette with picturesque variety and evident extravagance, rather than the unified, sober dignity that had characterised Schaw's royal works. The exotic mix of Northern and classical elements and the florid skyline must have given the mid-seventeenth-century Holyrood a Northern European feel not unlike the princely palaces of Denmark or Germany. One need only mention those of James VI's two brothers-in-law, Christian IV (such as Rosenborg) and the Elector Palatine (such as Schloss Heidelberg). This was the same court that was patronising Inigo Jones in London, yet the contrast could hardly be more striking. The difference must have been acceptable and deliberate – as if Scotland needed a more Northern, though no less splendid, architectural imagery.

Extensive repairs to the old church of Holyrood Abbey in preparation for Charles I's coronation were in a still more Gothic idiom, another instance of the Stewart court's enlightened and respectful conservation policy. William Adam recorded the west front of Holyrood Abbey, as it was restored by Sir James Murray, in his *Vitruvius Scoticus*.[135] The sum of £4,000 was spent on the church in 1624, and further repairs preceded Charles I's Scottish coronation in 1633.[136] (Meanwhile, Inigo Jones was restoring St Paul's Cathedral in London, but in an unmistakably classical style, again underlining the contrast between the self-consciously Northern bias of the Stewart king's Scottish buildings and the more Italianate image of their southern court.)

THE ROYAL GARDENS

Finally, we should remember the court's leading role in garden design. This was an outward-looking age – a time of expanding horizons, both internationally and locally. The royal palaces and castles now had oriels and huge glass windows from which to admire the views over the surrounding policies. The initial inspiration for Scotland's Renaissance gardens came from the court of France, where Italian and French gardeners had created intricate geometrical knot-gardens and parterres, extending the formal symmetry of the châteaux into their settings. The King's Knot at Stirling was probably Scotland's first Renaissance parterre, its geometry seen in bird's-eye view from the terraces and ramparts of the castle above (see Figure 2.18). It was first laid out by James IV in 1501; in the 1530s, James V installed a French gardener with three assistants. The massive earthworks, still visible today, seem to date from a later period, but documentation is lacking. Payments to the English gardener William Watts in 1628 for 'platting and con-tryving his Majesties new Orchard and Garden' may be related to a remodelling at that time.[137] The gardens at Falkland were also treated to 'platting and contryving ... anew' at the same date.[138] Royal garden buildings, too, could be innovatory. The real (*réal* or royal) tennis court at Falkland, built for James V in 1539, was

FIGURE 2.18   Stirling, King's Knot, 1501, remodelled 1628, aerial view.

one of the first in Britain, and was restored and re-equipped with balls and raquets for James VI's return in 1617 (see Figure 2.19).[139] The picturesque little building known as 'Queen Mary's Bathhouse' in the grounds of Holyrood Palace seems to date from the late sixteenth century, and once stood at the corner of the King's Privy Garden, facing the royal tennis court (see Figure 2.20).[140] Its role as a bathhouse has never been taken seriously, although the practice of taking hot baths in garden pavilions was not unknown in Renaissance Scotland: we need only think of the former bathhouse on the corner of the exquisite walled garden at Edzell Castle. The grounds of Linlithgow Palace, too, were equipped for leisure activities, with a bowling green, tennis court, and bow butts for archery.[141]

It was Charles I's return visit to Scotland in 1633 that provided the impulse for one of the smallest but most influential pieces of royal garden architecture, namely the sundial at Holyrood Palace, for which the King's master mason, John Mylne, was paid the handsome sum of £408 15s. 6d. Scots in the same year.[142] This is the earliest surviving example of a polyhedral sundial, an invention of remarkable scientific virtuosity pioneered in Scotland (see Figure 2.21). Each of the facets of the polyhedral sundial is excavated with cavities of various different shapes, each one containing a dial needle, numbering twenty-nine in all. The underneath faces are decorated with royal devices such as thistles and roses, as well as the initials of King Charles and his Queen Henrietta Maria. Not only is the dial itself an eye-

FIGURE 2.19 (*above*) Falkland Palace, Fife, real tennis court, 1539.
FIGURE 2.20 (*left*) Holyrood Palace, Edinburgh, 'Queen Mary's Bathhouse'.

FIGURE 2.21   Holyrood Palace gardens, sundial by John Mylne, 1633.

catching piece of stone-carving, formerly painted and gilded. Even more impressive
was the fact that every one of the twenty-nine needles told the same time, whatever
the time of day! The technology was greatly assisted by Napier's discovery of
logarithms in 1614, but it may have been the invention of that resourceful Aberdonian Davie 'Do A'thing' Anderson, who in 1596 'had devysit ane instrument,
of his own ingyne, to draw and mak dyellis or sone horolages'. A gilded and painted
stone sundial had already been made for the gardens at Falkland in 1629, but we
do not know what form this earlier dial took. By the year 1700, there were to be
at least forty-seven free-standing polyhedral sundials in Scottish gardens.[143]

CONCLUSION

It is one of the ironies of history that the Scottish court in the late sixteenth and
early seventeenth century was starved of funds for royal works, at a time when
there was an unprecedented building boom among the aristocracy, not to mention
the minor lairds and city burgesses. The stable, peaceful, political situation allowed
both agriculture and trade to prosper as never before, yet this wealth only reached
the court when begged or borrowed. Thus, the monarchy had scant resources for
architectural leadership and, after 1603, little immediate need to maintain the
Scottish households. Had it not been for the return visits of James VI in 1617 and
Charles I in 1633 and 1641, even less would have been done to embellish the early
Stewart palaces. But in spite of its impecunious state, the court of James VI seems

to have sensed its prominent role on the European stage, and the tendency to look to continental courts for inspiration continued to play an important role in feeding Scotland's visual culture with new ideas. The two main royal architects of the period, William Schaw and Sir James Murray of Kilbaberton, had different styles and aspirations. Schaw's work was infused with erudite classicism and restrained correctness, drawing on a wide range of Renaissance ideas gleaned from treatises as well as foreign travel. Murray's style had a more Baroque exuberance – he was, after all, a seventeenth century figure; his schemes were ostentatious and dynamic, with a sense of local historical tradition as well as an awareness of court culture across Europe.

After Murray's death in 1634, all regular provision for the maintenance of the Scottish royal palaces ceased. Their upkeep was in theory the responsibility of the hereditary keepers of each palace. These were distinguished members of the nobility, who were reluctant to spend their court pensions on the fabric of the royal seats. Even before the Civil War, the troubled years following the Covenant distracted royal attention, and revenues, from the need for routine repairs. In 1647, the masters of works of the time complained that the royal palaces 'this long tyme bygane have not bein sighted, visited nor repaired, altho it wes the old custome almost once evrie yeir to visite them'.[144]

In 1600, just two years before Schaw's death and three years before the court's move to London, the French visitor Henri Duc de Rohan had considered Stirling, Linlithgow and Dunfermline 'as worthy of commemoration as the most beautiful palaces in the world'.[145] By 1660, visitors were more likely to be impressed by the towns and industries than by the royal palaces: the English naturalist John Ray in about 1662, for example, dismissed Linlithgow Palace as 'a very good house, as houses in Scotland go'.[146] The years of civil war had dulled the splendour of James VI's palace blocks – at Dunfermline, Edinburgh Castle and Linlithgow – with their serene, symmetrical façades, central stair towers, flamboyant ornament and brightly painted stonework. The scene was set for Sir William Bruce, but that is another story.

CHAPTER THREE

The Countryside

Despite the growing prosperity of the burghs in the Renaissance period, Scotland was still a predominantly rural nation. Even in the later seventeenth century, 80–90 per cent of the population still lived in the countryside, and of these at least a quarter resided in the Highlands. Within this rural scene, however, there were marked differences in prosperity between one area and another. Several contemporary writers mention the flourishing farmlands of the shores of the Moray Firth: Bishop Leslie in 1578 marvelled at the 'orchardes, and fruitful gairdings' of Morayshire, where 'is the air maist hailsum, vncorrupte, temperat, thair cludis and rain mekle les than in ony vthir place, and thairfor sa gret incresse and plentie of cornes amang the nobilitie of the cuntrey'.[1] Fertility and high agricultural revenues encouraged the building of a series of fine Renaissance houses along this coast – including Boyne, Cullen, Pitullie, and Pitsligo.[2] The Central Lowlands also prospered, and Leslie remarked that 'Gentimenis places and gret palices ma sal ye find in na place than in Fife.'[3] Landowners could augment their farming revenues by exploiting the coal-mines and engaging in salt-panning – Sir George Bruce of Culross owned no fewer than forty salt pans.[4]

The period 1560–1660 witnessed a major redistribution of land-holding in Scotland, as church lands passed into lay ownership.[5] Before the Reformation, about one-third of the total land area was held by the church, but already in the early years of the seventeenth century many monastic estates had been granted to lay commendators. It was during the reign of James VI that most of the abbey lands were transformed into secular estates. Before 1600, monastic holdings were often granted to the descendants of the original lay commendators, while after the court's move to England others were granted to favourite courtiers. The number of Scottish peers rose from 49 to 92 between 1585 and 1625.[6] The new peers, known as 'lords of erection', formed the core of King James's administration, especially after his move south, supporting the King with loyal service.[7] Ambitious and wealthy, these lords of erection were also eager to express their royal links in the style, heraldry and decoration of their buildings.[8] They were impatient to transform old abbey buildings into noble country seats that implied an ancient right to the lands. Sir John Scott of Scotstarvit wrote of Newbattle Abbey, for instance: 'And the father and son did so metamorphose the buildings that it cannot be known that ever it did belong to the church, by reasin of the fair new fabric and stately edifices built thereon … instead of the old monks has succeeded the deer.[9]

Not only did the feudal titles of the church estates pass into secular hands, but the smaller tenancies were also feued out to lay feuars during the sixteenth century, reaching a peak in the 1550s and 1560s. Only 3 per cent of these new feuars were members of the nobility, the majority being minor lairds and tenant farmers.[10] Those tenants who could afford the initial down-payment thereby acquired a hereditary right to their land, paying a fixed annual feu-duty from then on. It was becoming increasingly common to pay rents in cash rather than kind, and high inflation in the later part of the century favoured these new feuars.

The growth of the power of the laird class was one of the most significant social changes in the Scottish Renaissance. Although the rural middle class was more parochial in outlook than the burghers and merchants in the towns, there was social mobility between the two groups. Some wealthy merchants invested their profits in the land, especially around the larger towns, while some of the more educated rural gentry moved to the towns to enter the professions.[11] The growth in wealth and confidence of the laird class encouraged them to request representation as a separate 'estate' in the Scottish Parliament, a right that was finally granted in 1640.[12] In their buildings, the smaller lairds emulated the great houses of the lords of erection and the older nobility, if on a reduced scale, for they shared the desire to portray themselves as long-established landowners.[13]

In a period of rapid social change and growing prosperity, the personal display of wealth and prestige helped to define and perpetuate social and political hierarchies. Architectural identity was an eloquent clue to the position of the proprietor. Some landowners even exceeded their own resources in their zest for personal display. The twelfth Earl of Crawford, for instance, was confined to Edinburgh Castle at the request of his family for the last ten years of his life to restrain his extravagance,[14] while Sir David Lindsay, as we shall see, ruined himself creating his wonderful Renaissance garden at Edzell Castle (see Figure 3.41).

Together with the older aristocracy, the new peers were educated, urbane and well-travelled Europeans. William Lithgow wrote in 1628: 'Now as for the nobility and gentry of the kingdom, certainly, as they are generous, manly and full of courage; so are they courteous, discreet, learned scholars well read in the best histories, delicate linguists, the most part of them being brought up in France or Italy.'[15] This chapter will show, however, that their intellectual sophistication did not make them eager to imitate French or Italian culture *en bloc*; on the contrary, it brought with it a subtle awareness of national identity and tradition that was to be reflected in their buildings, however inventive and innovative the architectural solutions.

Noblewomen had little opportunity to travel. On account of the poor state of the country roads, which were only passable on foot or on horseback, women were often marooned on their rural estates for long periods, especially during their child-bearing years.[16] Printing made knowledge more portable, but even among the aristocracy, women's libraries were modest and mainly restricted to religious and domestic subjects.[17] Noblewomen could, nevertheless, become actively involved in managing the family estates and buildings: Jane Gordon, Countess of

Sutherland, for instance, built herself a house on the Sutherland coast from which to supervise her mining, salt-panning and fishing operations.[18]

In this age of display, the most conspicuous builders were also the most powerful. There were the members of the ancient aristocracy, such as the Earls of Huntly, Atholl, Argyll and Mar, whose wealth lay chiefly in the inherited possession of vast rural estates. There were the great industrial entrepreneurs such as Sir George Bruce of Culross. And there were those in positions of political authority, however short-lived, such as Regent Morton (see Figure 1.1) and Chancellor John Maitland of Thirlestane. After 1603, the King's favoured courtiers became the principal builders – these included Sir George Home, first Earl of Dunbar; Alexander Seton, first Earl of Dunfermline; and Sir Thomas Erskine, first Earl of Kellie. The innovations of men such as these permeated down through the land-owning classes by a combination of emulation, family rivalry and class identity. So fundamental and distinctive were the architectural changes in Scottish country house building in this period, that it seems essential to try to characterise the innovations in general terms, rather than to examine selected houses in turn. We shall begin, like any visitor, at the point of arrival.

THE APPROACH

In Renaissance Scotland, as we have seen, almost everyone travelled on horseback or on foot. Unblinkered by coach windows, horseborne travellers were able to enjoy the distant silhouettes of the great houses. Lower walls might be screened by trees or the contours of the hills, but the skyline profile of a far-away château served as a guiding beacon, its chimneys billowing with smoke and its windows glowing in the hours of darkness.

The term 'château' is used here deliberately to allude to the new typology of the country houses of the Scottish Renaissance. Although these were no longer castles in the medieval sense, castellated forms still carried the imagery of feudal power, chivalric honour and knightly virtue, across Europe as well as in Scotland.[19] Inigo Jones's design for Oberon's Palace for Ben Jonson's masque *The Fairy Prince* in 1611 – a soaring castle with crenellations and bartizans – shows the same sensibility to these knightly overtones.[20]

Popular histories of Scotland like to dwell on the unrest and bloodthirstiness of the country's past. Apart from natural causes and accidents, family feuds probably now presented the most serious danger to life,[21] but the numbers involved were tiny compared with the large numbers of lairds and merchants living peaceably and prosperously. Moreover, bloodfeuds could not be prevented by living in a fortress. Admittedly, gypsies, 'witches' and robbers were feared: William Forbes is supposed to have said of Corse Castle, completed in 1581, 'Please God I will build me such a house that thieves will need to knock at ere they enter.'[22] But such intruders as these could be deterred without full-scale military force.

After 1603, with the end of the threat of English invasion, the need for security became even less pressing. Indeed, Alexander Seton, first Earl of Dunfermline,

boasted in a Latin inscription on his garden wall at Pinkie House that he needed no
fortifications:

> D.O.M. For himself, for his descendants, for all civilized men, Alexander
> Seton, lover of mankind and civilization, founded, built and adorned his villa
> and gardens and these out-of-town buildings. Here is nothing warlike, even
> for defence; no ditch, no rampart. But for the kind welcome and hospitable
> entertainment of guests a fountain of pure water, lawns, ponds and aviaries.[23]

The castle style, though, still had its attractions for visual and semiological – even
patriotic – reasons. In 1632, Sir Robert Ker advised his son William, Earl of
Lothian, on the rebuilding of his house at Ancram: 'By any meanes do not teke
away the battlement, as some gave me counsale to do ... for that is the grace of
the house, and makes it look lyk a castle, and hence so nobleste, as the other would
make it looke lyke a peele.'[24] Although, as we shall see, English elements were
being incorporated, Scottish houses still looked recognisably distinct from their
English counterparts. In 1636, the English visitor Sir William Brereton remarked:
'By the way, I observed gentlemen's (here called lairds) houses built all castle-
wise.'[25] And this was still the impression formed by English visitors after the
Restoration. As late as 1689, Thomas Morer observed that:

> The houses of their quality are high and strong, and appear more like castles
> than houses, made of thick stone walls, with iron bars before their windows,
> suited to the necessity of those times they were built in, living then in a state
> of war and constant animosity between families.[26]

DEFENCE

In reality, the threat of invasion by a foreign power in seventeenth-century Scotland
was non-existent, even if civil unrest was to recur in mid-century. Moreover, the
introduction of gunpowder weaponry had made the fortification of the medieval castle
redundant. Tall buildings were not easily defended against full-scale military attack, for
they could be easily demolished by low-level bombardment. Had the threat been a
serious military one, 'castle-wise' houses would not have been built in the sixteenth
and seventeenth centuries. The tops of towers, turrets and bartizans – crenellated and
machicolated – were no longer used by defenders armed with boiling oil, molten lead
or crossbows. Roof-top rooms were more likely to be used by the owner and his
guests for enjoying the view than to house garrisons of defenders (see Figure 3.1).

Since life was now more stable, firearms aimed horizontally by guards at the
doorway offered simpler, more effective security. Gunloops were often exotically
shaped, as if to advertise their decorative, rather than functional, role: pretty
examples can be seen at Tolquhon, Carnousie and Corse. None the less, penetration
was not easy for the casual intruder. A heavy iron yett would protect the entrance,
usually side-hung inside the main door (several can still be seen, for example at
Elcho and Craigievar). At Balvenie, a hefty double yett blocked the entrance pend
into the courtyard (see Figure 3.2). Windows at ground-floor level were normally

FIGURE 3.1 (*upper*)   Claypotts Castle, Angus, 1569–88.
FIGURE 3.2 (*lower*)   Balvenie Castle, Banffshire, Atholl Lodging, 1547–57.

small and few in number. Even on the first floor, the larger windows would be protected by hefty iron grilles (see Figure 3.25). As the Yorkshireman Thomas Kirke wrote in 1679, 'they look more like prisons than houses of reception'.[27]

The most impregnable houses of all were the cliff-top palaces built on promontories into the sea, linked to the mainland only by narrow causeways. There is a chain of such castles along the east coast: Dunottar (see Figure 3.3), Slains, Findlater and Girnigoe are the most impressive examples. But evidence suggests that these castles were by this time appreciated as much for their dramatic settings as for security. Indeed, the Ogilvies of Deskford abandoned Findlater Castle when they built a new house, more accessibly sited, at nearby Cullen in 1600.

As the seventeenth century progressed, the enthusiasm for traditional stronghold architecture gradually waned. Some new houses made no attempt to appear castle-like. The 1685 inventory of the House of the Binns (see Figure 3.4) near Linlithgow suggests an almost modern security system: 'all the doors within & without the house have pass locks on them which answear to open with the pass kies. And all the presses & studies within the house answer to the litle pass kie.'[28] In addition, the windows were protected by shutters and 'iron cruiks and bands' and 'stenchelled & tirlied' (fastened), but the house had no military trappings. Significantly, its early seventeenth-century builder, Thomas Dalyell, had been a successful butter merchant who had married the daughter of the Master of the Rolls and followed the King to London. He had no ancient ties to the land and was eager to show off his fashionable, Anglicised taste.

After the Restoration, English visitors began to notice that the newer houses looked more familiar. Thomas Kirke remarked in 1679, 'Some few houses there are of late erection, that are built in a better form, with good walks and gardens about them.'[29] Similarly, in 1689 Thomas Morer wrote, 'Now they begin to have better buildings, and to be very modish, both in the fabrick and the furniture of their dwellings.'[30] William Bruce at Balcaskie, Thirlestane and Holyrood was to show brilliantly how old and new could be reconciled, but some house-owners were less happy with the 'castle-wise' legacy. At Glamis, for example (see Figure 3.23), Patrick, third Earl of Strathmore, declared that 'there is no man more against these old fashions of tours and castles than I am'.[31] His judicious modernisations, begun in 1669, were sensitive and effective, however. Defoe was rapturous about Glamis: 'when you see it at a distance it is so full of turrets and lofty buildings, spires and towers, some plain, others shining with gilded tops, that it looks not like a town, but a city ...'[32]

ROOF-TOP DISPLAY

How could the great landowner of the late sixteenth and early seventeenth centuries express his power and domination architecturally, across the fields, forests and moors of his estates? Having lost their defensive function, roof-top towers could become more flamboyant. Bartizans projected daringly from the wall-head, supported on skilfully carved corbels. Gargoyles in the form of cannons, as at Craigievar and Castle Fraser (see Figures 3.27 and 3.5), alluded to their extinct military use.

FIGURE 3.3 (*upper*)   Dunottar Castle, Kincardineshire, from the air.
FIGURE 3.4 (*lower*)   The House of the Binns, West Lothian, view from the south, 1621–30, remodelled in the castellated style in the early nineteenth century.

Spacious roof-top terraces on top of square or round towers, such as those at Castle Fraser and Craigston (see Figures 3.5 and 6.1), were graced with elegant balustrades instead of crenellations. Dormers in the roofspace, or half-dormers thrust up through the eavesline, were decorated with intricately carved classical pediments, rich in allusions to the status of the family (see Figure 3.7). As in the period before 1560, roof-top ornament could be used to create unity between older structures and their new additions.[33] After 1600, the more daring masons used broken pediments, and the dormers were surmounted by finials and obelisks. Carved decoration was often based on the coats of arms or initials of the owner and his wife (see Figure 3.18), or on patriotic motifs such as thistles, fleurs-de-lis and, after 1603, the Tudor rose. Triangular gables were more popular for dormers than segmental pediments because they could be stretched upwards into prominent equilateral triangles (see Figure 3.30), sometimes flanked by spiky finials or urns. Triangular and segmental pediments could even be combined one inside the other, as in the eavesline dormers at Newark Castle, dated 1597 (see Figure 3.6).[34] Whereas the castellated language attested to the historic roots of the family, whether real or mythical, the modernity of the building would also be proudly advertised by placing the date on a dormerhead or over a doorway.

Wall-head sundials, functionally useful and scientifically sophisticated, were also dated and decorated. Turrets might be roofed with French-style cones or Germanic ogee domes, some covered, mermaid-like, in fish-scale slates (see Figure 3.7). There were open roof-top lanterns, as at Castle Fraser and Glamis (see Figure 3.23); and every dome or tower would be topped by a finial, a flag or a weathercock. Since stone-carving was expensive, dressed stone was placed where it was most conspicuous. Thus at Craigston, the parapet at the top of the façade is decorated with richly sculpted panels (see Figure 6.2); and at Huntly, the top storey, finished in smooth ashlar, proudly bears the names of the Marquis of Huntly and his wife Henrietta Stewart in outsized Roman letters (see Figure 3.8).

The Castles of Mar were characterised by their ornate corbels meandering unpredictably around the base of the top storey, as if to delineate the start of all the fun (see Figures 3.5, 3.16 and 3.27). By contrast, smokestacks were robustly plain and rectangular, or occasionally cylindrical, as at Glamis (see Figure 3.23). Along the garden front at Pinkie, a row of outsized, plain, solid chimneys is unapologetically lined up, belying the sophistication of the interior of Alexander Seton's *villa suburbana* (see Figure 3.9). From the eaves of Hamilton Palace, built in the 1590s, rose four outsized chimney stacks crowned with alternating triangular and segmental pediments (see Figure 3.10). At Grangepans near Bo'ness (a house built for John Hamilton in 1564 and now sadly demolished), the gable-head chimneys were aligned diagonally – three on each of the end gables and one on the central stairtower. William Wallace at Winton House introduced a more flamboyant type of chimney, with tall, slender stacks arranged in groups and richly carved, (see Figure 3.9), but these were little imitated in the wind and rain of the Scottish climate.

Two factors have tended to blur our sense of the Scottish Renaissance's fascination with skyline ornament. First of all, many of the great houses have since

FIGURE 3.5 (*above*)   Castle Fraser,
Aberdeenshire, detail of the north
front, signed and dated '1617 I Bel.'
FIGURE 3.6 (*left*)   Newark Castle,
Port Glasgow, the east wing, doorway
dated 1597. The entrance arch is off
the picture to the left.

FIGURE 3.7   Winton House, East Lothian, remodelled by William Wallace, 1620–7.

fallen into ruin; and with the loss of the roof, dormers and bartizans have been truncated or even disappeared. At Huntly, for instance, an attic storey of spiky dormers, visible in Nattes' drawing of 1799, has since completely vanished (see Figure 3.8). Secondly, the removal of harling from the walls of these great houses has reduced the prominence of the dressed stone. It is abundantly clear from many old water-colours and engravings that random rubble was not left unprotected in a sixteenth- or seventeenth-century house of any stature. It was the Victorian conception of the rugged baronial that led to the stripping of many of the walls of Renaissance houses, whether ruined or inhabited. Only in Deeside, where the attractive muted peach colour of the local harling has remained popular, have many châteaux preserved the characteristic juxtaposition of fine dressed stone and fleecy textured rendered walls (see Figure 3.16).

FIGURE 3.8   Huntly Castle ('The House of Strathbogie'), the south front, the top storey originally dated 1602.

GEOMETRY AND FORM

This was not yet the age of the formal, straight, tree-lined avenue which controlled the axis of the visitor's arrival and framed his view. Renaissance country houses could often be approached – or at least glimpsed – from many different angles, and their designs wilfully exploited the three-dimensional geometry. There were perplexingly unexpected juxtapositions of shapes: square cap-houses corbelled out from round towers (see Figure 3.1), cylindrical bartizans perched on wall-head corners (see Figures 3.16 and 3.27), towers radiating out at intriguing angles, and crow-stepped gables, some wilful in their asymmetry, some perversely colliding with roof-top turrets (see Figure 3.26). The element of surprise was part of the artistry, like an elusive Elizabethan 'device'; the classical desire for symmetry did not become a pervasive design principle in Scotland until after the Restoration.

Although the verticality of the Scottish Renaissance country house was inherited from the fortified medieval castle, it was often retained deliberately for reasons of display rather than out of a conservative fear of innovation. As we shall see, the emphasis in interior planning was moving towards a more horizontal arrangement of rooms, but this was only reluctantly expressed externally. There were some notable experiments in horizontality: Regent Morton's Aberdour Castle in Fife spread out in elongated fashion along the upper slope of his terraced gardens, with a gallery from which to enjoy the views across the Firth of Forth. The old Palace of Scone was a mere two storeys high, with little roof-top interest apart from its

FIGURE 3.9 (*upper*)   Pinkie House, Musselburgh, Midlothian, the garden front, *c.*1607–22.
FIGURE 3.10 (*lower*)   Hamilton Palace, Lanarkshire, the entrance front, drawn by Isaac Miller, *c.*1677.

gabled centre-piece and framing gables at either end, (see Figure 3.11). In Orkney and Shetland, only the very grandest houses were tall because of the windy climate; in the Northern Isles, the ordinary manor houses were remarkably prophetic of the Scottish mainland's eighteenth-century laird's house, with their gable-ended monopitch roofs, sometimes even supported by hefty buttresses, as at the Old Haa of Burravoe in Shetland, (see Figure 3.12). But on the mainland there was a reluctance to enjoy horizontality in country houses. John Mylne's design for Lord Somerville's house at the Drum, south of Edinburgh, built in 1584–5, was criticised because its 'outward forme' was not 'modish, being built all in length in forme of a church'.[35]

PLAN

A century ago, in their magisterial five-volume study, *The Castellated and Domestic Architecture of Scotland*, MacGibbon and Ross classified Scotland's Renaissance houses (those of their so-called 'Fourth Period') according to different plan types, ranging from the simple tower-house or keep, through the L-plan and Z-plan to the courtyard plan and various anomalous layouts.[36] Although their analysis may have overemphasised the defensive factors behind the choice of plan, the terminology remains useful. Moreover, the variety contained in these categories, as well as the large number of anomalies that defied classification, belie Sir John Summerson's dismissive remark that the range of design in Scottish houses of the period was narrow.[37]

The most magnificent of the Renaissance the châteaux were the courtyard palaces: but Seton and Hamilton Palaces have disappeared, and Boyne, Pitsligo and Balvenie now lie in ruins. Courtyard plans had royal associations in Scotland, Linlithgow Palace being the most conspicuous example (see Figure 2.17). (Holyrood Palace had inherited the courtyard plan from its monastic function (see Figure 2.15)). Even simple medieval tower-houses had often had walled enclosures attached, with ancillary buildings such as bakehouses, brewhouses and stables around them. It was the feat of the Renaissance to incorporate old and new structures into a coherent, more organised form. Foreign treatises, Serlio's in particular, published courtyard plans with evident royal associations, such as that of the palace of Poggio Reale in Naples.[38] Foreign travel, too, exposed patrons to models to be emulated. Almost every prominent Renaissance *Schloss* in Germany, for example, had a quadrangular courtyard plan with corner towers.[39] Some Scottish houses consciously attempted to introduce foreign innovation in their planning: a little-known example is the tantalisingly unfinished Barnes Castle, set on a ridge amid the fertile lowlands of East Lothian, and begun for a member of the Seton family who had been a courtier to Philip II of Spain.[40] A family chronicle records that Sir John Seton of Barnes became a gentleman of Philip II's chamber and master of the household, in which office he 'carried the golden key at his syde, in a blew ribbing'.[41] With its projecting square corner towers, the plan evoked the Spanish royal palace at the Alcazar in Toledo, rebuilt in 1535 and again remodelled between

FIGURE 3.11 (*upper*)   Scone Palace, Perthshire, sixteenth century, engraving of 1775, before the remodelling of 1802.

FIGURE 3.12 (*lower*)   Old Haa of Brough, Burravoe, Yell, Shetland, archway dated 1672, shown before the recent restoration.

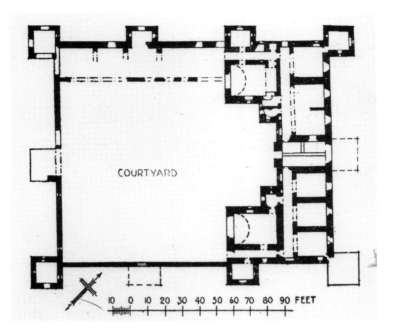

COURTYARD

10 0 10 20 30 40 50 60 70 80 90 FEET

FIGURE 3.13   Barnes Castle, East Lothian, begun before 1594, plan.

1543 and 1570.[42] Sadly, John Barnes died in 1594, leaving his Spanish-style dwelling unfinished (see Figure 3.13).

Even when four sides of a courtyard were not built up, the dramatic possibilities of the entrance pend were fully exploited. The house itself might comprise one, two or three wings of the courtyard, the other sides being surrounded by high walls.[43] The archway through the barmkin wall framed the approach, often precisely outlining the doorway to the house itself, demarcated by its heraldic display in one or more carved stone panels above, as at Newark (see Figure 3.6). Over the outer archway would be another heraldic panel, or even – as at Earlshall and the Bishop's Palace, Orkney – a corbelled oriel. In some courtyard palaces, such as Crichton, the entrance pend might even pass beneath the great hall, a bold arrangement anticipated by the original entrance to Linlithgow Palace. Balvenie, following the royal precedent of Holyrood, was entered through an archway beneath the main state apartment (see Figure 3.2). Some entrances, such as that of Rowallan – inspired by a third royal palace, namely Falkland – consisted of a French-style towered gatehouse.[44] Others, Tolquhon for instance, were approached through gatehouses on the wing facing the main living areas, in the manner of English Tudor country houses. At Seton Palace, the twin-towered entrance was placed on the diagonal, like the Château de Chaumont in the Loire (see Figure 3.14).

SYMMETRY

It is a commonplace that the European Renaissance required buildings to be symmetrical, whether in plan or elevation. In practice, even in Italy, consistently

FIGURE 3.14   Seton Palace, from an engraving in Grose's *Antiquities of Scotland*, vol. I,
described as 'having been drawn a great many years ago'.

symmetrical internal planning was rare in domestic buildings before the time of
Palladio, except perhaps in Venice where a degree of symmetry was a structural
necessity. In England, as Robert Smythson's architecture showed, the traditional
medieval arrangement of the hall entered from the side of the screens passage made
symmetry difficult, unless the hall were aligned perpendicularly to the main
entrance, the solution adopted at Hardwick Hall.[45]

Traditional Scottish tower-house plans, too, were ill-adapted to symmetry. In
the typical L-plan house, the great hall block was much larger than the jamb, and
only by making the two wings of equal size and providing an entrance through an
angle turret between could symmetry be achieved. The outstandingly successful
showpiece is, of course, Glamis, although centuries of modification were needed
to reach this point (see Figure 3.15).[46]

A Z-plan house only has symmetry if both corner turrets are of identical size
and shape, and even then the axis lies inconveniently through the diagonal: Claypotts
(see Figure 3.1), Notland and Glenbuchat all display approximately matching corner
towers. A more regular approach could be created by forming a French-style deep
basse-cour in front, masking the asymmetry of the Z-plan behind. This was the
solution adopted at Castle Fraser, where the forecourt was erected between 1592
and 1618. The master mason John Bel proudly signed the great roofline coat of
arms, dated 1617, which forms the climax of the entrance vista, (see Figure 3.5).

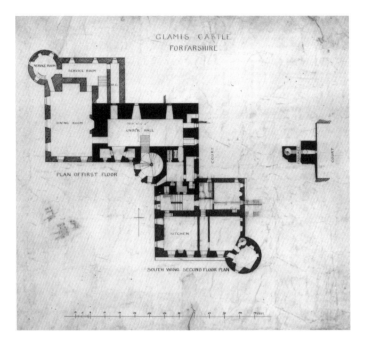

FIGURE 3.15   Glamis Castle, Angus, plan.

But even at Castle Fraser, the entrance remained in its traditional place, tucked into the foot of the right-hand 'Michael Tower'.

As we saw in Chapter Two, the new wings of the royal palaces had symmetrical façades with central stairtowers. This set a precedent which only very gradually filtered down the social scale. The central stairtower with apartments evenly distributed on either side offered the potential for a more regular building type, but it is intriguing to see how often in Scotland the symmetry was wilfully denied. At Lamb's House at Leith (see Figures 4.57 and 4.58) and Saughton House at Stenhouse – both of which had central stairtowers – the façade designs exploit the unexpected play of irregular shapes and lopsided gables, as we shall see in Chapter Four.

It was the U-plan, or double L-plan, which was most easily regularised, but even the most emphatic symmetry in plan could be teasingly thwarted in elevation. A spectacular example is Castle Stewart near Inverness, built in about 1625, where one of the two towers has a roof-top terrace with an ogee-ribbed lantern at one corner, while the other tower is gabled and clutched by bartizans.

Two of the earliest attempts at elevational symmetry were at Fyvie and Craigston. Fyvie was remodelled for Alexander Seton, first Earl of Dunfermline, who bought the estate in 1596 (see Figure 3.16). His architect may have been none other than the royal master of works, William Schaw. Only the south front is symmetrical, but it has a dramatic central focus in the form of a twin-towered gatehouse oversailed by a great roof-top archway. This monumental triumphal arch must have

FIGURE 3.16   Fyvie Castle, Aberdeenshire, the south front, remodelled for Alexander Seton,
Lord Fyvie, later first Earl of Dunfermline, from *c.*1598, by William Schaw?

been admired by John Urquhart who soon afterwards adopted this theme for the
centre-piece of his castle at Craigston, built in 1604–7 (see Figure 6.2).

The three-dimensional massiveness of Fyvie and Craigston was less appropriate
in a suburban context. In 1622, the royal master of works James Murray built
himself a house at Baberton, near Edinburgh, in a symmetrical double L-plan and
decorated with courtly buckle quoins and carved pediments, with the flanking
towers topped by ogee domes. The two side wings of Pitreavie in Fife, built in
about 1630, were topped by matching Dutch-style curvilinear gables. And at the
Binns (as we shall see, later in this chapter) the symmetrical U-plan (see Figure
3.4) was made delightfully meaningful by balancing the men's and women's service
wings on either side of the *basse-cour*. In short, we can see that consistent symmetry
was not always practical, and only rarely attempted, but it was often disregarded
in an artful, almost self-consciously mannerist way, to allow dramatic three-
dimensional massing, multiple axes and contrived geometries.

ENTRY

The principal doorway of a Scottish Renaissance house was not a large one (a
sensible security precaution), but it was given prominence by the frame and usually
by at least one heraldic panel above. Door frames were of smooth-cut masonry,
typically with robust roll mouldings, emerging crisply from what was normally a
rendered wall surface. Even on the plainest doorway, the lintel might carry an
inscription or moralising motto.

The most ostentatious heraldic display of all is to be found over the entrance to

FIGURE 3.17   Huntly Castle ('the House of Strathbogie'), heraldic frontispiece over entrance portal, dated 1602.

Huntly Castle (see Figure 3.17). The doorway, dated 1602, is set at the foot of a cylindrical stairtower, with armorial panels piled up the face of the tower. The design follows a logical hierarchical order. Over the doorway are the arms of the first Marquis of Huntly and his wife. In the level above, we find the royal arms of Scotland and Denmark, with the initials of King James and Queen Anne (the Queen was a close friend of the Marchioness). The top tiers of this 'frontispiece' are filled with Catholic religious imagery (later defaced by a zealous Covenanter). Finally, the triumphant figure of St Michael overcoming Satan, again since mutilated, stands on the apex of the crowning ogee arch.

As a rule, the door frames themselves were rather plain, in contrast to the flamboyant ornament at roof level, but there are some notable exceptions. At Newark Castle, the main doorway, dated 1598, has a broken pediment with a triple cornice, supported on fluted pilasters. From the gap at the apex of the pediment rises a finial topped by a fleur-de-lis (see Figure 3.6). Later variants on

FIGURE 3.18   Ochiltree Castle, West Lothian, the entrance portal, *c*.1610. From a photo of
c.1892.

this theme can be seen at Northfield House (the doorway is dated 1611), with its
finials at either end of the pediment as well as in the centre, and at Auchans in
Ayrshire, where a broken segmental pediment was surmounted by three obelisks
in relief.[47] The entrance to the Earl's Palace at Kirkwall is flanked by monumental,
fluted half-columns and topped by a richly carved lintel supporting tiers of heraldic
panels framed by swelling baroque-style balusters. Perhaps the oddest doorway in
a Scottish Renaissance laird's house was the porch at Ochiltree Castle. Over the
porch, two pediments stood side by side, with the initials and coat-of-arms of the
owner on one side and those of his wife on the other, while a third, plain pediment,
slightly recessed, peered out through the gap in the middle (see Figure 3.18).
   The doors themselves were usually solid oak boards, but their surfaces were
heavily studded and embellished with large iron hinges. Occasionally, the door
itself might be richly carved: a fine example from Terregles House in Dumfriesshire,
dated 1601, survives at Traquair.

Typically in Renaissance Scotland, the main door of a country house was at the foot of the main staircase. Thus, reception formalities would be performed upstairs in the great hall, if not outside the building. During the century 1560–1660, however, we begin to notice experiments in alternative entry layouts. There were two main innovations. First, in Morayshire and the surrounding areas, the Conns of Auchrie began to introduce formal entrance halls. At Delgaty, Towie Barclay and Gight, for instance, the doorway opens into a small vestibule with a Gothic ribbed vault. The vaulted ceiling would probably have been painted and gilded to create a rich effect. From the hall, one entered a corridor, over 10 feet long at both Towie Barclay and Gight, which in turn led to the foot of the great stair. The second innovation, significantly after 1603, under the impact of English practice, was to place a main reception room, known as a 'Laigh [low] Hall', on the ground floor. Conspicuous examples of this solution are the House of the Binns, near Linlithgow, and the Argyll Lodging in Stirling.[48] Of course, we should not forget that the west wing of Holyrood Palace had had a 'Laigh Hall' since the 1530s, but this was raised on a low basement and entered through the central pend, not directly into the hall. More significantly, the principal apartments in the palace block at Stirling were on the ground floor.

GROUND-FLOOR ACCOMMODATION

Except in houses with laigh halls, the ground floor was principally a service area. Here one would find the kitchen, the wine cellar, the store-rooms for fuel and provisions, and only occasionally in these more tranquil days a prison. As a rule, the ground-floor rooms were stone-vaulted, although a few lairds' houses, such as Fountainhall in East Lothian (see Figure 3.19), had wooden-roofed ground floors. Since the maximum span of a stone barrel vault was around 20 feet, this became the traditional limit to the width of a residential block. During the Renaissance, experiments were made to break out of this formula by adding a vaulted corridor alongside the row of vaulted service rooms (see Figure 3.20). The inspiration for this solution may have been the royal palaces. At Linlithgow, Falkland and probably Holyrood, inner skins with vaulted corridors surmounted by galleries had been added in the first half of the sixteenth century. The practical advantages of a ground-floor corridor were obvious: providing direct access to each vaulted chamber without having to pass through the kitchen or store-rooms. Furthermore, the addition of the lower corridor allowed the broadening of the reception rooms above, though the length of available timbers to span the ceilings of the upstairs rooms was still a constraint.

Perhaps the most sophisticated corridor plan was that of Drochil Castle in Peeblesshire, a huge Renaissance palace begun by Regent Morton (see Figure 1.1) and probably still unfinished when Morton was executed in 1581 for his supposed part in the murder of Darnley (see Figure 3.21). This castle has an ostensibly Z-plan with round towers at diagonally opposite corners, but the main block is over 50 feet wide with two parallel ranges of vaulted rooms, separated by a broad central passage with an entrance at either end. The same arrangement is repeated

FIGURE 3.19   Fountainhall, East Lothian, the garden front.

on the first floor, with the great hall along one side of the central corridor, and a row of three separate rooms on the other.

In the great Scottish houses of the late sixteenth and early seventeenth centuries, the vaulted ground-floor service rooms now seem dark, damp and depressing, especially in ruined castles; but with the walls plastered and whitewashed, and the hearths and lamps blazing, they would have been much more cheerful. The typical kitchen had a huge vaulted fireplace across one end of the room. In most cases, baking was done in the kitchen, in a baking oven at the side of the main hearth, but the largest houses had a separate bakehouse, and often a brewhouse as well. Some kitchens still preserve their stone sinks with wastepipes.

In a few cases, living accommodation was provided on the ground floor. A pioneering example can be found in the lodging of the fourth Earl of Atholl at Balvenie, where a set of chambers on the ground floor extends the diagonal of the courtyard into the very corner of the angle turret (see Figure 3.22). These four rooms are well lit, and each one has a fireplace and a garderobe. The approach from the courtyard is through a stately door at the foot of the inner corner tower, skilfully exploiting the dramatic possibilities of the diagonal vistas. These rooms must have been used by friends or very privileged servants of the Earl. A similarly dignified ground-floor steward's room can be seen on the ground floor of nearby Huntly Castle, but since the fourth Earl of Atholl married the daughter of the fourth Earl of Huntly the connection is not surprising.

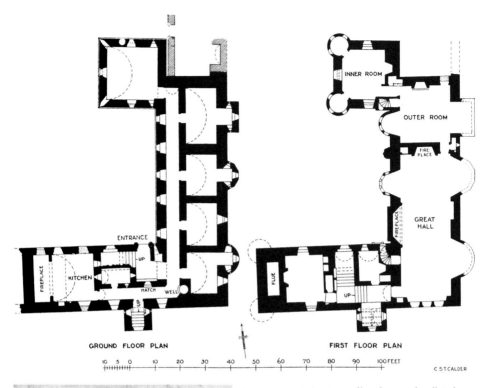

GROUND FLOOR PLAN   FIRST FLOOR PLAN

C S.T.CALDER

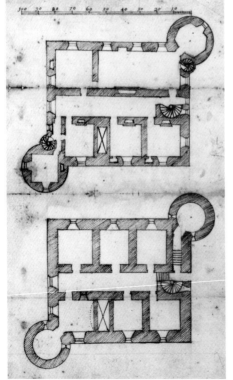

FIGURE 3.20 (*above*)   Earl's Palace, Kirkwall,Orkney, 1606, the ground- and first-floor plans.
FIGURE 3.21 (*left*)   Drochil Castle, Peeblesshire, the first-floor (above) and ground-floor plans drawn in 1663.

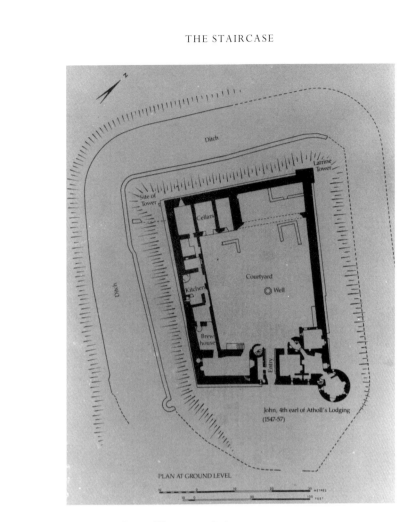

FIGURE 3.22   Balvenie Castle, Banffshire, ground-plan.

Finally, we should remember the wings of lodgings added to the most palatial Scottish houses, where whole households of visitors could be accommodated. This was an English practice dating back to Tudor times, but in Scotland Holyrood Palace was already provided with wings of lodgings. At Dunottar Castle, beside the Earl Marischal's quarters at the seaward end, a range of ground-floor lodgings, surmounted by a long gallery, forms the west side of the courtyard, looking out on to the bowling green behind (see Figure 3.3).

THE STAIRCASE

Many medieval Scottish castles had been entered by external wooden staircases to the first floor, easily removable in time of attack. Those with ground-floor entrances had tightly twisting, narrow turnpike stairs, preferably tucked into a re-entrant angle where they could be defended from the wings on either side. How would the design of the staircase respond to the increasing stability and ceremonial of the

FIGURE 3.23   Glamis Castle, Angus, the entrance front.

Renaissance age? Wooden ladders outside the building were hardly decorous, and no one could make a grand entry from a defensive turnpike stair.

The most obvious result of this new security was that staircases became wider. Two or more people could now ascend side-by-side, or pass each other in opposite directions. Palladio recommended a minimum of 4 feet for the width of a staircase,[49] but Scotland did not need a treatise to provide this common-sense advice. The staircase was becoming a focus for display – the wider, the higher, the better lit and the more ornate the better. In houses of any importance, the principal staircase was now invariably of stone.

The simplest way of modernising the traditional formula was to keep the stair in the re-entrant angle, rising to the top of the building, but to increase its size. Braemar Castle (1628) is a well-known example, although the top of the stairtower has lost its original French-style, conical roof. Its builder, the Earl of Mar, almost betrayed the simplicity of the solution when he described it as 'A great body of a house, a jam and a staircase.'[50] An even more surprising updating of medieval practice is seen in Delgaty Castle, erected in the 1570s, probably by the local family of masons, the Conns of Auchrie. Here, the turnpike staircase is indeed broad and spacious, yet it is a mural stair, contained within the mass of the masonry of the great tower.

One of the most impressive variations on the traditional formula is the grand turnpike stair at Glamis, completed in 1606 (see Figures 3.15 and 3.23). This spacious staircase has a hollow newel in the centre, with an opening on every level. According to Billings this was originally used for drawing water to the upper floors.[51] Harry Gordon Slade has pointed out that Lord Glamis had visited the

FIGURE 3.24   Fyvie Castle, Aberdeenshire, the great staircase, from Billings, *Baronial and Ecclesiastical Antiquities*, vol. II.

Continent just before the stairtower was erected, and it is surely to Europe that we should look for the inspiration for this new enthusiasm for imposing, ceremonial staircases.[52] MacGibbon and Ross pertinently compared the magnificent stone staircase at Fyvie Castle, completed in 1603 (see Figure 3.24), with that of the Château de Chaumont on the Loire, yet emphasising its 'palpably Scottish' character.[53] Its sequence of ascending ceiling arches supported on delicate corbels and the richly carved decoration of the central newel are indeed impressive, reaching a climax at the summit where the ceiling is vaulted in a star pattern. Nor should one forget the impact of sheer size, each step being almost 9 feet wide. The form is also ingenious, for the walls of the staircase are rectangular inside as well as outside. This staircase was built for Alexander Seton, Earl of Dunfermline, and was most probably designed by the royal master of works William Schaw. A great stone stair of comparable splendour can be seen at Notland Castle on the island of Westray in Orkney.

Scalloway Castle

FIGURE 3.25   Scalloway Castle, Shetland, 1600. Reconstruction sketch by William Dodd, 1971.

   The most characteristic staircase arrangement in a Scottish Renaissance house was more complex than any of those just mentioned. More typical than a single principal stair serving every floor was a broad, spacious ascent to first-floor level only. Two fine examples were built for the Forbes family at Lickleyhead (1629) and Pitsligo (where the stairtower is dated 1603),[54] both of them spiral staircases with gentle gradients and high vaulted ceilings. In such an arrangement, the space over the staircase hall would be occupied by living areas, although some of the earliest experiments were awkward – at Glenbuchat, for example, the staircase cuts into one of the first-floor rooms, leaving a rudimentary bedroom shaped like a bitten biscuit.

   Gradually, meanwhile, the idea began to take root that undefended staircases could be straight rather than spiral.[55] Single straight flights to the first floor, as if the medieval straight mural stair had burst out of the confines of the wall thickness, can be seen at Craigievar (see Figure 3.27), Craigston (see Figure 6.3) and Ochiltree, to name but a few. These examples are still fairly narrow and steep, but with a scale-and-platt stair (short flights with landings), straight stairs could be far more impressive. The finest of this type are the truly regal ceremonial staircases built by the notorious Earl Patrick Stewart, first at Scalloway Castle in Shetland (1600) (see Figure 3.25), and then in his palace at Kirkwall in Orkney (1607), under the direction of his master of works Andrew Crawford (see Figure 3.20). Scale-and-platt stairs could also be used to fill up a space between two wings of different ages, giving access to each and thus obscuring problems caused by different floor levels. This solution was adopted at Glamis in the sixteenth century, before the erection of the great turnpike (see Figure 3.15).

The logical consequence of the introduction of the scale-and-platt stair was to vaunt it shamelessly by carrying the ascent to the roofline, or even above, and topping it with an ostentatious classical balustrade. The first experiment was probably the square tower, designed by William Aytoun – Wallace's successor as master mason to Heriot's Hospital – at Innes House in Morayshire, built between 1640 and 1653, and imitated at Leslie Castle in Aberdeenshire in 1661.

Why did the main staircase so often stop at first-floor level in Renaissance Scotland? The answer can only be surmised, but it is related to the disposition of public and private spaces within. Usually, the main stair led directly to the great hall, the main reception room of the house, to which any visitor who was admitted had access. This was probably also the route for bringing food from the kitchen on the ground floor. Feasts were carried upstairs with glittering pageantry by liveried servants accompanied by musical fanfares. Smaller access stairs to the kitchens or wine-cellars were not uncommon; but although these might have been adequate for carrying down the remains of the meal, they were not suited to large-scale hospitality.

Beyond the great hall, rooms became increasingly private. From the hall, the typical arrangement provided a series of small spiral staircases giving access to private chambers or apartments on the upper floors, the number of subsidiary staircases obviously dependent on the size of the building and the complexity of the plan. A remarkably subtle arrangement can be seen at Elcho, near Perth (see Figure 3.26). These secondary stairs preserved the legacy of the medieval plan, in which internal ascent only began at first-floor level, but now that walls were thinner and less impregnable, turnpikes could no longer be contained within the wall thickness. Instead, they were pushed out centrifugally beyond the plane of the main structural walls. This three-dimensional planning is one of the most fascinating aspects of Scottish Renaissance house designs. A building such as Craigievar is difficult to envisage from conventional plans and sections, and can only have been designed using models in the round (see Figure 3.27). The secondary staircases provided the excuse for dramatic embellishment to the outside of the building, precariously projecting on ornately carved corbels, as at Fordyce (and sometimes even perversely reaching down almost to ground level, as at Ferniehurst). Charles McKean's choice of the phrase 'expressed staircases' is aptly ambiguous![56] At roof-

FIGURE 3.26 (*above*)   Elcho Castle,
Perthshire, late sixteenth century, from
Billings, *Baronial and Ecclesiastical
Antiquities*, vol. II.
FIGURE 3.27 (*left*)   Craigievar Castle,
Aberdeenshire, sketch made in 1948
before the modern reharling.

FIGURE 3.28 Newark Castle, Port Glasgow, the north facade from River Clyde.

top level, the stairtowers offered further scope for display in the massing and detailing of their turrets.

There is one further development in staircase design in the Scottish Renaissance which deserves comment because of its royal associations. This was the placing of a staircase tower in the centre of a long façade, a solution we have already seen in the royal palace blocks at Dunfermline, Edinburgh Castle and Linlithgow. Sometimes, these were stairs from first floor upwards only, for example at Newark Castle (see Figure 3.28), but they were often extended down to the ground floor, as at Fountainhall (see Figure 3.19), Grandtully and Corse Castle. In all of these cases, the main entrance is on the other side, and it is the garden front (or the river front at Newark) that is rendered symmetrical by the addition of a central tower. At Tolquhon Castle, the main residential block facing the gatehouse has a projecting central tower, containing a staircase from first-floor level upwards. There is also an intriguing series of houses with a central staircase on the entrance front, classified by MacGibbon and Ross as T-plan houses – Farnell in Forfarshire (mid-sixteenth century), Grangepans near Bo'ness (1564) and Luffness in East Lothian (1584) are rural examples, while Lamb's House in Leith (see Figures 4.57 and 4.58) and Stenhouse in Edinburgh adopt the same arrangement. The virtue of the central stair in houses such as these was not so much a desire for symmetry as the flexibility offered by access to two different rooms at each landing. Less pretentious, but uncannily prophetic of the eighteenth century laird's house, are the few Renaissance houses in which a single straight flight runs straight up through the middle of the main block of the house from a central doorway. This arrangement was to be found at Duntarvie in West Lothian, and Fernielee in Selkirkshire, both now ruined.

THE GREAT HALL

Still the hub of the family's hospitality, the great hall was the scene of lavish entertainment, although some English visitors were shocked to find bowlfuls of steaming porridge on the tables. In 1598, Fynes Moryson reported: 'Myself was at a Knight's House, who had many servants to attend him, that brought in his meate with their heads covered with blew caps, the Table being more than halfe furnished with great platters of porredge, each having a little peece of sodden meate.'[57] Moryson was even more surprised to see that the servants then sat down with the rest of the company, and relieved to discover that the porridge was for them! The top table was given a stew of chicken with prunes instead. In the houses of the nobility, meat, fish, game and good wine were plentiful. In the year 1590, the household of Duncan Campbell of Glenorchy consumed 90 beeves (fed oxen), 20 swine, 200 sheep, 424 salmon and 15,000 herrings, as well as large quantities of butter and cheese.[58] The rent in kind paid to the Marquis of Huntly in 1660 included 167 cattle for slaughter, 483 sheep, 316 lambs, 167 young pigs, 14 swine, 1,389 capons, 272 geese, 3,231 poultry, 700 chickens and 5,284 eggs.[59] On his visit to Scotland in 1618, John Taylor, the 'Water Poet', was struck by the hospitality he encountered there. He remarked that a typical country landowner, though dressed in homespun clothes:

> keepes and maintaines thirty, forty, fifty servants, or perhaps more, every day releeving three or four score poor people at his gate: and besides all this, can give noble entertainement for foure or five days together, to five or six Earles and Lords, besides Knights, Gentlemen, and their followers, if they bee three or foure hundred men and horse of them; where they shall not only feede but feast, and not feast but banket.[60]

Every house from the largest palace to the smallest laird's house had a great hall. In older houses that were converted or extended in this period, the medieval hall usually continued to serve as the main ceremonial reception room, although occasionally – at Crichton for instance – the old hall seems to have been abandoned in favour of the newer state rooms. The size of the hall could vary enormously, from the grand scale of the great hall at Huntly (43 feet long, 29 feet wide and 16 feet high) or the 55-foot long dining hall of the palace block at Dunottar Castle, to the more domestic scale of the numerous laird's houses that surrounded Edinburgh, such as Roseburn House (1582) where the hall is less than 15 feet wide. Even the largest halls faded into insignificance in comparison with their royal counterparts – the great Lyon Chamber at Linlithgow Palace is about 100 feet long.

The great hall in Renaissance Scotland was lit by large windows, set in splayed window embrasures to admit yet more light. Sash windows were unknown before the late seventeenth century,[61] and many windows still had fixed glazing, with the panes set in lead in the upper half of the opening, and the lower half closed by wooden shutters which could be more easily opened and closed than glazed casements (see Figure 3.10). This type of window has been restored at Culross Palace. How many of the richer houses had fully glazed windows at this period is difficult to determine.[62] Rothiemay's engraving of the west front at Holyrood suggests that by the 1640s the great windows were entirely of glass (see Figure 2.4). Larger windows, such as those at Huntly and Balvenie, were protected by fixed iron grilles.

The window embrasures served as alcoves for private conversation or for admiring the view, and were often fitted with window seats, and perhaps with aumbries for keeping objects such as books. The hall was heated by at least one great fireplace, with a stone surround, roll moulded or embellished with classical ornament. The hall chimneypiece of Newark Castle at Port Glasgow (1597) is based on fireplace designs in Serlio's treatise.[63] A similar fireplace can be seen at Spedlin's Tower in Dumfriesshire, but differences of detail suggest it was not necessarily the work of the same mason. In the grander houses, a heraldic panel decorated the overmantel. The great armorial display over the hall fireplace at Craigievar is in plaster rather than stone, but since the royal arms are represented, it was probably originally gilded and painted like the heraldry in the royal palaces (see Figure 3.29).

Craigievar still preserves its screens passage, with the minstrels' gallery above, concealing the top of the staircase down to the kitchen. This arrangement was a legacy of the medieval great hall, allowing food to be brought in with theatrical splendour and musical fanfares, but the elegant fluted pilasters and delicate carved ornament on the wooden screen betray its later date (1612–26). At Craigievar, the Renaissance wooden panelling stretches right around the lower walls of the hall. Above this point, the walls would have been hung with tapestries, contrasting in texture and colour with the rich, three-dimensional ornament of the white plaster ceiling above. Some halls, as at Culross Palace, had wooden panelled walls up to cornice level. The ceilings, whether painted or plastered, were one of the most spectacular achievements of the Scottish Renaissance. We shall return to these later in this chapter.

THE APARTMENT

The medieval Scottish laird had sought peace and privacy in his solar or great chamber, a secluded room leading off the great hall, either at one end or on the

FIGURE 3.29   Craigievar Castle, Aberdeenshire, the Great Hall, from Billings, *Baronial and Ecclesiastical Antiquities*, vol. I.

floor above. It was during the Renaissance period, on the Continent as well as in Britain, that the apartment, or suite of private rooms independent of the great hall, evolved from this initial search for privacy. The grander the lifestyle, the more rooms in the apartment, each chamber within the suite being more private than the last. Visitors were admitted only as far as their status allowed; indeed, in seventeenth-century Rome, the social gradations were so complicated that etiquette manuals were needed to establish the hierarchies.[64] The bedchamber was usually the last in the sequence, with the exception of small closet-like rooms, used as studies, charter rooms, oratories, or servants' rooms at the end. The apartment was not necessarily arranged in a straight *enfilade*: in Tuscany, at the Sassetti villa at Montughi (begun in the 1460s) and the Medici villa at Poggio a Caiano of *c.* 1485, each corner block contained a suite of rooms in a circular pattern, a solution imitated at François Ier's Château de Chambord. But the important point was that the apartment should be laid out *horizontally*, and it was this new horizontality that rendered the Scottish medieval tower-house nearly redundant in Renaissance Scotland.

To qualify as an apartment, rather than a lodging, the suite had to have at least three rooms: typically a withdrawing chamber, a bedchamber and a closet. In the case of a married couple in the house of a prominent noble, husband and wife would each have a separate apartment, either one above the other, connected by a private staircase between the bedchambers, or on the same floor on different wings of a courtyard, again connected between bedchambers. Once again, the lead had been taken by the court: the royal palaces had provided separate apartments for king and queen from at least the time of James V. Bedchambers were the principal living rooms by day as well as by night.

Within a single block, the introduction of the double-pile plan allowed the principal suite to lie alongside the dining hall on the same floor. The earliest Scottish examples seem to be Culross Abbey House of 1608 and the palace block of Edinburgh Castle, as it was enlarged in 1615 (see Figure 2.6). In both these cases, the chimneys are contained within the central spine wall. The double-pile plan was anticipated in Regent Morton's Drochil Castle (1570s), with its broad first-floor corridor (see Figure 3.21), an arrangement perhaps inspired by continental examples such as the Château of Chenonceau in the Loire begun in 1513. At Drochil, however, the three living rooms on the opposite side of the corridor from the great hall, each provided with a fireplace and garderobe, are not interlinked and must have been separate lodgings.

The best suite is often called the 'state apartment' because it would have been used by honoured guests such as visiting royalty. A splendid survival of two superimposed apartments can be seen at Huntly, lofted up high above the great hall. Traces of the former magnificence of these rooms can be seen in the splendid stone fireplaces and fragments of rich plaster friezes, dating from the years following the Earl's elevation to Marquis in 1599 (one of the fireplaces is dated 1606, and the external inscription originally bore the date 1602).[65] The Marquis himself would probably have occupied the top floor, distinguished as the state apartment on the outside by its smooth ashlar masonry, outsized inscriptions and huge, elaborate oriel windows (see Figure 3.8).

A favourite location for the bedchamber of a state apartment, as seen at Huntly, was in a corner tower. Indeed, there is strong evidence that huge corner towers were built on Renaissance great houses specifically for this purpose. Long misunderstood as defensive bastions, circular towers offered panoramic views over the estates and landscape. Charles McKean has ingeniously shown how, at Pitsligo for example, the tucking of windows into the inner edges of the corner tower, near the flanking walls of the main block, was not a means of providing covering fire, but simply a way of ensuring the best lighting for the bedchamber from east and south.[66] Bartizans, too, made spectacular settings for bedrooms and closets.[67] Comfort and aspect were much more important considerations than most historians have so far realised. The delightful turret bedrooms often had large windows with attractive stone frames, as if to advertise their gracious, unmilitary use – for instance, on the corner bartizan at Elcho Castle. In other cases, the windows were exotically shaped, such as the oval windows in the bartizans at Lickleyhead and Castle Fraser (see Figure 3.5). Charles McKean has also shown how the shape of the turret rooms changed during the Renaissance, from square bedrooms in cylindrical towers, to circular bedrooms in round towers, and finally to rectangular rooms in square towers.[68]

FIGURE 3.30   Caerlaverock Castle, Dumfriesshire, the Renaissance wing inserted into the thirteenth-century triangular courtyard, 1634.

We should pause to mention some of the ways in which medieval tower-houses could be updated to provide the horizontal apartments that the changing lifestyle demanded. A new wing could be tucked into the precinct of a fortified castle – at Caerlaverock Castle, for instance, a Renaissance wing with richly carved classical pediments, huge windows and smooth ashlar masonry in the rich – red local Dumfries sandstone was inserted into its tiny triangular courtyard in about 1634 (see Figure 3.30). Alternatively, a new wing could be attached to the side of an older tower-house, as at Edzell, where the house was gradually extended around the barmkin wall to create a courtyard plan. A less practical, though showy, alternative was to add extra accommodation on the top of an older tower. This was the solution adopted at Preston in East Lothian, but the house seems to have been abandoned soon afterwards, Sir John Hamilton's more modern replacement built alongside in 1628 proving more suitable.

Not all Renaissance houses had full-scale state apartments. On the simplest scale is the example of the priest's house at Dunottar of 1574, a miniature version of a Renaissance laird's house known as the Waterton Lodging. Over the hall and kitchen on the ground floor was a private chamber reached by a spacious spiral stair. A tiny newel to the cap-house gave access to a little attic. At the other extreme are the houses with half a dozen or more individual private rooms scattered around the turrets and attics, each provided with a garderobe, and reached by secluded small spiral staircases. At Lickleyhead, for instance, there are seven private rooms on the upper floors, and Elcho Castle has a proliferation of upper lodgings reached by three separate stairs, probably each originally divided into two rooms, all provided with fireplaces and with garderobes on the north side (see Figure 3.26).

THE GALLERY

The origins of the gallery can probably be traced back to France in the fourteenth and fifteenth centuries. The first French galleries were covered wooden walkways over stone cloisters or loggias.[69] Later, superimposed open loggias of stone appeared, as in the Louis XII wing at Blois, before eventually becoming transformed into long, ceremonial, enclosed rooms such as the gallery of Francois Ier at Fontainebleau. The earliest surviving English example seems to be the gallery wing at the Vyne in Hampshire, an oak gallery over a stone one, probably completed by 1531. In Scotland, galleries in the form of linking corridors were to be seen in the royal palaces of James V's time. The gallery-corridor at Linlithgow, with its overtly Tudor windows, may even date from the reign of James IV and his Tudor queen. The gallery at Falkland, which runs along the courtyard front of the south wing, was erected under James V. It was common practice in Renaissance France for galleries to connect with chapels. At Holyrood, too, there are documentary references to a gallery on the north side of the main court.

By the late sixteenth century, the gallery in Scotland had become an independent room rather than a corridor. Its function was to provide a place for indoor exercise, for admiring the view and for the display of works of art. Compared with the celebrated long galleries of Elizabethan England, the few surviving Scottish examples are modest in size, but they were impressive both in siting and decoration. The gallery at Pinkie House – the villa of the first Earl of Dunfermline, Alexander Seton, James VI's Lord Chancellor – is on the second floor, with a row of east-facing windows down one side overlooking the walled garden, and a great English-style bay-window at the south end. The interior is some 75 feet long. As we have seen, the outside of this wing is dour and understated (see Figure 3.9), but the interior would have been a riot of festive colour. The elliptical wooden vault is richly painted with emblematic scenes set amid Renaissance-style ornament.[70]

Scottish long galleries were normally situated under the eaves, whether across the top of a lofty palace or at first-floor level along a low, purpose-built wing. The gallery at Earlshall, over 50 feet long, extends right across the second floor of the main block of the house, begun in 1546 (see Figure 3.31). It has a flamboyant painted ceiling of about 1620, again covering an elliptical wooden ceiling.[71] Another example of a long gallery flanking a formal garden is to be found at Regent Morton's house at Aberdour in Fife, while the Earl Marischal's gallery at Dunottar, above the lodgings already mentioned, overlooked the bowling green (see Figure 3.3). Perhaps the most surprising Renaissance gallery in Scotland, though modest in scale, is the roof-top gallery at Craigievar. Despite the advantages of its height, the windows are small and the ceiling is plain, though it may once have been painted. To take full advantage of the view, one would have had to climb to the roof-top terrace, but the gallery offered a useful recreational area and may have been used for sittings of the barony court.

Some great houses had wooden galleries projecting from their walls. At Hamilton Palace, there was a wooden balcony at first-floor level, across the centre of the entrance front (see Figure 3.10). Traces of the wooden fixings for such balconies can be seen at Craigmillar, Girnigoe and Drochil, amongst others.

ORIEL WINDOWS

In an age of increasing security and structural confidence, oriel windows provided a magnificent opportunity for both house-owners and master masons to show off. The technical virtuosity of an oriel window, daringly supported on corbels, was emphasised by elaborate stone-carving on the corbels and over the windows. One of the most ostentatious of these displays is to be found in the Earl's Palace at Kirkwall, where the great hall and withdrawing chamber are lit by huge corbelled oriels on one side and by bay-windows of equal splendour on the other (see Figure 3.20). The corbelled projections on the east side of the palace block at Edinburgh Castle originally supported oriel windows, offering a dramatic view of the city below (see Figure 2.14). The pretty oriel of the gatehouse at Falkland Palace has already been mentioned in Chap. Two (see Figure 2.2).

The oriel offered scope for the roof-top expression and geometrical surprise so characteristic of the period. For instance at Pitullie Castle near Fraserburgh, now a ruin, there were diagonally set oriels splayed across the corners of the top of the main tower, shown in James Giles's early nineteenth-century view. The higher the placing of the oriel, the more daring it appeared. At Maybole Castle in Ayrshire, the panelled room at the top of the staircase tower, probably of the early seventeenth century, is lit by a three-light corbelled oriel set in a smooth ashlar gable (see Figure 3.32). Attention has already been drawn to the row of dramatic oriels across the top of the south front of the Earl of Huntly's palace at Strathbogie (see Figure 3.8), anticipated more modestly in the Atholl Lodging at nearby Balvenie (see Figure 3.2).

From within, the oriel window might offer a semi-private alcove for conversation or reading. In a town house, an oriel could provide much needed extra space as well as display, but in the country the importance of the view over the landscape was paramount. In this outward-looking age, the oriel was one of the most flamboyant symbols of the ever-broadening cultural scene. The oriel window in the great hall of the cliff-top palace of Girnigoe in Caithness must have offered a spectacular view of storm-lashed cliff scenery. More traditionally, oriels sometimes indicated the presence of oratories, especially if their windows had Gothic forms, as in the king's and queen's oratories at Linlithgow Palace. Similarly, the diminutive

FIGURE 3.31 (*above*) Earlshall, Fife, the interior of the gallery showing the painted ceiling, dated 1620.

FIGURE 3.32 (*left*) Maybole Castle, Ayrshire, showing the corbelled oriel, from Billings, *Baronial and Ecclesiastical Antiquities* vol. III.

little oriel on the second floor of the Bishop's Palace in Elgin may have lit a private prayer-alcove or chapel.

CEILINGS

The century 1560–1660 coincides with the flowering of the painted ceiling in Scotland.[72] Fortunately, many have been preserved in fine condition, hidden under suspended plaster ceilings when the fashion faded in the Restoration period. In the 1790s, the author of the *Statistical Account* was evidently amazed by the vigorous, colourful ceilings at Huntly Castle: 'Indeed most of the apartments are still in tolerable preservation; particularly the ceilings, which are ornamented with a great variety of paintings, in small divisions, containing many emblematical figures, with verses, expressive of some moral sentiment in doggerel rhyme.'[73] The medium was a water-soluble tempera paint, producing a brightly coloured, matt surface. The paint was applied either to the beams and the tongued-and-grooved boards that rested on them, or to a wooden vault nailed on to a hidden structure. Vaulted ceilings are usually found in the houses of the wealthier patrons – the most impressive surviving painted vaults are probably those of the long galleries of Earlshall in Fife (see Figure 3.31), and of Alexander Seton's Pinkie House (see Figure 3.9), mentioned earlier in this chapter.

In ceiling design, the influence of the court was once again decisive. Mary Queen of Scots' apartment in Holyrood Palace has one of the earliest known painted ceilings, datable to 1558–9, as well as a broad frieze in subtly shaded 'grotesque' patterns. The delicacy of these grotesques reflects a taste that pervaded Europe in the sixteenth century, inspired by the remains of antique painted decoration. The name 'grotesque' alludes to the grotto-like nature of the Roman archaeological sites where they were studied. The painted decoration of Mary Queen of Scots' rooms at Edinburgh Castle reveals a more robust approach than that of her Holyrood apartment, with boldly illusionistic strapwork cartouches reminiscent of the French court style. This was, after all, a court stronghold rather than a sophisticated suburban villa.

Among the surviving Scottish painted ceilings, huge variations of style, quality and refinement make generalisation difficult. The ceiling from Prestongrange in East Lothian, now at Merchiston Tower in Edinburgh, is not only one of the earliest – it is dated 1581 – but it is also one of the most accomplished and sophisticated (see Figure 3.33). The fantasy element of the grotesque theme is perfectly captured, and the execution is superb. The colours are based on subtle shades of terracotta, pink and white. Like Holyrood, this was a former monastery, converted to gracious living for the powerful ecclesiastic-turned-courtier Mark Ker of Newbattle and his wife Helen Leslie.[74]

We know little of the painters who executed these flamboyant decorative schemes, but the personalities and tastes of the patrons are vigorously conveyed. Mark Ker's overtly conjugal lifestyle while still Commendator of Newbattle makes the presence of bold, priapic figures in the Prestongrange grotesques less surprising.[75] By contrast, Sir George Bruce, the industrial entrepreneur who exported coal and salt to the Low Countries, decorated the vault of his little second-floor

FIGURE 3.33 Painted ceiling dated 1581, from Prestongrange, East Lothian, now in
Merchiston Tower, Edinburgh.

gallery at Culross Palace with moralising stories explained by two-line texts.
Whereas Bruce's inscriptions at Culross are in the vernacular, inscribed in Gothic
lettering, reflecting his Northern European orientation, the gallery of the Rome-
educated Alexander Seton at Pinkie House is strewn with inscriptions in Latin and
Greek. While the Culross scenes are arranged in rectangular panels like a comic
book, those in the gallery at Pinkie are contained in elaborate feigned coffering in
varied geometrical patterns, richly embellished with strapwork and heraldic
displays. Both ceilings used emblem books to provide both visual and textual
sources, but Seton's display of erudite, humanist erudition expresses a Mediterranean culture far removed from Bruce's dour, Puritan moralism.[76]

Even at Prestongrange, we see one of the characteristics that gives these Scottish
ceilings their individuality, that is, the practice of outlining the forms with black
lines. This feature is more evident in the bolder, less refined examples, such as the
Nine Nobles Room at Crathes Castle where the vigorous outlines give the swag-
gering heroes the air of stained-glass figures (see Figure 3.34). The ceiling depicts
the famous 'Nine Worthies', a series well known across Europe. It consisted of
three classical heroes (Hector, Julius Caesar and Alexander the Great), three
biblical ones (David, Judas Maccabeus and Joshua) and three from the Middle Ages

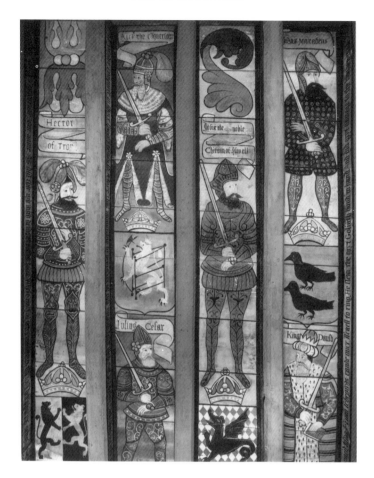

FIGURE 3.34   Crathes Castle, Kincardineshire, the painted ceiling of the Nine Nobles Room.

(Arthur, Charlemagne and Godfrey de Bouillon). A tapestry of these heroes at the Château de Langeais in the Loire celebrated the marriage of Charles VIII and Anne of Brittany, and the series was engraved by Nicholas de Bruyn in 1594.

Walls, too, were sometimes painted. Impressive examples survive at Kinneill House and at Huntingtower, as well as in the gallery of Provost Skene's house in Aberdeen.[77] The English painter Valentine Jenkin was employed at Hamilton Palace in 1627, and for the same family at Kinneill in 1634.[78] Original early seventeenth-century wooden wall panelling, recently discovered at the Binns, was painted with illusionistic mouldings and gold stars at the corners.[79]

After 1603, plaster ceilings began to make their appearance in the great houses of Scotland.[80] Aesthetically, this English import brought a drastic change, as exuberantly three-dimensional white plasterwork, — often with drooping pendants penetrating far into the room space — began to supersede the two-dimensional polychromy of the painted ceiling. However, the ceiling remained a focus for the display of family roots, loyalties and moral principles. Support of the Union could

FIGURE 3.35 House of the Binns, West Lothian, detail of the ceiling of the King's Room, *c*.1630.

be advertised – as at the Binns and Winton House – by the incorporation of thistles, Tudor roses, fleurs-de-lis and harps in the ceiling plasterwork. Even the Nine Worthies, or rather, selected heroes from their band, remained popular. David and Alexander were the favourites, both sharing their names with past Kings of Scotland, while the biblical David was one of the images of kingship adopted by James VI and I.[81] Roundels depicting the heads of David, Joshua, Alexander and Hector figured on the moulds used by the bands of travelling plasterers (see Figure 3.35). These Worthies appear, for instance, in the ceilings at Balcarres in Fife and at Craigievar (see Figure 3.29), doubtless emulating the ceiling executed in 1606 in the Old Palace at Bromley-by-Bow, possibly a royal hunting lodge of James VI and I.[82] This rich plasterwork decorative scheme, now in the Victoria and Albert Museum in London, was effective in establishing this taste in court circles.

Some of the plasterers are known by name. A certain John White ('Quhytte, Jhone') was paid £100 'in part payment of his plaister wark' at Winton, and his moulds were also used at Pinkie and at Moray House in Edinburgh.[83] Another team executed the plaster ceilings at Glamis, Muchalls and Craigievar in the 1620s. Some of the iron moulds used by the plasterer Alexander White, paid in 1630 for work at the Binns, are still preserved in the house.[84] The technique required long training and virtuosic skill, enabling rich, high-relief ornament (made of a mixture of lime, sand, water and chopped animal hair) to be suspended from wooden laths nailed to the joists.

The basis design of most plaster ceilings was a pattern of interlocking ribs, rectangular or v-shaped in section, dividing the ceiling into complex geometrical compartments. The ribs were interwoven with the intricacy of a knot-work garden design, overlapping each other in swiftly flowing lines. Relief patterns extended into the friezes (as at Winton and the Binns) (see Figure 3.36) and armorial overmantels (such as the huge display at Craigievar) (see Figure 3.27). The plasterwork was rarely painted, except perhaps for the most ostentatious heraldic displays. The whiteness of the relief, lime-washed to create a brilliant, uniform surface, gave an air of classical dignity inspired by the stuccowork and relief carvings of the ancient world. White ceilings made rooms lighter, illuminating the wall-tapestries and bed-hangings, where painted ceilings would have competed with them. The deliciously meringue-like texture and colour of the plaster, apparently as malleable as royal icing, yet wrought into tautly organised geometrical designs, allowed Scotland's early seventeenth-century plasterwork to embellish the soaring vault of a great hall as successfully as the low ceiling of a tiny bedchamber.

FURNISHINGS

Many of Scotland's Renaissance country houses are now rubbly ruins, some overgrown, some fossilised in state care. Many of those that are still in use have since been altered, and it is the interiors that have most often been lost. Few still have Renaissance furniture, and even the most sensitive restorations, such as that by Lorimer at Earlshall in Fife, have inevitably – and rightly – had to respond to more modern uses.[85] To imagine how Scotland's Renaissance interiors looked and felt, one has to linger in the occasionally almost unaltered house, Craigievar being an outstanding example, or in those houses, such as Towie Barclay, now occupied by sensitive, restoring enthusiasts.[86] In addition, we have the good fortune that furniture, like architecture, was zealously inscribed with dates and the owners' initials and coats-of-arms.

Using the evidence of objects in museums and galleries, written descriptions, inventories and surviving decorative schemes, we can thus begin to build up a picture of a typical Scottish Renaissance interior. We have already noted the richness of ceiling decoration and chimney pieces. Walls of important rooms would have been panelled with wood or plastered, and covered with tapestries or leather hangings if not painted. In 1559, Sir William Hamilton at Newton in Ayrshire owned 'Thre fyne arress warkis' as well as another twelve 'grosser'.[87] At Fountainhall in East Lothian (see Figure 3.19), once the country home of the wealthy Edinburgh merchant William Dick of Lauder, Flemish tapestries were discovered still *in situ* under the plaster.[88] Sixteen tapestries were to be found at Hamilton Palace in 1607, but by 1623 these had been replaced by gilt leather.[89] Eleven hangings of

FIGURE 3.36   House of the Binns, West Lothian, the King's Room, showing the plaster ceiling
and the frieze, c.1630.

gilded leather were listed among the contents of the Palace of Huntly during the
reign of Mary Queen of Scots.[90] By 1681, these 'Spanish leather' hangings, hitherto
mostly imported from the Low Countries, had become so popular that a monopoly
was granted to an Edinburgh manufacturer, Alexander Brand.[91] The panelling or
tapestries provided insulation, and softened the acoustics of the room, as well as
adding an element of dignity and richness.

Some of the carpentry of the period was as ornate as the richest carved stonework,
and often similar in style. The Renaissance wooden panels at Craigston, for instance
(see Figure 3.37), probably originally from Cromarty House, resemble the relief
panels in the garden wall at Edzell (see Figure 3.41).[92] As we shall see, the Edzell
panels were inspired by German engravings, and the Craigston panels also appear
to be the work of German or Netherlandish woodcarvers. The tradition of skilled
woodcarving of early sixteenth-century Scotland, seen in the Stirling ceiling roundels as well as in the so-called Montrose panels now in the National Museums of

FIGURE 3.37 Craigston Castle, Aberdeenshire, the carved wooden panels of St Matthew and St Luke, possibly from the old Cromarty House.

Scotland, was gradually transformed during the next hundred years by the introduction of classical framing elements and details. But the change was not a sudden one, for the delicate, naturalistic vine, flower or leaf patterns of late Gothic ornament were equally fitted to the stylised 'grotesque' designs of the Renaissance.

Furniture was of oak or pine, or even occasionally of West Indian mahogany, and carved with similarly hybrid classical/naturalistic decoration. The surviving pieces are dark-stained and varnished, but presumably the oak and pine were originally light in colour. The warm, light surface of the woodwork, soon softened by the patina of use, would have offset the polychromy of the textiles and painted ceilings, and contrasted effectively with the crisp whiteness of the plasterwork.

The characteristic chair was the *caqueteuse*, a high-backed wooden armchair used for dining or for conversation (as the name suggests).[93] Its back was carved in relief, with initials, date, heraldry or classical motifs such as pediments or fluted

FIGURE 3.38   Wardrobe said to have belonged to Mary Queen of Scots.

pilasters in any combination. One of the finest collections of *caqueteuses* is that preserved at Trinity Hall in Aberdeen. Chairs of this type were not upholstered, but inventories mention colourful velvet and embroidered cushions.[94] As well as tables of various sizes, there were large upright wardrobes, some with ornate carved doors. A fine example is the cupboard of Mary Queen of Scots (now in the National Museum of Antiquities in Edinburgh), which has Renaissance carved panels incorporating the motif of the classical head in a roundel which we have already seen at Falkland Palace and in the Stirling ceiling heads (see Figure 3.38). The iron hinges and lock of the cupboards are also intricately wrought with a baluster detail.

Beds were of several types. The simplest were box beds, like those still to be seen in the attic servants' bedroom at Craigievar, set in curtained alcoves in the walls. Many servants slept on folding mattresses on the floor. Since bedchambers were often used by day, folding beds in the wall panelling were a useful space-saving alternative: a bed of this type has survived at Newark Castle at Port Glasgow. The English visitor Fynes Moryson in 1598 was clearly surprised: 'Their bedsteads were then like Cubbards in the wall, with doores to be opened and shut at pleasure, so as we climbed up to our beds.'[95]

In the grander houses, beds were stately four-posters, hung with colourful valances and curtains of velvet or silk often inlaid with embroidered panels.[96] A fine four-poster bed dated 1594, as well as an Orcadian version of 1641, can be seen at Crathes Castle. The bedhangings listed at Newton in Ayrshire in 1559 were coloured blue, green, red and yellow, contrasting with the sombre hues of much of the clothing recorded in the inventory.[97] At Huntly in 1562, the colours of the bed-curtains included yellow, crimson, blue, green and violet, this rainbow-like spectrum glittering with gold embroidery.[98] Apart from two black beds, presumably for those in mourning, the bed hangings at Hamilton Palace in 1607 were green, red, yellow, orange, blue and brown.[99] A valance from the marriage bed of Sir Colin Campbell of Glenorchy's House at Balloch, dating from about 1550 and illustrating the story of Adam and Eve, can still be seen in the Burrell Collection.[100]

Chests (kists) and presses for storing clothes and documents were often placed at the foot of the bed. Like the tables, they would be covered with carpets or rugs, oriental in origin or at least in inspiration. Mary Queen of Scots owned 'Saxtene turkie tapies contening sevin greit and nine small.'[101] A splendid survival is the famous Persian-style Strathmore carpet from Glamis Castle, with the same family monogram as the ceiling of the great hall, which is dated 1620.[102] This huge woollen carpet, over 5 metres long, still preserves its vivid colours, predominately bright red. It was probably made in England. The High Hall at the Binns in 1685 had '3 tables with 3 large carpets'.[103]

Not only carpets but also the finer textiles and trimmings were imported from England or from the Continent, especially France and Holland. By contrast, embroidery was a home industry – a popular recreation for women, however highly born, and Taylor the Water Poet remarked that spinning and weaving were done by Scots lairds' wives and daughters as well as by the servants.[104]

Finally, we should mention the silverware, for Scotland had excelled in the craft of metalwork since the Celtic period. Surviving silver pieces of the time, such as the Galloway mazer, are beautifully crafted and sophisticated in design.[105] The quantities of silverware were also impressive – at Hamilton Palace in 1623 almost a hundred silver plates were listed in the inventory.[106] By 1685, there were as many as five dozen silver or silver-mounted cups at the Binns, as well as numerous other objects such as boxes, candlesticks, salt-cellars and even whistles. The inventory records a dozen knives and over three dozen spoons – but only one fork![107] Silverware was not only functional, but also provided a reserve of capital for investing surpluses.[108] For everyday fare, many households used pewter: the household of Sir William Hamilton at Newton in Ayrshire in 1559 was equipped with no fewer than 280 pewter dishes.[109] More modestly, the contents of Patrick Robertson's house at Finmouth in 1560, valued at £40, included a dozen pewter plates and trenchers (but only three silver spoons).[110]

OUTBUILDINGS

The range of estate buildings in Scotland in the century 1560–1660 is impressively wide, though the thatched or turf-roofed outhouses that are known from some older views (at Leith Hall for instance) have been lost. Stables, brewhouses and bakehouses, for instance, were to be found at the larger landowners' houses, usually within the courtyard for security.

One of the most complete accounts of the outbuildings of a major Renaissance house is to be found in the inventory of the House of the Binns (see Figure 3.4). The list was made in 1685, after the death of General Tam Dalyell, but it describes the house and outbuildings erected by his father Thomas Dalyell and his mother Dame Janet Bruce.[111] The house is dated 1621 on one of the pediments, and the hall fireplace is dated 1622. The entrance court was flanked on the west side by a women's service wing, with a pewter store, dairy and granary below, and sleeping quarters for female servants above. To the east were the menservants' quarters with the stables, brewhouse and bakehouse. The west courtyard arch, on the women's side, is surmounted by a broken pediment bearing the initials IB, for Janet Bruce, the mistress of the house, while Thomas Dalyell's initials, TD, are on the pediment over the gateway on the men's side. The byre, work-horse stable, barns and hen house were probably more discreetly placed in a separate court at the back.

At the Binns there was a laundry, but in general the facilities for washing were limited. English visitors in the period were not impressed by the personal hygiene of the Scots, complaining of lousy beds and of the Scottish practice of stamping the steeping laundry with bare feet (see Figure 4.31).[112] Sophisticated bathing was a rare luxury. We have already mentioned Queen Mary's bathhouse at Holyrood (in Chap. Three); the bathing pavilion on the corner of the walled garden at Edzell incorporated a furnace to provide hot water.

Some of the ancillary buildings were for food supply – including the doocot (dovecote) to ensure all-year-round eggs and meat. A doocot was sometimes even incorporated into a gable of the house itself, for instance at Northfield House in East Lothian. The doocot might be set into the barmkin wall, as at Newark at Port Glasgow (see Figure 3.28), or perhaps within a walled garden, such as the lectern doocot at Preston tower. The design of the doocot provided an excuse for architectural experiment: as well as the common lectern and beehive types, there were picturesque variations, including the dormered doocot at Glamis, and the beehive doocot with a monopitched roof encircled with crow steps at Ecclesiamagirdle at Bridge of Earn.[113] Stenhouse in Edinburgh still has a chicken house at one end of the ground floor, with nesting boxes inside and little pointed arched openings in the outside wall. Beehives were a useful asset: early examples can be seen in the walls at Tolquhon and Midmar, both in Deeside.

One of the most remarkable survivals from the period is the salmon house at the mouth of the River Ugie, still serving its original purpose for netting and oak-smoking salmon (see Figure 3.39). The skew is dated 1585 and bears the arms of the fifth Earl Marischal, who also built nearby Inverugie Castle. Documents record that the Gordons of Huntly had a stone salmon-curing house at Helmsdale which cost £16 to repair in 1617.[114]

Of recreational outbuildings we have tantalising glimpses from records of the period. There were bothies in the Highlands for summer stalking and shooting.

FIGURE 3.39   The salmon house of the Earls Marischal on the Ugie Estuary, near Peterhead,
1585. The sixteenth-century building is on the right.

When hunting with the Earl of Mar in 1618, Taylor camped at 'small cottages built
on purpose to lodge in, which they call Lonquhards'.[115] There they feasted on fresh
fish and game roasted on spits or boiled in cauldrons over the bankside hearth, and
washed down with ale, wine, sack and brandy. Lowther recorded in 1629 that the
Marquis of Huntly's eldest son used to 'familiarly go in the mountains after the
deer 80 miles a day'.[116] At the more gracious end of the spectrum, at Edzell one
could enjoy delicate sweetmeats in the delightful banqueting pavilion on the corner
of the walled formal garden (see Figure 3.41).[117]

   In a hilly country of high rainfall, water-mills provided a useful source of power,
especially as forests became depleted. The seventeenth-century water-mill just
below Boyne Castle, a plain but substantial rubble building, is a typical example. In
Orkney and Shetland, the water wheels rotated horizontally rather than vertically,
although none of the surviving mills dates from earlier than the eighteenth century.
In the Lowlands, those landowners who were lucky enough to own coal-mines
could use their own solid fuel for industrial purposes, especially salt-panning. A
full treatment of the industrial archaeology of Renaissance Scotland lies outside the
scope of this book, but we must remember that industrial expansion as well as
progress in farming methods provided the economic background to the domestic
architectural innovations that we have seen in this chapter.

COTTARS' DWELLINGS

Again, a complete account of vernacular traditions of the period is impossible in a book of this length, but a brief mention is important to balance our view of the houses of the nobility and lairds. Outside the towns, almost nothing survives of the housing of the rural poor from the late sixteenth and early seventeenth centuries. Subsequent depopulation of the Highlands and the provision of 'improved' estate cottages in the Lowlands have left only archaeological remains. Travellers' accounts of the modest standard of housing in the countryside were, however, probably little exaggerated. John Ray, for instance, though not a sympathetic visitor, may have been reporting a realistic situation when he wrote of the rural housing of East Lothian: 'The ordinary country houses are pitiful cots, built of stone, and covered with turves, having in them but one room, many of them no chimneys, the windows very small holes and not glazed.'[118]

The poor still had little security of tenure, and their virtually biodegradable housing, made of rubble stonework and roofed with turf, was almost as quick to build as to pull down (as another jaundiced English traveller remarked).[119] Only the roof timbers were valuable, and these could be removed and reused whenever the family was forced to move. As late as 1769, Thomas Pennant commented that the houses of the rural poor 'look at a distance like so many black mole-hills'.[120]

Almost every rural family kept a cow, and many had a pig in the summer months, to be slaughtered and salted for the winter.[121] In the Lowlands, the cow could remain out-of-doors for most of the year, but in the Highlands many cottages were byre-houses with two rooms, one of which served as an animal shelter. This was a widespread practice all over Europe at this time, with the dual advantages of warmth and security.

It is easiest to reconstruct the appearance of rural vernacular housing of our period in depopulated Highland glens where the sites are not overlain by later land-use developments. For example, the Royal Commission's recent survey of Glen Shee has shown evidence of intensive cultivation of the lower slopes of the valley from the Spittal of Glenshee to Dalmunzie.[122] Remains of shielings on the upper slopes show that the hills were used for summer grazing of sheep. The lands of Dalmunzie, recorded in a charter of 1510, were under the feudal superiority of the Earl of Atholl, while the 'Spitale of Glenshe' is mentioned in a document of 1542.[123] The housing in the fermtouns of both Spittal of Glenshee and Dalmunzie took the form of rectangular buildings of one or two rooms, with one three-compartment house in each settlement (see Figure 3.40). The houses were of turf-covered stone, and of not inconsiderable size, even the smallest being at least 6 metres long and over 3 metres wide, although we do not know much about the number of occupants in each house. Several of the houses had rounded corners, a traditional Scottish practice which suited both the building methods and the windy climate. Between the two fermtouns were scattered farmsteads or little groups of buildings clustered around enclosed yards. Most of the settlements had a kiln, probably for drying grain, and there was a quarry at Dalmunzie.[124]

Space does not allow us to consider here the regional variations in vernacular

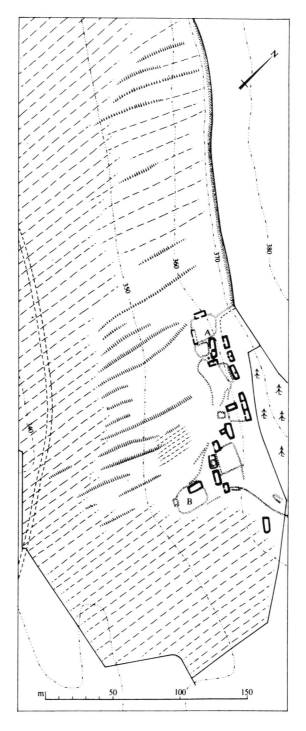

FIGURE 3.40   The former fermtoun at Spittal of Glenshee, Perthshire, archaeological survey.

building, such as the Hebridean blackhouses or the idiosyncratic 'planticrues' of Shetland (circular, stone-walled, doorless enclosures for cabbages). There is a continuum of regional tradition running from prehistory through the Pictish and Viking periods into historical times which deserves fuller discussion, but in our period continuity was more significant than innovation in the case of the rural poor.

RECREATION

Hunting, hawking and fishing were not the only sports of the Scottish country landowner. Ballgames, too, were a favourite pastime, and their range and variety at this time is impressive. Some needed costly facilities, especially tennis, which was limited to the wealthy élite. 'Real' (that is, *réal* or royal) tennis required a large-scale building, in the form of an open court surrounded by high walls equipped with galleries and mural orifices. The tennis court at Falkland Palace, built for James V in 1539, is the oldest surviving real tennis court in Britain (see Figure 2.19). The tennis court at Holyrood faced the entrance to the little pavilion now known as Queen Mary's Bathhouse (see Figure 2.20). Bowling greens, too, needed a prepared surface, perfectly levelled with immaculate, velvety lawns. Defying the rugged cliff-top site, the Earls Marischal even indulged in a bowling green at Dunottar Castle (see Figure 3.3). One of the most admired was to be seen at Heriot's Hospital in Edinburgh, likened to 'a green carpet' by a French visitor, Jorevin de Rocheford, in 1661 (see Figure 4.27).[125] At Cowane's Hospital in Stirling, completed in 1639 (see Figure 4.61), the bowling green occupied almost the entire garden space.[126]

In contrast to tennis and bowling, golf and football could be played on any stretch of well-drained, open ground. By tradition, Mary Queen of Scots is believed to have imported golf from France, but in reality the game is mentioned in Scotland as early as 1457.[127] Its closest continental parallel is the game of 'kolf', played in the Low Countries on both dry land and ice.[128] Coastal dunes, then as now, were favoured by golfers. Mary Queen of Scots played on Seton Sands, as well as on the shores of the loch at Linlithgow.[129]

Although football was a game played in all ranks of society, it aroused continual disapproval. From the fifteenth century onwards, laws of the Scottish Parliament tried unsuccessfully to forbid both football and golf, in an attempt to encourage the devotion of time and energy to archery.[130] Even James IV, however, is known to have bought two footballs in 1491.[131] The diffusion of sporting activity down through the social scale is engagingly recorded in a letter of Sir Robert Gordon to his brother, the Duke of Sutherland: 'Cherish your countreymen and train them up in all kynd of honest exercise, such as hunting, ryding, archerie, shooting with the gun, golfing, jumping, running, swimming and suck lyk. Eschew the footeball as a dangerous and unprofitable exercise.'[132]

Archery was regarded as the most suitable recreation, although in reality gun-powder warfare had long limited its military usefulness. Archery grounds, known as *bow-butts*, were to be found in the grounds of major castles, as well as on the outskirts of burghs. At Linlithgow, for instance, the *bow-butts* lay on the east side of the palace, visible from the windows of the royal kitchen where the boy cooks

were allowed to use old targets as shields to protect them from the spitting fat![133]
Even women were to be seen on the *bow-butts* – Mary Queen of Scots practised
archery with her ladies-in-waiting in the park at Holyrood Palace.[134]

GARDENS

The arts of horticulture and garden design developed rapidly in the Renaissance.
Inspired by the literary descriptions of the gardens of antiquity, villa owners across the
whole of Europe created elaborate formal gardens embellished with statues, fountains,
sweet-smelling arbours and formally planted knot-gardens. The Scottish Renaissance
garden fits into this whole spectrum, reflecting the same desire to tame and improve
on the delights of the natural world.[135] In Scotland, however, these ideals had to be
modified to take account of the harshness of both climate and terrain.

We have already remarked on the impressive range of sporting activities.
Whereas the Ottoman sultans in the Topkapi Palace in Istanbul relaxed by resting
in shady garden pavilions open to the faintest sea breezes, and Roman popes and
cardinals picnicked under trellises of vines beside their garden fountains, the Scottish
country landowners gained little pleasure from staying still in their gardens.
Recreation was active, and the formal gardens were walled to protect plants and
people alike from cold winds. Walls had the further advantage of keeping out wild
rabbits – Scotland had little need of the artificial warrens and fish-ponds of
continental Renaissance parks.[136]

Garden walls were usually of rubble masonry, using local stone, which helped
to attune them to the colours of the landscape and the soil. The walls had no
defensive function, the lintel of the portal of the walled garden at Earlshall proudly
declaring: 'HERE SHALL YE SEE NO ENEMY BVT WINTER AND ROVGH WEATHER'.[137]

The finest surviving walled garden of the Scottish Renaissance is to be found at
Edzell Castle in Angus (see Figure 3.41). Here the walls are of a particularly pretty
local sandstone veined in red and white. The garden was the creation of Sir David
Lindsay whose arms are displayed – together with those of his wife – over the door
in the garden wall, dated 1604. The slender colonnettes that once articulated the
rhythmic bay system along the walls have long since disappeared, but their bases,
capitals and ornamental 'waists' remain. In the centre of each bay, pedimented
niches project above the coping – were they intended for busts or urns? The orifices
in the walls in a chequer-board pattern give added relief and interest – were they
supposed to hold plants, as they do, most appealingly, today? It has been pointed
out that they create a gigantic representation of the fess chequy of the Lindsay
arms.[138] And what was the function of the holes rimmed by seven-pointed stars
(another family emblem) high up on the wall – perhaps to encourage nesting birds?
Three sides of the garden are decorated with boldly sculptured relief panels – the
cardinal virtues on one side, the liberal arts on another, and the planetary gods on
the third. These deities are known to have been based on a German engraved
source (Lindsay's German connections are also evident in his procurement of two
German mining engineers to work the mineral reserves on his estate).[139] The

FIGURE 3.41 (*upper*)   Edzell Castle, Angus, the walled garden, 1604.
FIGURE 3.42 (*lower*)   Gowrie House, near Perth (demolished), 'The Monk's Tower', summer house on the banks of the River Tay. From Grose, *Antiquities of Scotland*, vol. II.

FIGURE 3.43   Pinkie House, Musselburgh, East Lothian, the Doric fountain, c.1607–22. Photo of c.1910–20.

patron's ambitions exceeded his resources, alas, and he died in 1610 'in extra-ordinary debt', without having decorated the fourth side of the garden wall.'[140]

Garden pavilions offered shelter from wind and rain, rather than from sun and heat. On the banks of the River Tay in the garden of Gowrie House near Perth stood a little oval summer house (Fig. 3.42), probably built for the first Earl of Kinnoull who died in 1634 (he is commemorated in a huge monument in the nearby church at Kinnoull, which will be considered in Chapter Five). Francis Grose recorded that its interior room had a 'coved cieling [sic], in which are coarsely painted the twelve signs of the Zodiac, the Heathen Gods and Goddesses, and the arms, crest, and cyphers of the Hay family'.[141] The walled garden at Edzell has a tiny banqueting house at one corner, and there are archaeological traces of a bathhouse with a hot-water supply at another.[142] On a brisk summer's day in Angus, a hot bath and a feast of sweetmeats offered delectable attractions.

Fountains were less tempting. A rare exception is the splendid monumental Doric fountain in front of the entrance to Pinkie House (see Figure 3.43).[143] We have already seen how its owner Alexander Seton, first Earl of Dunfermline, had been educated in Rome, noting his garden inscription which clearly indicates that he was an admirer of the imagery of the Roman *villa suburbana*. As if to advertise Seton's royal connections as Chancellor of Scotland, the fountain is surmounted by a gigantic crown like the fountain installed for James V at Linlithgow Palace (see Figure 2.1).

The aspect of the garden had to be as sunny as possible – at Edzell the garden was placed on the south side of the tower-house, avoiding its shade just as most medieval monastic cloisters lay on the sunny side of their churches. Climatic factors discouraged the blurring of the boundary between house and garden that we see so vividly in the loggias of Roman Renaissance villas, but a few houses did have arcades overlooking the garden. At Huntly Castle, the late eighteenth-century *Statistical Account* records that:

> Many people, still in life, remember to have seen a range of pillars, supporting an arched roof, which seemed to have been intended as a cover for such as inclined to take the air, or a view of the garden which lay before the Castle: there being a door that had led to it, from the upper hall, on a level with it.[144]

Steep slopes were tamed by ambitious terracing: surviving Renaissance terraces can still be seen at Castle Campbell, Aberdour Castle and behind Culross Palace. Costly earthworks were needed to level and buttress these terraces, as we learn from the earliest surviving Scottish gardening manual, *The Scots Gard'ner* by John Reid. He recommends box hedges as the border for flower beds, surrounded by gravel walkways where one could stroll even in damp conditions.[145] The flower beds were planted in elaborate geometrical designs similar to those illustrated in Book IV of Serlio's treatise.[146] Reid stresses that plants of similar colour should not be planted side-by-side, creating a riot of colour far removed from the soft palette of the gardens now to be seen, for example, at Crathes Castle.[147] Twentieth-century planting at Pitmedden and Edzell has attempted to restore the original appearance of the Renaissance parterres, while the Renaissance art of topiary has been revived in the gardens at Earlshall.

Similarly formal planting characterised the vegetable gardens. According to John Reid, 'The Kitchen Garden is the best of all Gardens.'[148] Here, too, Reid recommended complete symmetry, matching each plot of one crop with a matching bed on the opposite side. Rapid advances were taking place in the art of improving and manuring the soil: Reid's recipe for compost is impressive. He recommends filling a great pit with 'dungs, Vegetables, and soils ... ferns, weeds, leaves, soot, ashes, sticks, saw-dust, feathers, hair, horns, bones, urine, scouring of pondes, ditches, blood, pickle, brine, sea-water, the cleansing of the House of Office & c'.[149] Scientific interest also extended to botany. Species of fruit and vegetables were imported from all over Europe – quince from Portugal, cauliflower seeds from Crete, asparagus, parsnips, currants, peaches and cherries from Holland, and leeks from France.[150]

The most remarkable and distinctive manifestation of the Renaissance spirit of scientific enquiry in Scottish gardens was the virtuosity of the sundials. Often, sundials were to be seen perched high on the walls of buildings, both public and private, but they also provided impressive centre-pieces in formal parterres. The most ingenious format was the polyhedral sundial, mounted on a column, on which every face of the polyhedron tells exactly the same time. MacGibbon and Ross identified three types, based on the shape of the polyhedron – the lectern, the obelisk and the facet-head.[151] The various faces are usually hollowed out in concave circles or even heart shapes. A total of 330 free-standing garden sundials are known in Scotland, no fewer than 47 of them sundials datable to before 1700.[152] The mathematical calculations depended on the discovery of logarithms, first published by John Napier in Edinburgh in 1614 (see Figure 1.3). One of the earliest and most elaborate of these polyhedral showpieces was the sundial at Holyrood Palace, carved by the royal master mason John Mylne for the Scottish coronation of Charles I in 1633 (see Figure 2.21). This monument, already described in Chapter Two, stands over 3 metres high, with 29 dials on the upper surfaces of the polyhedron and heraldic devices on the lower surfaces. It was originally richly painted and gilded. Even more ostentatious is the crown-topped sundial at Glamis Castle, standing 7 metres high on a base supported by twisting columns and shield-bearing lions, which has a total of 84 dials (see Figure 3.44).

If the Scottish Renaissance 'Pleasance' or pleasure garden was as enclosed as the medieval *hortus conclusus*, the introspective character of the gardens of the Middle Ages was a remote memory. The parterres were walled for protection from the elements, to exclude rabbits, and even – as at Edzell – for flamboyant heraldic display. This was not an inward-looking age, however; oriels, long galleries, roof-top terraces and bedroom towers were designed with views in mind. Unimproved nature was appreciated as much as formal pleasure gardens. In 1656–7, a visitor from Cambridge, Richard Franck, was stunned by the wild beauty of the setting of Dunottar Castle, where 'nature has finished what she had to do, and has left nothing for the artist to practise, save only to adorn the natural excellency'.[153]

GENERAL ARCHITECTURAL TRENDS

This chapter has sought to examine broad themes in rural architecture, rather than attempt a building-by-building chronological account. The decision to follow this procedure was taken reluctantly, because it disregards the arrangement of the other chapters in this book. On the other hand, it seemed essential to set architectural developments within the context of changes of lifestyle in the countryside. This chapter has tried to characterise those common trends that unify our period and distinguish its châteaux both from earlier, more fortified structures, and from the symmetry, the monumental classicism and the grand vistas of the great houses of the Restoration.

Several other considerations supported this approach. Many houses – indeed, almost all those built on the same site as their predecessors – incorporated older structures into their fabric. This makes the dating of innovatory features highly uncertain. Similar difficulties result from the extent of later remodellings and

FIGURE 3.44   Glamis Castle, Angus, the garden sundial.

alterations. The ruined state of many of the rural buildings offers further hazards
to the historian – both physical and intellectual. Most tragic of all is the almost
complete obliteration of many of the finest Renaissance palaces of the Scottish
nobility. Among these are such important examples as Hamilton (see Figure 3.10),
Seton (see Figure 3.14), Dunbar, Dumbarton and Scone (see Figure 3.11), as well
as the so-called Wrychtishouses near Edinburgh[154] and the house of the Campbells
of Glenorchy at Balloch. Newbattle Abbey, Dalkeith Palace[155] and Blair Atholl have
been transformed out of all recognition. The loss of such impressive buildings –
those which set the trends followed by lesser nobles and lairds – makes it difficult
to pinpoint the sources of architectural innovation.

   A cultural obstacle should also be mentioned – one that is in some ways peculiar
to this period. Medieval castles can be analysed to some degree in terms of military
considerations; and a regard for established canons of correctness informs the

'polite' architecture of the late seventeenth and eighteenth centuries. By contrast, the period of this book is one in which such strictures of taste and function were disregarded as often as they were obeyed. This was an age in which the Renaissance cult of the individual fostered the expression of personal or family identity through visual display. Wilful eccentricity, the luxury value of exuberant ornament, and an admiration for technical virtuosity tended to encourage experimentation. Such memorable design solutions as the lofted oriels at Huntly set within an outsized inscription had no imitators, merely competitors in panache (see Figure 3.8).

This love of dazzling display acted out a dialogue with traditional design solutions, especially in the country where the expression of an ancient right to the lands helped to assure the landowner's status and prestige in the area. Thus, for instance, Alexander Seton, first Earl of Dunfermline, when granted the lordship of Fyvie in 1598, remodelled the house by creating a grand symmetrical façade with a huge triumphal arch in the centre (see Figure 3.16). A family chronical boasts that Seton had been given a Jesuit education in Rome, where he was renowned as a humanist scholar and 'had great skill in architecture and herauldrie'.[156] Yet, Seton's contribution to Fyvie is neither *all'antica* nor Italianate, but adheres closely to the style of traditional Aberdeenshire castellated houses. Only its emphatic symmetry betrays the patron's classical leanings. Even at Pinkie, his *villa suburbana* at Musselburgh near Edinburgh, a Scottish solidity pervades the dour masonry and sturdy chimneys of the garden front (see Figure 3.9). If a continental bent was to be expressed at all, it was more likely to be French than Italian, as one can see in Seton Palace, the family's principal country seat (see Figure 3.14). On his visit to Scotland in 1769, Thomas Pennant wrote of Newbattle Abbey that 'like most other houses of the *Scotch* nobility, [it] resembles a *French Chateau*.'[157]

Nevertheless, it would be too bashful to conclude this chapter without attempting to detect some broader architectural trends within the period. The most conspicuous development in architectural language was the increasing fondness for elaborate strapwork ornament, particularly after about 1620, the date of the completion of William Wallace's influential new wing at Linlithgow Palace. Carved pediments above windows and dormers were an expression of wealth and prestige, but also offered scope for heraldic displays (see Figure 3.7).

In terms of layout and syntax, the gradual increase in stability allowed a more open lifestyle. 'Laigh' halls began to appear, especially after 1603, and staircases became broader and better lit, especially to first-floor level. Scale-and-platt stairs in particular became increasingly popular. Apartments arranged horizontally offered more privacy and could express subtle gradations of hospitality. Access corridors increased the width of service areas, allowing the enlargement of the chambers above. The increasing popularity of the courtyard plan, inspired by the royal prototypes of Linlithgow and Holyrood (see Figure 2.17 and 2.15), is a development that one can easily underestimate because of the loss of such prominent examples as Hamilton Palace (see Figure 3.45). In general terms, an increase in the size and scale of landowners' houses in the period reflects the increasing prosperity of the age, as the rural economic base expanded into mining, trade and manufacture.

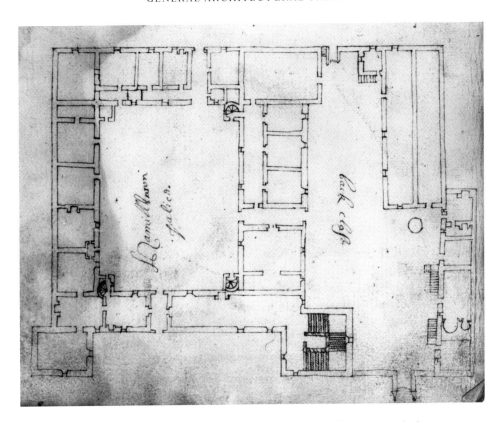

FIGURE 3.45   Hamilton Palace, Lanarkshire, the plan drawn by Isaac Miller, *c.*1677. Rebuilt
from 1822, demolished 1919.

In the country, the influence of the court remained fundamental, even after
1603, when James VI's courtiers followed the King to London. Some signs of
English influence can, of course, be detected in Scotland after 1603, especially in
the rich plaster ceilings of the first half of the seventeenth century. But even these
had a royal source in Bromley-by-Bow, which justified their adoption as a Stewart
feature rather than as an English one. The courtly medievalism of Scotland was
paralleled in English visual culture in the same years, but although the same pattern
books were in circulation north and south of the border, the great houses of the
Scottish nobility retained a strong sense of national identity.

Of the Three Estates, the nobility was the most deeply rooted in tradition
architecturally. Nobles and lairds, especially those granted former church lands,
needed an imagery of feudal tradition to stabilise their rights to their new estates,
just as much as they sought trend-setting modernity. The historian who seeks to
impose a logical or sequential pattern on this complex interaction of ideals can
hardly do justice to the richness of invention that it embodies.

CHAPTER FOUR

The Burghs

In 1647, James Gordon of Rothiemay was paid 500 merks by the burgh of Edinburgh for his 'paines and travellis' incurred in making the 'draught of the Toun' (see Figure 4.1).[1] His impressive bird's-eye view of Edinburgh was published in the same year, to be followed in 1661 by that of the largest town of his native region, Aberdeen. In Gordon's views, each building was depicted with apparently minute accuracy (see Figure 4.18); and yet the clear structure of the original medieval feuing pattern survived to control and organise the layout. The towns were displayed as ordered, coherent macro-organisms, within which individuals could flourish and display their own identity. These maps were Scotland's first accomplished cartographic celebration of the new civic consciousness which characterised the Renaissance period throughout Europe. The association between an ordered townscape and an ordered society can be traced back to the writers of antiquity, most notably Cicero.[2] As we have seen, Scotland was a major European centre of scholarship in the fifteenth and sixteenth centuries, and an awareness of the authority of classical antiquity was fostered by the expansion in printing and publishing. The inscription on the new building of Edinburgh University, dated 1617, makes explicit reference to Roman precedent with the opening words 'SENATVS POPOLVSQVE EDINBVRGENSIS ...'

The need to give a visual imagery to the townscape was stimulated by the rapid increase in travel, both national and international. Scottish merchants travelled

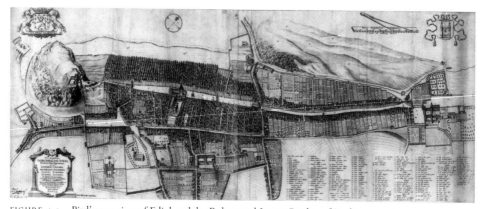

FIGURE 4.1   Bird's-eye view of Edinburgh by Robert and James Gordon of Rothiemay, 1647.

throughout Europe, while their towns were visited by numerous foreigners – merchants, diplomats, churchmen, adventurers, and scholars among others. A town had to be recognisable, and its plan easily understood, in order for a visitor to assimilate the experience, or for a citizen to describe his home-town to others.

It is important to remember that Scotland's burghs – whether medieval or later foundations – were formally planned from the start. A street plan was devised, the position of the public buildings decided, and the street-frontages were feued out to the prospective inhabitants.[3] The layout of each burgh was designed to take account of local landmarks and topography, but all shared the same characteristic subdivision into long, thin plots, arranged perpendicular to the main street, or streets. The simplest layout (Edinburgh being the most famous example) was the single main thoroughfare, widening in the centre to make space for a market (see Figure 4.1).[4] Edinburgh and its suburb, the Canongate, were not 'ribbon-developments', growing up haphazardly along an existing road. The main street was deliberately created to link the castle to Holyrood Abbey – it led no further in either direction. This 'Royal Mile' served as the setting for ceremonial and mercantile activity, rather than as a line of communication. In some burghs, such as Old Aberdeen, Haddington or Lauder, the main street forked at one end to make a Y-shape. The plan of Dundee, roughly a St Andrew's Cross, was described in 1678 by the Revd Robert Edward as resembling 'a human body, stretched on its back with its arms towards the west, and its legs towards the east'.[5] In an ingenious display of self-conscious humanism, he likened the church to the head, and the market-place to the belly, with the market cross at the navel. Glasgow began as a simple intersection of north–south/east–west streets near the cathedral. As the city expanded in the Renaissance period, the centre of gravity moved southward towards the Clyde, to focus on a second *quadrivium* at the centre of the merchant city which almost exactly repeated the form of the original ecclesiastical centre.[6] Old and New Aberdeen show a similar distinction between the cathedral town to the north and the merchant city further south towards the harbour.

Reading travellers' accounts, we can sense the need of visitors to define the character of each Scottish town. Edinburgh offered the most memorable first impression, with its densely packed tenements piled up on either side of the High Street, visible from far away. In the words of Thomas Pennant: 'The view of the houses at a distance strikes the traveller with wonder; their own loftiness, improved by their almost aerial situation, gives them a look of magnificence not to be found in any other part of Britain.'[7] The Royal Mile was typically described as a 'broad and very faire street' (by Fynes Moryson); 'the goodliest street that ever mine eyes beheld' (by Taylor the Water Poet); 'the glory and beauty of the city' (by Sir William Brereton); and 'the most spacious, the longest, and best inhabited street in Europe' (by Defoe).[8] Leith's waterfront offered a similarly imposing frontage: 'Scotland cannot present you with a more pleasant port; for here the houses and structures are large and lofty, and the pier like a gnomen directs to the tolbooth', wrote Cambridge-born Richard Franck in 1656.[9] This comment by Franck shows how much the traveller appreciated an easily understood plan-form. Glasgow had

the most flamboyant array of steeples, each one topped by a great gilded weathercock erected at the expense of the burgh council (see Figure 4.2). Whether outside
the town or within its precincts, the visitor would notice roof-top embellishments
and steeples, which not only enlivened the skyline but also aided orientation.[10]

Local materials contributed to the individuality of the townscape.[11] Perhaps the
best-endowed city in this respect was Aberdeen, with its silvery-white granite
masonry. At the opposite extreme was the textile-manufacturing town of Kilmar-
nock, disparagingly described by Franck as having 'such ugly houses, as, in my
opinion, are but little better than huts … all built so low that their eaves hang
dangling to touch the earth'.[12] In Caithness and Orkney, the local flagstones split
so thinly that they could not only be laid in layers in the walls but also used as roof
tiles. Red sandstone quarried in the south-west, as well as in other quarries down
the east side of the country, allowed an unusually colourful townscape in towns
such as Dumfries, Dunbar and Arbroath. Most of Scotland is endowed with good
building stone, but the cost of masonry was still relatively high because of the
amount of skilled labour involved.[13] Ashlar masonry was confined to the buildings
of highest prestige, while rubble masonry was generally harled or limewashed.
Slates and red clay pantiles were used increasingly to roof town houses from the
seventeenth century onwards.[14] In Edinburgh, local by-laws required fire-proof
materials: from 1621 onwards, all new buildings in Edinburgh's High Street had
to be roofed with slate.[15] Wooden galleries extending the space inside the house
were especially common in Edinburgh, where a royal decree of 1508 had encouraged the erection of timber frontages, projecting up to 7 feet forward into the
street, in order to clear trees from the Borough Muir (see Figure 4.3).[16]

Gates and walls could give visual coherence to a townscape, but few Scottish

FIGURE 4.2   Glasgow from the south, from Slezer's *Theatrum Scotiae*.

FIGURE 4.3   Edinburgh, Skinner's Close, drawn by James Drummond, 1856, showing timber galleries.

towns were completely walled. In 1521, the historian John Major singled out Perth as 'the only walled town in Scotland',[17] but this was an impression enhanced by the *castrum*-like rectangular shape of the town (see Figure 4.4).[18] These walls have now disappeared, but they were still intact in 1655 when Thomas Tucker described Perth as 'an handsome walled towne, with a citadell added thereunto of late yeares' – referring to the newly built Cromwellian fortress.[19] Edinburgh's Flodden Wall, begun after the traumatic defeat of 1513 at the hands of the English, enlarged and replaced the earlier walls, but it did not prevent the Earl of Hertford's invasion in 1544.[20] Stirling was neatly wrapped in walls, built in 1547–8 'for resisting of oure old innemeis of Ingland', and improved in 1574, giving its dense and complex street pattern a more definable shape.[21]

The most advanced fortifications built in Scotland in the sixteenth century, though from the ground the least impressive, were the star-shaped ramparts of Leith, begun by the French in 1548 to protect Mary of Guise and her court (see Figure 4.5).[22] The design emulates the angle-bastioned fortress of the Fortezza da Basso outside Florence, begun in 1534 with a similar objective, namely to protect the Medici Grand Dukes from an internal uprising. The architect of the Fortezza da Basso was Antonio da Sangallo the Younger, but the strategy seems to have been proposed by Filippo Strozzi.[23] It can be no coincidence that the designer of the Leith fortifications in 1548 was Filippo Strozzi's son, Piero, a military expert at

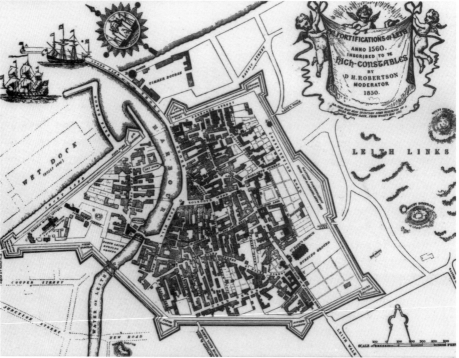

FIGURE 4.4 (*upper*)   Perth, plan by J. Rapkin, vignettes by H. Winkles, mid-nineteenth century.
FIGURE 4.5 (*lower*)   Leith, fortifications begun in 1548, map from David Henderson Robertson's
Sculptured Stones of Leith, Leith, 1850.

the French court, who directed the work from a sedan chair because of an injury. The defences were deliberately mutilated as soon as Leith capitulated to the Protestants in 1560,[24] but remnants of the low angle bastions and the earthen banks and ditches survived for centuries. Even in 1655, the English customs official Thomas Tucker was to observe that 'The towne of Leith is of it selfe a pretty small towne, and fortifyed about.'[25] It was not until the 1650s that Cromwell's men built similarly modern fortifications, for instance in the citadels overlooking the harbours of Ayr and Inverness.

Most towns were in fact surrounded by simple boundary walls, rather than modern defensive ramparts, not to repel invasion but to enable the control of merchandise entering and leaving the burgh. Travellers and merchants were held up at the town gates (usually called ports or bows) for the payment of customs dues and tolls. The only Scottish Renaissance town gate to have survived is the West Port of St Andrews (see Figure 4.6), built in 1589 by the Fife mason Thomas Robertson, who was directed to use Edinburgh's Netherbow Port as the model.[26] The Netherbow, which defined the lower limit of Edinburgh's High Street, was demolished as a traffic obstruction in 1764.[27] The appearance of this courtly, French-style gateway, with its conical turrets and tall steeple, is known from old engravings, and from its remaining fragments preserved at Huntly House (see Figure 4.7). The steeple – equipped with a great bell, newly recast in Middelburg, and the burgh clock, newly restored and painted – was erected when the gateway was repaired and embellished in 1606–9.[28] Archways stood at either end of the stone bridge at Stirling, but these, too, have been removed.[29] Glasgow's 'orna-mental ports', admired by Franck in 1656, were soon to be swept away to allow the passage of wheeled traffic.[30]

It was the arch of the town gate which framed the visitor's first glimpse into the town as he lingered, awaiting permission to enter. Forced to contemplate its imagery, as one might pause to admire the frontispiece of a seventeenth-century book, the traveller would absorb the implications of its architectural form and its heraldic displays. The West Port of St Andrews, for instance, carried the Royal arms – the town, though founded by David I in about 1130, was not ratified as a royal burgh until 1620.[31] Likewise, the arms of the City of Edinburgh, displayed on its civic buildings and still to be seen on the Tron Church (see Figure 5.15), portray a battlemented castle, again celebrating the feudal origins and royal status of the burgh. On his royal entry into Edinburgh in 1579, the young James VI was welcomed with a triumphal arch 'qhuarupon was erectit the genealogie of the kings of Scotland'.[32] In 1616, payments were made to the French artist Benjamin Lambert for a portrait and royal arms of James VI to adorn the Netherbow 'in remembrance of his Majestie and of thair sincere affectioun borne unto him'.[33] Unfortunately Lambert died in the course of the work, and the statue was completed by John Mylne.[34] For the entry of Charles I into Edinburgh in 1633, 109 kings of Scotland were painted on the west end of the Tolbooth by the celebrated Scottish portrait painter George Jameson.[35]

This was a period when the towns, like the court and feudal lords, were searching

FIGURE 4.6 (*above*)   St Andrews, Fife, West Bow, 1589. From a photo of *c*.1870.

FIGURE 4.7 (*left*)   Edinburgh, Netherbow Port, demolished in 1764. From William Maitland, *History of Edinburgh*, Edinburgh, 1853.

for their own antiquity. The need for a visible history was intensified by the
Reformation, which had created a disorientating fracture between past and
present.[36] When Edinburgh welcomed James VI in 1617, the city's welcome
oration traced its own foundation back to 331 BC.[37] Similarly, David Buchanan's
Latin description, written to accompany Rothiemay's map of Edinburgh of 1647
(see Figure 4.1), devotes a lengthy section to claiming a Hebrew etymology for
the city's name.[38] It was not enough simply to adopt the decorative embellishments
of Roman classicism as a superficial veneer to town buildings – Scotland wanted
its own history, not a history grafted from outside.[39]

The synergy between the church and the burghs, fostered by their shared
Calvinist principles, gave these two groups a strong political voice in Parliament in
the century following the Reformation. This chapter will explore the ways in which
the confidence and economic security of the burghs was expressed in the assurance
and solidity of their architecture. The burgh council was led by the Lord Provost,
usually a leading burgess, but in some towns (Peebles, for example) this office was
held by a member of the leading local land-owning family.[40] The council was re-
elected annually, but some members might be retained from the old council – four
in the case of Aberdeen – to ensure continuity.[41] The leading councillors were the
baillies and the Dean of Guild. In the larger towns, the magistrate with the greatest
direct impact on the townscape was the Dean of Guild, who was responsible for
matters such as boundary disputes, materials, repairs to municipal buildings and
obliging feuars to repair or replace derelict structures.[42] The rest of the council
was made up of representatives of the craft incorporations and the merchant guilds,
in varying proportions.[43] Whereas in Perth the craftsmen were the majority group,
a port such as Dundee was dominated by its merchants.[44] The balance was further
complicated by the involvement of the country landowners in trade. Mercantile
lairds were especially prominent in Aberdeen and the North-East – we need only
think of 'Danzig Willie' Forbes of Craigievar – but in the ports along both sides of
the Firth of Forth, too, the aristocracy exported salt and coal from their estates.[45]

Although the burgh share of national taxation was never more than one-sixth,[46] the
Incorporation of Royal Burghs was a politically powerful faction in Renaissance Scotland,
able to raise capital more easily than any other social group. Some royal burghs
established in the twelfth century – such as Cullen or Inverurie – were, by now, small
villages little bigger than a fermtoun. Indeed, as late as the eighteenth century, 90
percent of the population of Scotland would still be living in fermtouns.[47] Nevertheless,
most of the towns with a good harbour and a productive hinterland prospered, despite
the ups and downs in trade and farm-yields. Almost every east coast port flourished,
and a series of new royal burghs founded along the coast of Fife by James VI (Culross,
Burntisland, Dysart, Earlsferry, Anstruther Easter and Wester, and Kilrenny) gave
further encouragement to North Sea trade.[48] The foundation of sixty-four new burghs
of barony in the Lowlands between 1600 and 1650 attested to the growing indus-
trialisation of the coal-mining areas.[49] Urbanisation hardly impinged on the Highlands,
except for the three towns founded by Act of Parliament in 1597 to maintain order –
namely Fort William, Campbelltown and Stornoway.[50]

The largest city, both in terms of population and volume of trade, during the period of this book was Edinburgh, with a population estimated at about 30,000 in the seventeenth century.[51] In 1594, using the share of national taxation as the yardstick, the next four towns in order of size were Dundee, Aberdeen, Perth and Glasgow (see Figures 4.31, 4.24, 4.4 and 4.2).[52] The rise of Glasgow is the most remarkable success story, for by 1670 it had risen to second place, its prosperity swelled by the increasing importance of trade with Ulster and the New World and the development of manufacturing industries.[53] Even small towns could grow out of all recognition. In 1655, Thomas Tucker remarked of Bo'ness that 'This port, next to Leith, hath of late beene the chiefe port one of them in Scotland',[54] whereas Sir Robert Sibbald recalled in 1698 that: 'There was a gentleman died since the year 1660 who remembered that ther was bot one house where now ther is the town of Borrowstoness.'[55] Bo'ness was ideally placed to import goods from the Baltic or Holland and transport them overland to Glasgow and the South-West.[56]

TOLBOOTHS, TRONS AND MERCAT CROSSES

The three essential elements at the heart of a Scottish burgh were the tolbooth (or town hall), the mercat cross and the town kirk. These were the symbols of the political, economic and spiritual life of the community respectively. The erection of a tolbooth could be funded either by the feudal superior, or more commonly by the burgh council.[57] At Fraserburgh, according to the charter of erection dated 1613, the tolbooth, mercat cross and harbour were provided by the superior, Sir Alexander Fraser.[58] At Stonehaven, by contrast, the tolbooth was improvised in about 1600 from a former warehouse belonging to the superior, the Earl Marischal.[59] At Peterhead, the Earl Marischal was even less munificent, obliging the feuars – once their number reached thirty – to build the tolbooth at their own expense, or else to pay him 200 merks for the construction.[60] Edinburgh needed special taxes and loans to pay for its public works, whereas by the early sixteenth century the rapidly growing burgh of Glasgow seems to have funded its municipal building projects from revenue income. The rapid turnover of councillors meant erratic patronage, with little consistent architectural policy, unless funds were available to carry a scheme through without interruption.[61]

The principal function of the tolbooth was to provide a council chamber and court room, but it might also serve a wide variety of other uses, ranging from the town prison to the local school.[62] No Scottish tolbooths survive from the medieval period, but we do know the appearance of part of the first recorded tolbooth in Edinburgh, the 'Belhous' founded after the fire of 1386, which stood at the north-west corner of the town kirk of St Giles (see Figure 4.8).[63] This was a tall, narrow, gabled stone house, with a conically roofed stairtower to the south, and flamboyant gothic niches on the north side facing the High Street.

The provision of a new tolbooth in Edinburgh was one of the first resolutions passed by the town council under the Protestant Congregation on 19 June 1560, anticipating the first assembly of the new Parliament in August of the same year.

FIGURE 4.8   Edinburgh, sketch by the Revd John Sime, showing from left to right: the Luckenbooths on the north side of St Giles, the old 'Belhous' begun in c.1386, and the tolbooth, built in 1609–10.

The initial plan, to build 'ane fair Tolbuith for serving of the town in their affairs and all other necessar rooms' in the west end of St Giles, also proposed 'ane scole for their barnes' at the east end, leaving room between for the 'preiching and ministration of the sacraments'.[64] This conversion was carried out in 1562–3, starting with the demolition of part of the old tolbooth, so that its timbers could be reused.[65] The work was interrupted by a financial crisis, but the necessary money was raised to avoid offence to the Queen 'becaus hir hieness had commandit the samyn to be endit with all deligence'.[66] The Queen's impatience probably reflected her recognition that her political survival depended on the proper use of Parliament, for which the tolbooth would provide premises of suitable dignity.

The erection of a new tolbooth in Leith in the same years likewise involved Mary Queen of Scots, who was feudal superior of the port where she had arrived in Scotland just two years earlier. Here, once again, she became impatient with the burgh council of Edinburgh, who tried to block the project in 1563, claiming their own right to the superiority of Leith.[67] In 1564, she issued a defiant order to Edinburgh to allow the citizens of Leith to erect their tolbooth 'for it is oure will that the samyn be biggit'.[68] The tolbooth no longer survives, but nineteenth-century views reveal its flamboyant, European character (see Figure 4.9). At one end of the first-floor council chamber, a courtly oriel topped by heraldic beasts projected boldly, supported on ostentatious corbelling just above eye level. String

courses meandered anarchically across the façade, which was topped by a crenellated
parapet pierced by gargoyles in the form of cannons. The external forestair would
have been used for public proclamations as well as to enhance the ceremonial
dignity of the council functions.[69] The placing of the hall over the pend parallels
the same arrangement in the former west wing of Holyrood Palace, (see Figure
2.4). An ostentatious heraldic panel asserts the royal patronage, which Queen Mary
was to relinquish just two years later when she agreed to hand over the superiority
of Leith to the burgh of Edinburgh in return for a loan of 10,000 merks.[70]
Showy oriel windows were characteristic of Northern European town halls in the
Renaissance period – one could cite the example of the Rathaus of Altenburg, built
in the very same years (1562–4), which has two corbelled oriels overlooking the
town square. But in the Leith tolbooth, the oriel window also expressed feudal
lordship, evoking the bay-window at the high table end of a royal or noble hall.

    Tolbooths were obliged by Act of Parliament to possess a belfry and a bell, but the
appearance of the former 'Belhous' at Leith is uncertain.[71] The tolbooth of nearby
Musselburgh was erected in 1590 (see Figure 4.10), but the adjoining bell tower, like
that of Edinburgh, is reputed to be earlier – a tradition supported by the survival of
the clock given by the Dutch States in 1496. The eccentric profile of this tower, likened
by Colin McWilliam to 'a slated and static model of a Dutch windmill', suggests a
conscious attempt to celebrate Netherlandish trading links.[72] Although the solid ashlar
façade of Musselburgh's tolbooth is much less flamboyant than its Leith predecessor, it
adopts the same broad scheme of the external forestair to the first-floor meeting room,
over a ground floor containing prison cells and a pend to the back of the site. But
instead of courtly splendour, this building exhibits the dour solidity of post-Reformation
burgh values, superseding the old order almost literally by the reuse of stonework from
the nearby chapel of Our Lady of Loreto.

    The tolbooth of Edinburgh's suburb, the Canongate (see Figure 4.11), was
almost exactly contemporary with that of Musselburgh. It bears an inscription to
Sir Lewis Bellenden, the feudal superior of the burgh, and the date 1591 on the
tower entrance, while the great heraldic panel in the centre of the façade carries a
dedication to James VI on its pediment.[73] The basic layout again echoes that of
the Leith tolbooth, with a forestair – originally perpendicular to the façade – to the
first-floor council room, and a stately oriel, here topped by thistle finials, at the
other end of the chamber. As at Leith and Musselburgh, a pend leads through to
the rear of the building, in this case piercing the base of the tower. The four
pedimented dormers on a corbelled parapet across the roofline were rebuilt in the
restoration of 1875, when changes were also made to the doors and windows of
the ground floor, once the prison cells. The Canongate tolbooth is dominated by a
bell tower projecting forward into the street, and rising high above its roofline, as
at Musselburgh. Here, too, we find, in the profile of the spire, early signs of the
Dutch influence that was to be so prominent in Scottish tolbooth architecture,
though it is compromised by the French–Scottish conical bartizans at the corners.[74]
And here, too, we have a literal legacy of the North Sea trading link in the survival
of a bell made in 1608 by Jan Burgerhuys of Middelburg.[75]

FIGURE 4.9 (*upper*)   Leith, tolbooth, 1564, from a drawing by S. R. Burns in the possession
of Charles McKean. Demolished in 1823.
FIGURE 4.10 (*lower*)   Musselburgh, East Lothian, tolbooth, 1590.

FIGURE 4.11 (*upper*)   Canongate, Edinburgh, tolbooth, 1591.
FIGURE 4.12 (*lower*)   Kinghorn, Fife, former tolbooth, from MacGibbon and Ross, *Castellated and Domestic Architecture*, vol. V.

Whereas the towns we have considered so far were old-established communities eager to celebrate their own long history, the east coast of Scotland was sprouting new burghs in the later sixteenth century. Some towns were, of course, older foundations, such as the fishing port of Crail, where a Dutch bell dated 1520 (preserved in the tolbooth) is still symbolically tolled every evening at ten o'clock.[76] The tolbooth adopts the arrangement, already seen at Musselburgh and the Canongate, of a bell tower with an adjoining wing housing the council chamber.[77]

This was a period of much experimentation, however. Some tolbooths, such as at Stonehaven and Culross, lacked bell towers.[78] Older structures were often incorporated, whether for economy or for symbolic reasons. One of the most curious examples is the former tolbooth of Kinghorn in Fife, recorded by Mac-Gibbon and Ross, which seems to envelop an older church within its bulky construction (see Figure 4.12).[79] Its architectural idiom is that of a lordly tower-house rather than a municipal building, with a huge round tower at one end capped by a corbelled rectangular cap-house. If Kinghorn literally swallowed up a church tower, the top of the steeple of Kirkcudbright tolbooth was partly built of stones from nearby Dundrennan Abbey, and the tolbooth of Elgin – erected in 1605 – was 'biggit wt. stanes frae ye kirkyard dyke'.[80] The hall wing of the latter (which later acquired a Venetian window and double forestair) flanked a solid, Dutch-looking tower with a curiously tapering corbelled turret at one corner.

The close relationship between the kirk and the burgh could even result in a combined kirk and tolbooth. We have already seen how the west end of St Giles was fitted out as a tolbooth in 1562–3. At Pittenweem, the kirk tower – rebuilt in about 1588 – housed the tolbooth and the grammar school;[81] and at Fordyce in Banffshire, the tower of St Talorgan's Church – dated 1661 on the belfry – served as the town prison, reached by a forestair to the first floor.

The tolbooth that was eventually constructed in Edinburgh was not in the Kirk itself, but against the west flank of the old 'Belhous', part of which had been demolished leaving an unsightly scene of dereliction. In 1581, the council deplored the old tolbooth now 'lyand waist', and resolved to rebuild it using a supply of stone from Inchcolm Island, but the craft deacons opposed the scheme.[82] The project was revived in 1597, when a proposal to build a new church in the Kirk o'Field was dropped in favour of returning the west end of St Giles to ecclesiastical use, and 'the bigging of the Tolbuith qhair it wes of auld'.[83] In 1598, it was lamented that the site of the old tolbooth still lay waste 'to the greitt skayth and deformities of the haill toun'.[84] In that year the burgh resolved to raise £20,000 for the scheme, and in 1600 they agreed to build a new tolbooth 'for administration of Justice abone the waster Kirk of this burgh', presumably this time outside, rather than inside St Giles.[85] But the project again fell dormant until 1609, when the master mason Andrew Symsoun was commissioned to erect a new prison 'in the auld tolbuith be west the present tolbuith quhair the grund is presentlie red'.[86] In 1632, under pressure from Charles I to restore St Giles to a single church, the burgh again resolved to remove the council chamber and courts from the High Kirk 'to be buildit upone the hie streit above the new tolbuith'.[87] In the event, however, the courts were accommodated in the new Parliament building, to be discussed later in this chapter. Edinburgh's tolbooth was first and foremost a prison.[88]

Thus, the tolbooth that we know from nineteenth-century views seems to have consisted of a late fourteenth-century 'Belhous' and an adjoining building erected in two stages in 1609–10. It projected westwards along the High Street, extending the line of the Luckenbooths – the row of shops and tenements which enveloped the north side of St Giles – and enclosing a new civic space in front of the west end of the kirk (see Figure 4.13). If Walter Scott's *Heart of Midlothian*, published the year after the tolbooth's removal in 1817, offered a literary elegy, most of the nineteenth-century, posthumous engravings were equally romanticised in their picturesque irregularity.[89] By contrast, the most carefully observed of Nasmyth's drawings clearly shows the tolbooth as a five-storey block, nearly symmetrical in elevation (see Figures 4.8 and 4.13).[90] With its central stairtower (conically roofed like that of the Belhous) facing the new square, the tolbooth was a reduced version of the formula that we have already seen used in royal palace blocks of the late sixteenth and early seventeenth centuries. The masonry quoins around the windows on the north side suggest that the building was harled, in contrast to the ashlar finish of the Belhous, but string-courses between each storey gave order to the elevations, counteracting the strong verticality. The two-storey extension with its roof-top balcony over a row of shops was added to the west side in 1633, to serve as a ceremonial stage during the visit of Charles I.[91] It was at this time that George Jameson was commissioned to paint the portraits of 109 Scottish kings, mentioned earlier, to decorate the west end of the tolbooth.[92]

The use of a simplified palace-block design for Edinburgh's tolbooth, responding to the increasing desire for classical symmetry and regal dignity, represented an appealing alternative to the asymmetrical formula of Leith tolbooth and its successors. An awareness of Dutch town halls with central stairtowers reinforced the trend, for these offered an image of Calvinist public morality and frugal prosperity, two qualities emulated in Scottish burghs. The old tolbooth at Linlithgow was apparently recorded in 1667 when designs for its replacement were presented to the burgh by John Mylne, the royal master mason. Whereas some of these drawings show Mylne's proposed scheme (in the event his design was not executed because his death intervened),[93] others depict a thick-walled, three-storey palace block with a central bell tower, gabled dormers and a projecting wing to the rear (see Figure 4.14).[94] This alternative would have seemed old-fashioned in 1667 and appears to represent an earlier structure. Whereas in Linlithgow the royal associations of the palace formula would have been recognised, at Dunbar, a port that depended on trade with the Low Countries, the North Sea imagery predominated (see Figure 4.15).[95] The tolbooth, dating from about 1650, has an octagonal stairtower in the centre of the façade, recalling Netherlandish models such as Gennep and 's Heerenberg, a link underlined by its dumpy, Dutch-style spire, brick-red stone and capped crow steps.[96]

Whereas Edinburgh vacillated and procrastinated over the rebuilding of its

FIGURE 4.13   Edinburgh, tolbooth, 1609–10; Belhouse from *c.*1386; and the east front of St
Giles, from the south-west. Drawing by Alexander Nasmyth, just before their demolition in
1817, in the collection of Mrs Sylvia Stevenson.

tolbooth, Glasgow burgh council was decisive and efficient. In 1625, 'all in ane
voice' they set about procuring stone and acquired a thousand salvaged ships'
timbers.[97] Early in 1626, the old tolbooth was demolished and the foundation stone
for the new one laid.[98] The following year, the master of work John Boyd was paid
£100 'for his bounthethe and deligens in building the Tolbuithe'.[99] By 1628, the
painter Valentine Jenkin had been paid for gilding the weathercock and coats of
arms, and the clock maker had completed the clock for the tower.[100] The tolbooth
itself was demolished when it was rebuilt by Thomas Hamilton in 1813 (this
structure, in turn, was demolished in *c.*1921), but the steeple survives (see Figure
4.16).[101] Its height (126 feet) is all the more impressive when one remembers that
the tolbooth itself, five storeys high, reached to the level of the top-most string-
course, just below the clock.

The layout adopted in the Glasgow tolbooth was not that of the symmetrical
palace-block type, but addressed older prototypes with its external stair at one end
and bell tower at the other. The crenellated parapet (like that of Leith tolbooth)
and the corbelled, square turrets at the roofline also asserted the antiquity of the
burgh. The architectural language, however, was absolutely up-to-date. The façade
articulated by ornately pedimented windows and string-courses emulated the newly
built north wing of Linlithgow Palace, completed by William Wallace in 1620,
while buckle quoins were becoming a fashionable detail in Scottish buildings with
court connections in this period.[102] Similar, square, bartizan-like turrets were to

FIGURE 4.14   Linlithgow tolbooth, drawn by John Mylne, 1667. From Mylne, *Master Masons*.

be found on the newly rebuilt royal palace block at Edinburgh Castle. The regal imagery was underlined by the crown spire, recalling the kirks of Linlithgow and Edinburgh. Glasgow was a merchant city, but it was also an ancient royal burgh, eager to outdo the capital, then as now. A generation later, in 1656, the Cambridge traveller Richard Franck still wrote admiringly of this 'stately tolbooth, a very sumptuous, regulated, uniform fabrick, large and lofty, most industriously and artificially carved from the very foundation to the superstructure, to the great admiration of strangers and travellers'.[103] Even Defoe was to describe the building as 'very noble and very strong', whereas he dismissed the Edinburgh tolbooth as 'a miserable hole'.[104]

   Like the tolbooth, the mercat cross was an important symbol of burgh authority, asserting the trading privileges of the town.[105] Most mercat crosses of this period were stone shafts, usually polygonal, raised on a stepped platform and topped by a heraldic beast or coat of arms.[106] Examples of this type from the late sixteenth and

FIGURE 4.15   Dunbar, East Lothian, tolbooth, seventeenth century.

early seventeenth centuries can be seen at Clackmannan, Crail, Anstruther Easter, Fraserburgh and Inverkeithing, amongst others, though all of these have been moved or partly remodelled.[107]

The most elaborate mercat crosses were those raised above a flat-roofed platform from which public proclamations could be made (see Figures 4.17 and 4.19). The windowless interior of the drum had no function other than to house the stair, although the guards who kept watch at Edinburgh's tolbooth at night may have used the shelter. The mercat cross of Edinburgh played an important part in royal entries:[108] for the entry of Mary Queen of Scots in 1561, four 'fair virgynis' representing Fortune, Prudence, Justice and Policie welcomed her from the platform, while wine gushed from the gargoyles below.[109] When James VI visited the burgh in 1600, the drum was hung with tapestry, and the King himself sat on the cross during the sermon.[110] For the proclamation of the restoration of the monarchy in 1660, the whole burgh council 'in their riche robbis' stood with the heralds on

FIGURE 4.16   Glasgow, tolbooth steeple, 1626 (rest demolished in 1921).

the platform, 'the Croce being richly clad'.[111] Executions were held there, and severed heads, including that of Montrose in 1650, were even occasionally displayed on the cross.[112] (Brereton saw the Earl of Gowrie's head on the Leith tolbooth in 1626.[113])

In 1616–17, anticipating the visit of James VI, Edinburgh's mercat cross was moved from its original spot west of St Giles – now constricted by the new tolbooth – to a more spacious site further down the High Street, to the east of the church (see Figure 4.18).[114] The base was probably remodelled at this time, to judge by the confident classicism of its Ionic order framing arches borne on smaller Tuscan pilasters (see Figure 4.17). At about the same time, the little burgh of Preston (to the east of Edinburgh), on James VI's route from London, erected an even more accomplished version, with panelled Tuscan pilasters framing elegant shell niches (see Figure 4.19). Cannon-like water-spouts drain water from the platform, which is enclosed by a demure attic parapet.

If the mercat cross provided a symbolic monument to fair trading, the tron, or

FIGURE 4.17   Edinburgh, mercat cross, moved and probably remodelled in 1616–17. Engraved
by A. Cameron before its removal in 1756.

public weigh beam, enabled its practical implementation. Scots merchants would
have been familiar with the splendid weigh houses of Dutch ports, such as those of
Haarlem (1598) and Hoorn (1609), where giant balances hung in lofty arcaded
halls. In Scotland's burghs, however, the public scales were normally suspended
modestly from a vertical post in the open air. An example can still be seen at
Stenton in East Lothian. Edinburgh was most ambitious in this respect, with two
trons, one towards the Netherbow, near where the Tron Kirk now stands, and the
'Over Tron' or 'Butter Tron' further up the High Street at the Over Bow. The
upper tron was rebuilt in 1612–14, but it was reputedly destroyed by Cromwell;
the appearance of its successor, the 'Butter Tron', demolished in 1822, suggests
that much of the early seventeenth-century building may, in fact have survived the
Cromwellian ravages (see Figure 4.20).[115] The only surviving seventeenth-century
weigh house in Scotland seems to be the little two-bay wide building in the Fife
village of Ceres, identified by the pair of scales carved in relief over the door (see

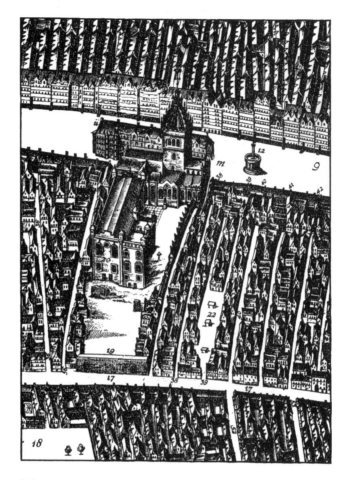

FIGURE 4.18   Edinburgh, detail of Gordon of Rothiemay's bird's-eye view of 1647, showing
St Giles with the tolbooth to the west, the mercat cross to the east and Old Parliament House
to the south.

Figure 4.21). This unassuming cottage, punctuated by rolled skews like inverted
commas, seems to have served as a tolbooth as well, for it has jougs beside the
door, and a basement cell at the back.

   Scotland's tolbooths, trons and mercat crosses of the post-Reformation period,
as we have seen, expressed a wide range of aspirations and references. Towns that
were growing rapidly through trade were eager to give the impression of a long-
established history, even if this were virtually non-existent, as in the case of Bo'ness,
whose tolbooth (now lost) was described by Pennant as being 'in the form of a
Castle'.[116] Glasgow, too, alluded to older traditions, as we have seen, while the
tower of New Aberdeen's tolbooth, built in 1615, displayed the corbelled bartizans
of nearby tower-houses. Others – such as Musselburgh, Dunbar, and Clackmannan – made reference to Netherlandish trading associations, especially in the
shapes of their towers. And although the burghs were dominated by the burgess

FIGURE 4.19   Preston, East Lothian, mercat cross, *c.*1617. Photo from *c.*1950.

class of merchants and craftsmen, promoting a community-based Calvinist morality, none the less the more powerful among them did not hesitate to allude to their royal connections, whether in architectural language or heraldic displays.

SCOTLAND'S PARLIAMENT

As we have seen, Edinburgh's tolbooth was used for parliamentary assemblies from the time of Mary Queen of Scots onwards. It was not until the reign of King Charles, between 1633 and 1639, that a Parliament building was finally erected. Although the royal master of works Sir James Murray directed the work and probably designed the building, it was the burgh of Edinburgh which had to finance the project from public subscriptions and repeated large loans.[117] This – rather than the tolbooth or the university – was Edinburgh's premier building project, proudly described by Buchanan as a *palatium*.[118]

The building was refaced in the early nineteenth century, but its original appearance is know from the views by Gordon of Rothiemay (see Figures 4.22 and

FIGURE 4.20   Edinburgh, 'Butter Tron', the upper weigh house, 1612–14, rebuilt or repaired in c.1660, drawn before its demolition in 1817 by D. Somerville.

4.18) and Elphinstone.[119] Fragments of the original façade can be seen at Arniston in Midlothian,[120] while the main hall with its splendid hammerbeam roof – the work of John Scott in 1637–9 – still survives inside (see Figure 4.23).[121] The site was steeply sloping and restricted, but its location was important, for it completed the civic square in front of St Giles framed on the north side by the new tolbooth (see Figure 4.18). The building was in the form of an L-shape, with a turnpike stair in the angle. The great hall was at first-floor level, raised over a 'laigh hall' entered by the grand portal facing St Giles, beneath Alexander Mylne's life-size figures of Justice and Mercy (see Figure 4.22).[122] This doorway is very similar in style to the rusticated portals of Glasgow University, begun just three years before (see Figure 4.25), while its diamond-rusticated pilasters recall a design in Francini's newly published treatise.[123] Elements drawn from other recent high-prestige buildings in the burghs include the ogee-domed stairtower, recalling those at Winton and Heriot's (see Figures 3.7 and 4.29), and the rectangular bartizans of Glasgow

FIGURE 4.21   Ceres, Fife, weigh house in the High Street, seventeenth century, from a
photograph of *c.*1889.

tolbooth and Edinburgh Castle (see Figure 2.14). Although the hammerbeam roof
revived the much older precedents of Westminster Hall and Edinburgh Castle, its
medievalism falls into place when we consider the awareness of historical allusion
that is so prominent in this period. Moreover, its ingenious carpentry displayed a
technical virtuosity that would not have failed to impress, especially given the low
pitch of the leaded roof above, hidden behind the roof-top parapet.

EDUCATION

Education was one of the most important elements in the Reformation programme
in Scotland, building on a basic educational structure previously in church hands.[124]
In 1560, Scotland already had three universities, Aberdeen, St Andrews and
Glasgow. Three more were to be established by the end of the century, namely
Edinburgh, Aberdeen's Marischal College, and a rival foundation by the Frasers of

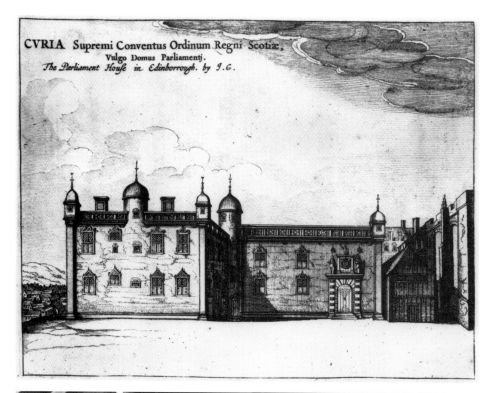

FIGURE 4.22 (*upper*) Edinburgh, Parliament House, 1633–9, designed by Sir James Murray of Kilbaberton. Drawn by Gordon of Rothiemay, 1647.

FIGURE 4.23 (*lower*) Edinburgh, Parliament House, the hammerbeam roof of the great hall by John Scott, 1637–9.

FIGURE 4.24   Old Aberdeen, from Slezer's *Theatrum Scotiae*. The university buildings are in the middle distance on the right.

Philorth in the newly founded port of Fraserburgh.[125] Though a serious proposal at the time, the last of these was too utopian to survive.

It is ironic that little building work was carried out at King's College in Old Aberdeen — Scotland's most distinguished centre of humanist scholarship in the period and the only one to teach Greek — until Cromwell's tower with its onion dome and crenellated parapet was added in 1658 (see Figure 4.24).[126] The pre-Reformation chapel and quadrangle, described by a French visitor in 1548 as 'sufficiently well ordered and equipped', were presumably splendid enough.[127] The Earl Marischal's university in New Aberdeen was founded on the site of the former Greyfriars' monastery, but its original buildings were replaced in the nineteenth century.

In the early seventeenth century, as printed books became cheaper and more plentiful, both St Andrews and Edinburgh universities erected new libraries — indeed Edinburgh burgh council, so often tight-fisted, donated 200 merks to St Andrews in 1613 towards the cost of 'ane common bibliothek'.[128] This library still survives on South Street, while much of the courtyard of St Mary's College behind is of the same period (1612–43).[129] Though much altered, this court has two fine towers, one ogee domed and one gabled, and the display of ornate strapworked pediments and heraldic panels hints at its former splendour.

Edinburgh University, founded in 1583, benefited greatly from the generosity of benefactors — both nobles and commoners — who gave money, books, instruments and even buildings, though the Marquis of Hamilton's claim to one of the buildings on the Kirk o'Field site was upheld in court, and the town had to pay him £3,000 to purchase the property back.[130] Two new buildings were completed in 1615–18 and 1642–6 respectively.[131] Such was the speed of acquisition of books that the earlier of these proved too small for the library, which was moved into the second building in 1646. Writing just afterwards, Buchanan, using the classical Greek term 'Academia', loyally described the university as 'magnificently enlarged and adorned with buildings' in his text to accompany Rothiemay's map.[132] But this panegyric comment was apparently as idealised as the view in the map itself. The buildings of Edinburgh's 'Tounis College' remained an improvised agglomeration loosely organised around two courts, until Robert Adam's new university was begun in 1789.[133]

As in the case of the tolbooths, Glasgow outdid Edinburgh in the provision of university buildings. The new college was begun in 1630, with a gift of 1,000 merks from the burgh, who donated a further 1,000 merks for library books.[134] This magnificent palace of learning, celebrated in Slezer's engraving of 1693 (see Figure 4.25), was on a new site further down the High Street, attesting to the shift of the town's centre of gravity from the cathedral to the merchant city. With its array of pedimented dormers, heraldic panels, polygonal, circular and square towers and strapwork ornament this was no utilitarian structure.[135] In 1636, Sir William Brereton remarked that 'there hath been collections throughout Scotland towards the building of this college, and much more money is collected than is needful thereof'.[136] The second court was completed in about 1660.[137] John Ray in 1662 considered its 'pretty stone building ... not inferior to Wadham and All Souls' Colleges' in Oxford,[138] but its conical turrets, polygonal oriel, floridly carved pediments and lofty clock tower gave it a North European air more reminiscent of a Danish or German palace than an Oxford college.

We know far less about school buildings in the aftermath of the Reformation than about Scotland's universities. The larger burghs already had grammar schools, but they were not fitted to their growing importance.[139] Edinburgh's High School was rebuilt in 1578 in the grounds of the former Blackfriars' monastery under the mason William Bikertoun (see Figure 4.26).[140] The building – a symmetrical gabled block with a projecting central jamb flanked by matching cylindrical stairtowers – was ready for occupation in the following year.[141] Its maintenance was the financial responsibility of the school master, who was obliged to keep it wind and watertight.[142] The first master in the new school lasted only five years, as a result![143] At this time, the Grammar School in Glasgow was still thatched; straw was bought for the repair of its roof in 1577.[144] In 1600, the council decided to rebuild the school, and the new building was begun in the following year under the master of works Thomas Pettigrew.[145] Even this building had short life, for in 1656 it was demolished and rebuilt yet again.[146]

Neither of these buildings has survived, and the one purpose-built school of the period which has remained in use ever since is hardly a typical case. This is the palatial Heriot's Hospital in Edinburgh, endowed in 1624 by the royal jeweller George Heriot, who had followed the King to London in 1603 (see Figure 4.27). Queen Anne of Denmark's appetite for jewellery was prodigious,[147] and enabled Heriot to make a fortune, which he bequeathed to the city of Edinburgh to found

FIGURE 4.25 (*upper*)   Glasgow University, begun in 1630, from Slezer's *Theatrum Scotiae*.
FIGURE 4.26 (*lower*)   Edinburgh, High School, 1578, demolished by 1777. From Grant's *Old and New Edinburgh*, vol. II.

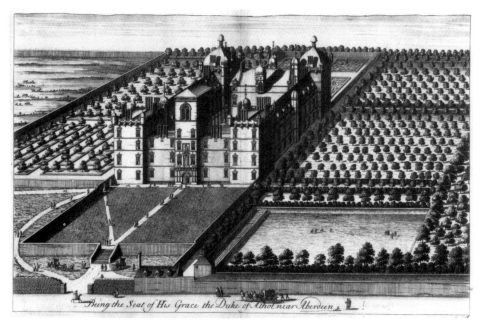

Being the Seat of His Grace the Duke of Athol near Aberdeen

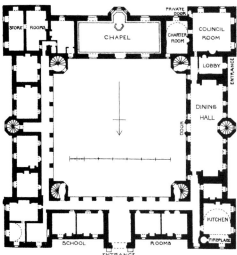

FIGURE 4.27 (*above*)   Heriot's Hospital,
Edinburgh, begun in 1628 by William Wallace
and continued after 1631 by William Aytoun.
From Slezer's *Theatrum Scotiae*, where the view is
given the wrong caption!
FIGURE 4.28 (*left*)   Heriot's Hospital,
Edinburgh, begun in 1628, the ground-plan.
From MacGibbon and Ross, *Castellated and
Domestic Architecture*, vol. IV.

an institution for the education of 'poor Orphans and Fatherless children of decayed
Burgesses and Freemen of the said burgh, destitute and left without means'.[148]
Heriot's executor, his nephew Sir Walter Balanquhall, then Dean of Rochester,
sent a plan from London, which seems to have been a version of the plan in Serlio's
book VII for a villa in Provence known as 'Il Rosmarino'.[149]

The building which rose above this *provençal* ground-plan (see Figure 4.28) was
no Mediterranean villa. It was a lofty courtyard palace which, like Glasgow
University, was in the North European idiom. We cannot tell who contrived the

overall design, although the Governors in 1627 specified that the new building was to 'conforme to ye paterne and prescript maid be ye said Deane of Rotchester'.[150] The royal master mason William Wallace was in charge of the project from the laying of the foundation stone in 1628 until his untimely death in 1631. After his death, Wallace's widow handed over his 'haill muldis and drauchtis' for the building in return for a pension from the hospital.[151] Wallace was succeeded by the master mason William Aytoun, whose portrait still hangs in the hospital. Aytoun was required to follow the prescribed design, supplying additional decorative details where needed. Indeed, the more daring style of ornament on the upper storey, where many of the pediments are broken, reflects the change of authorship, and thus suggests that the design of decorative detail, at least, was in the hands of the master masons.[152] The large number of masons' marks found on the building testifies to the scale of the building operation.

Heriot's Hospital is remarkable for the range of books consulted in its design. We have already mentioned the Serlian ground-plan; the fluted Doric pilaster order of the courtyard is also taken from Serlio's book VII, although the reader is unlikely to have studied the text which described this form as the 'Dorico bastardo', an allusion that was highly inappropriate in this case.[153] The refectory doorway (see Figure 4.29) is based on Vignola's design for his villa at Caprarola, published in his *Cinque Regole* in 1562, while the chapel doorway is taken from an absolutely up-to-date source, Alexandre Francini's treatise on architecture, published in Paris in 1631.[154] The northern treatises of Dietterlin and de Vries provided ideas for exuberant Mannerist detail such as textured rustication and buckle quoins. The correct succession of superimposed classical orders in the windows of the stair-towers (see Figure 4.29) suggests a conscious attempt to convey an erudite impression, but books were used as pattern books rather than sources of philosophical principles.

Despite its undisciplined eclecticism, Heriot's Hospital makes an emphatic architectural statement. That this is a palace is clear from the size and richness alone;[155] that it is a building with regal associations is evident from the employment of the royal master mason William Wallace, who developed the idiom of his newly completed north wing at Linlithgow Palace (see Figures 4.29 and 2.16). Indeed, this is one of the most conspicuous of the buckle-quoined buildings from the 1620s onwards, representing what Aonghus MacKechnie has described as a Scottish 'court style'.[156] In the richly embroidered stonework one can also imagine an allusion to the intricacy and splendour of Heriot's craft.

The building is not divorced from English Jacobean culture, however. After all, Balanquhall, like Heriot before him, was now living in London. In its medievalising elements — bartizans, gargoyles and machicolated corner towers — the building evokes the chivalric spirit of temporary festive scenery at the English court, such as Inigo Jones's masque design for Oberon's palace in 1611, or the magician's castle erected for the firework display celebrating the marriage of Princess Elizabeth to the Emperor Palatine in 1613.[157] If in the wedding scene ogee-domed turrets may have alluded to the Princess's German marriage, they were to become absorbed

FIGURE 4.29   Heriot's Hospital, Edinburgh, begun in 1628, the courtyard elevation towards
the refectory.

into the Jacobean vocabulary on both sides of the border. The imagery of knightly
pageantry was given permanent form in England in buildings such as Bolsover
Castle, begun by John Smythson in 1612, where the architect had recourse to a
range of continental treatises remarkably similar to those used at Heriot's – Serlio,
Dietterlin and Francini among them.[158] The interplay between medieval fantasy
and Renaissance control is subtle and complex, but at Heriot's the historical
allusions are subservient to the overriding air of authority. In the words of Thomas
Pennant, 'Herriot's hospital is a fine old building, much too magnificent for the
end proposed, that of educating poor children.'[159]

THE ARCHITECTURE OF COMMERCE AND INDUSTRY

As Scotland's trade expanded, an increasingly elaborate infrastructure of harbour
works, bridges, warehouses and industrial developments grew in parallel. Many of
the harbour works were financed by the great landowners, eager to find a safe port
from which to market their surpluses.[160] Thus the Earl of Winton, involved in
mining and salt-panning on his estates in East Lothian, constructed a new harbour
at Cockenzie.[160] Ingenuity was not lacking – Davie 'Do-A'thing' Anderson, the
probable inventor of the polyhedron sundial, gained great admiration for floating
away a great boulder at the mouth of Aberdeen harbour on the rising tide.[162] The

pumping mechanism at Sir George Bruce's under-sea coal-mines at Culross was so impressive that James VI was taken there on his return to Scotland in 1617.[163]

Co-operation between landowners and the burghs was remarkably effective. The Earl Marischal raised donations from both Edinburgh and Aberdeen for the new harbour at Stonehaven which he built in 1612.[164] The construction of the Isle of May lighthouse resulted from elaborate consultations held in 1635 between shipmasters of surrounding ports from Leith to St Andrews.[165] The lighthouse that was eventually constructed bears the arms of the feudal superior of the island, Alexander Cunningham of Barnes, and the date 1636.[166] Salt pans were extensive but architecturally unspectacular installations, which by the mid-seventeenth century stretched along both sides of the Firth of Forth. Further north, off the coast of Sutherland, a salt industry was established at Brora by the enterprising Jane Gordon, Countess of Sutherland.[167]

Of the industrial complexes of the period almost nothing survives. Edinburgh's mint or 'Cunzie House' in the Cowgate, erected in 1574 when minting was transferred to the town from the royal palaces, survived into the nineteenth century (see Figure 4.30).[168] The Cowgate at this time was no sordid back alley; in 1532 it had been described by Alexander Alesse as a street 'ubi nihil est humile aut rusticum, sed omnia magnifica'.[169] Edinburgh's brewery was much admired by Sir William Brereton in 1636: 'I ... observed there the greatest, vastest leads, boiling keeves, cisterns and combs, that I ever saw.'[170] Its site near the old university has recently been excavated, prior to the erection of the new Museum of Scotland on the site.

As in the Baltic ports the provision of storage space was essential, and to judge by written and graphic reports, warehousing in the larger ports such as Leith and Dundee was extensive, although not one warehouse from the period survives in either town today. As we shall see, some merchants' houses also had warehouse space, but the purpose-built warehouses must have been impressive. Defoe admired the tree-lined avenue between the town of Dundee and the harbour, with 'very good warehouses for merchandises, especially for heavy goods' along one side (see Figure 4.31).[171] One sixteenth-century warehouse has been preserved at Limekilns in Fife, a barn-like, rubble-built building with two superimposed, barrel-vaulted spaces, and a pediment above the door (apparently inserted later) bearing the date 1581 and the arms of the Pitcairn family.[172] At Peterhead, where the Earl Marischal founded a new port in 1593, a harbour warehouse preserves a pediment, dated 1616, from an earlier store on the site. Lerwick had piers with storerooms, known as 'lodberries', in front of the harbour-front houses. It is in Shetland that one of the most unusual commercial buildings from the sixteenth century still survives. This is the German merchants' booth at Symbister, on the island of Whaalsay, built in the shape of a boat to resist the waves on the seaward side (see Figure 4.32). A pulley hoisted fish into or out of the boats into the warehouse on the lower level, while an outside stair on the landward side led into the upper room. There was already a German 'booth' on Whaalsay in 1566 when it was attacked by pirates.[173] Merchants from the Hanseatic ports came each year to Shetland to buy stockfish.

FIGURE 4.30 (*upper*)   Edinburgh, the old mint or 'Cunzie House', 1574. From Grant's *Old and New Edinburgh*, vol. I.

FIGURE 4.31 (*lower*)   Dundee, the view from the east, from Slezer's *Theatrum Scotiae*.

The fish (ling or cod) was salted in the fishing boat, and then dried in buildings with slatted sides to allow the wind to pass through; an early example can be seen at Symbister near the Germans' booth. An English visitor in 1633 was struck by the extent of the trade with Hamburg and Bremen, but remarked that the herring fishing was done by Dutch sailors. He was unimpressed by the islands' burghs: 'There are several Towns in Shetland, so called, being about eight or ten houses together.'[174] Later in the seventeenth century, most houses were still roofed with turf and straw. Some were tiled with deals, but 'There are but only four Houses here thacked with slate.'[175]

Finally, we should mention the few guild halls of which we know the appearance. The former Skinners' Hall in Edinburgh is a sedate L-shaped building with a polygonal stairtower in the angle (see Figure 4.33).[176] The town's Tailors' Hall still stands, though much mutilated. Its coat-of-arms, engagingly decorated with a huge pair of scissors and dated 1644, is now in the courtyard at Huntly House. The Merchants' House in Glasgow, a palatial building on the Bridgegate, was built in 1659, but only its steeple remains, built in tiers like a German town spire.[177]

DOMESTIC BUILDINGS IN THE BURGH

The potential of buildings for expressing status – both the rank of the owner's class or social group, and the kudos of the individual and his/her family – was recognised throughout Europe. Renaissance treatises from Alberti onwards reveal a finely tuned awareness of the communication of social nuances through architecture. Meanwhile, the obsession with self-conscious image-making spread down through the social classes, as education, travel and trade expanded. The wide variety of Scottish town houses that survive from the century 1560–1660 is at first baffling, given the regional variations in materials, trading links and town size.[178] None the less, it is possible to distinguish general themes in the period; and the range of disparate elements within these broad categories reflects not confusion and uncertainty, so much as inventiveness and self-assurance.

In every royal burgh or burgh of barony, traces of the original feuing pattern remained. Along the frontage of the main street (or streets), the original feu widths still dominated the property boundaries, even if complicated by subdivision and amalgamation. As a general rule, houses would be built with their gable ends facing the street to allow more living space on each plot.[179] Access to the rear of each toft or land – as the plots were called – would be through a pend or close. Only in smaller burghs, where there was less pressure on the land, would one find small two-storey houses with the roofline parallel to the street, often with an outside stair to the upper dwelling.[180] Few survive from this period, as they would have been simple thatched cottages, but examples of a slightly later date can be seen in St Andrews, Falkland and Prestonpans.

One of the consequences of the regularised feu widths was that the possession of two or more adjoining plots was, in itself, a status symbol. Thus we find, in Renaissance mansions such as Moray House in the Canongate (see Figure 4.34) or the so-called French Ambassador's House in Musselburgh (see Figure 4.35), that

FIGURE 4.32 (*above*) Symbister,
Whaalsay, Shetland, German merchant's
booth, sixteenth century.
FIGURE 4.33 (*left*) Edinburgh, Skinners'
Hall, from Grant's *Old and New
Edinburgh*, vol. I.

the simple fact of the alignment of the roofline parallel to the street played a part in the display. In more densely built-up towns such as Edinburgh and Stirling, however, the larger houses became taller rather than wider, or extended further back from the street. An example is the late sixteenth- or early seventeenth-century house known as Darnley's House in Stirling, where status is expressed instead in the fine ashlar masonry and the three pedimented dormers straddling the eaves.[181] At the other end of the scale, even in Edinburgh, the most prosperous and crowded burgh of all, some houses were still thatched, many had precarious, projecting wooden galleries (see Figure 4.3), and others were completely dilapidated. In 1644, the burgh council was empowered to buy up derelict properties in order to improve the image of the city.[182] Significantly, this was just before Gordon of Rothiemay was commissioned by the council to make his celebrated bird's-eye view of Edinburgh, mentioned at the start of this chapter as a symptom of growing civic consciousness (see Figure 4.22).

SCOTTISH TOWN HOUSES: THE EUROPEAN DIMENSION

As we have already seen in the three previous chapters, there was also a highly developed awareness of national style in architecture in this period. Every Scottish traveller to Europe would absorb each new culture by comparing it with his own, and would come to realise the deeper social and religious values that each incorporated. Life was becoming increasingly cosmopolitan in the Scottish ports, and the more people travelled, the more they could understand the significance of borrowings from other cultures.

Even after the Reformation, France and Scotland enjoyed a close affinity, though this was complicated by religious factors.[183] France remained one of the most highly regarded places to educate young Scottish nobles, and French architecture retained its appeal as a purveyor of courtly dignity, in the town as in the country. The French *hôtel*, a town house arranged around three sides of a courtyard with the entrance in a screen wall along the street frontage, was the most relevant urban model. The finest example in Scotland is the Argyll Lodging in Stirling, converted from an L-shaped block to an *hôtel* from 1632 onwardst (see Figure 4.36). The patron was the powerful courtier, Sir William Alexander, for whom the site just below the royal castle would have been as eloquent as the sophisticated continental layout. His own son, Sir Anthony Alexander, one of the King's masters of works, executed the work.[184] The display of richly carved pediments in the 'court style' of Linlithgow Palace and Heriot's Hospital would have added to the effect of tasteful ostentation. At Acheson House in the Canongate another splendid *hôtel* survives, though on a smaller scale (see Figure 4.37). The courtyard is entered through a decorous roll-moulded gateway, leading to a portal surmounted by a broken pediment displaying the patron's initials, coat-of-arms and motto, with the date 1633. From the lane outside, passers-by would see a row of pertly pointed gabled dormers, topped with the royal emblems of the thistle, rose and fleur-de-lys, asserting the patron's loyalty to the Stewart court.[185] Thus Acheson's court position as a secretary of state to Charles I was emphatically flaunted. In Kirkwall,

FIGURE 4.34 (*above*)
Edinburgh, Canongate, Regent
Moray's House, *c.*1625. From T.
H. Shepherd's *Modern Athens:
Edinburgh in the Nineteenth Century*
London, 1829–31.

FIGURE 4.35 (*left*)
Musselburgh, East Lothian, the
'French Ambassador's House' in
the High Street, from a photograph
of *c.*1900.

Tankerness House still preserves its arched courtyard entrance, dated 1574, when it was the house of Archdeacon Gilbert Fulzie.[186] It became a more coherent *hôtel* when all the houses around the courtyard were bought in about 1630 by James Baikie, a merchant who had just acquired the estate of Tankerness and thus, no doubt, wished to express his transition to the laird class (see Figure 4.38).

Germany, meanwhile, appears to have been the inspiration for the courtly oriels that appeared in the Scottish urban scene in this period: examples may still be seen in Renaissance towns such as Freiberg, near Dresden. The oriels on the tolbooths of Leith and the Canongate, both burghs with strong royal connections, have already been mentioned (see Figures 4.9 and 4.11). In the towns, as in Scottish country houses of the period, oriel windows were symptomatic of a new openness and security, but the view was more likely to be man-made than the work of nature. In the towns, the spectacle worked both ways: not only would the occupant of the house survey the scene below, but he or she could also be viewed by spectators outside, framed like a picture by the stonework of the oriel. A sober example could be seen on a house overlooking Leith harbour, demolished in the late nineteenth century; the building was traditionally associated with Mary of Guise, but appears to have been of a slightly later date.[187] More dramatic was the oriel on Cardinal Beaton's house in Blackfriars' Wynd in Edinburgh, a square turret with a pyramidal roof projecting diagonally into the street, daringly corbelled to rest on a single stone column below.[188] The corbelled balcony across the front of Moray House in the Canongate could have served a similar purpose (see Figure 4.34).[189] Oriels in the town could alternatively provide a view, not of the street below, but to the landscape beyond. At the back of the so-called Queen Mary's House in South Street, St Andrews, is a polygonal oriel with large windows looking south over the gardens, corbelled below and panelled within (see Figure 4.39).[190] Later alterations to the roof suggest that the oriel may originally have supported a polygonal turret roof like that of Cardinal Beaton's house.

Holland was the fastest-growing mercantile nation in Europe in the seventeenth century. It was not only a familiar destination for Scottish merchants, but also represented a society which embodied the values that were admired in Scotland's urban culture.[191] The image of the worthy, frugal, devoutly Calvinist merchant, enshrined for us in portraits by Rembrandt and his school, seemed worthy of emulation, in architecture as in commerce. The boldly dated inscriptions and worthy mottoes, so conspicuous on both Dutch and Scottish town houses, are one of the most obvious signs of this empathy. Rows of crow-stepped gables charac-terised the street frontages in both countries, and some houses in Scotland even borrowed the capped crow-steps so characteristic of the Low Countries. Surviving examples can still be seen on Bruce of Auchenbowie's House in Stirling and on Dunbar Tolbooth (see Figure 4.15).

In Scotland as in the Low Countries, the idea of combining domestic and commercial premises was well established. For instance, the house built by Clement Cor in Advocate's Close in Edinburgh in 1590 has two warehouse entrances inscribed with pious mottoes at ground-floor level, and an outside stair to the living

FIGURE 4.36 (*above*)   Stirling, Argyll Lodging, remodelled 1632 onwards. From a photo of *c*.1880.

FIGURE 4.37 (*left*)   Edinburgh, Canongate, Acheson House from Bakehouse Close, 1633.

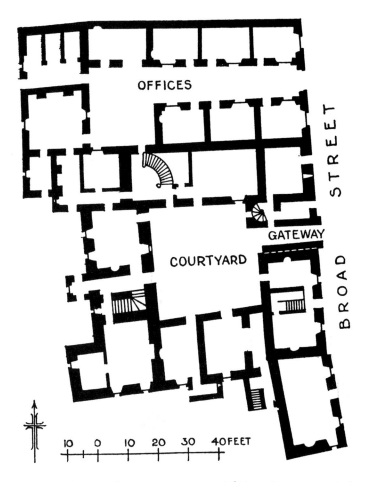

FIGURE 4.38   Kirkwall, Orkney, Tankerness House, 1574, with additional property acquired in c.1630, the ground-plan.

accommodation above (see Figure 4.40).[192] Robert Gourlay's house in Edinburgh, built in 1569, had expansive ground-floor warehousing lit by two tiers of tall windows, like Dutch harbour-front houses still to be seen in towns such as Hoorn (see Figure 4.41).[193] Yet, this house was considered distinguished enough to lodge King James VI on several occasions.[194] In Holland and the Baltic ports, pulleys projected from the gables of merchants' houses like branches of trees, ready to hoist merchandise into the attic storerooms. The siting of the warehouse at attic level was relatively rare in Scotland, where the ground floors were less liable to flooding. Only a few examples have survived, most notably Lamb's House in Leith and Bailie McMorran's House in Edinburgh (see Figures 4.57 and 4.56).[195]

   The influence of Italy on the townscape is less evident than that of France or Holland, reflecting the fact that in the post-Reformation period travel to Italy was less necessary (for churchmen and diplomats) and more difficult. Although Italy

FIGURE 4.39   St Andrews, Fife, Queen Mary's House in South Street, the view from the
garden showing the polygonal oriel.

boasted some of the largest cities in Europe, its culture and climate must have
seemed hardly relevant to the Scottish context. There was, of course, no shortage
of information about Italian architecture from printed books and treatises, while
Italian visitors were not unknown. Venetian glassmakers came to help establish Sir
George Hay's glassworks in Fife in the early seventeenth century,[196] and the role
of Piero Strozzi in the fortification of Leith has already been mentioned. In 1593,
another Italian, 'Bartolomeus Marques', presented a scheme to the burgh of
Edinburgh 'for bringing of the sey to the North loch', a utopian notion reminiscent
of earlier Florentine proposals to canalise the Arno.[197]

The most consciously Italianate development on the Scottish urban scene in the
period was the increasing popularity of street-level arcades, known as 'piazzas' in
recollection of the arcaded streets and squares of Italy. After the two great fires in
Glasgow in 1652 and 1677, stone frontages supported on arched pillars were

FIGURE 4.40   Edinburgh, Advocate's Close, Clement Cor's House, the warehouse doorways, dated 1590.

encouraged by burgh legislation (see Figure 4.42).[198] Edinburgh recommended the use of 'piazzas' in 1674, when they made stone a compulsory building material for new houses.[199] In both cities, these by-laws gave official sanction to a trend that was already well established. After the 1508 Act allowing timber galleries on the front of Edinburgh houses, many houses already had arcades at street level, but these were supported on wooden piers, and many were rickety and unsightly, not to mention the hazard of fire (see Figure 4.3). Examples of such wooden arcades survived into the nineteenth century, especially in the Cowgate.[200] A fine Edinburgh colonnade of fluted stone columns at the top of Warriston Close was exposed during repairs in 1848.[201] That the burgh condoned the replacement of timber galleries in stone is clear from cases such as the house in the Lawnmarket in Edinburgh known as Gladstone's Land (see Figure 4.43). This tenement was extended forwards twice in the early seventeenth century, once to rebuild the timber gallery in stone in about 1620, and once, after the house was acquired by

FIGURE 4.41   Edinburgh, Robert Gourlay's House, 1659 (demolished). From Grant's *Old and New Edinburgh*, vol. I.

the merchant Thomas Glaidstanes in 1631, to build a stone 'piazza' extending the building even further forward into the street.[202] A subtle balance between public and private power was achieved, and the town dignified by the arcade, at the expense of further encroachment into public space.

Outside Edinburgh and Glasgow, the most extensively arcaded town seems to have been Elgin, though here, too, many of the surviving examples are from the later seventeenth century. Dr Johnson remarked that 'there is sometimes a walk for a considerable length under a cloister, or portico, which ... seems to have been uniformly continued in the old city'.[203] Meanwhile, individual buildings with stone arcades were found in burghs throughout Scotland, apparently as a sign of classical dignity rather than to provide the citizens with shelter. One of the finest and most unusual was the house in the Greenmarket in Dundee, recorded by MacGibbon and Ross just before its demolition in the late nineteenth century (see Figure 4.44).[204] This house must date from after 1562 when the site was still under water; it seems to have been built by James Pierson who was Provost of Dundee in 1643–

FIGURE 4.42 (above)   Glasgow, seventeenth-century houses in the High Street, from a nineteenth-century postcard.

FIGURE 4.43 (left)   Edinburgh, Lawnmarket, Gladstone's Land, façade of 1631.

5. The house was approximately square in plan, with a spine wall beneath the ridge of the roof – a structurally sensible but uncommon solution at this date. It had cylindrical towers at three corners (only one of them a stair-turret, and all of them later truncated) and a grand scale-and-platt staircase in the fourth. The exposed frontages of the ground floor were continuously arcaded, apparently in the form of a blind arcade. The arches were small and numerous, supported on slender, fluted Tuscan pilasters, with a straight architrave running across each receded bay as if to render the arcade more classically correct. At the opposite end of the spectrum, the Glencairn Lodging in Dumbarton, known as the 'Glencairn Great Tenement', rises above a trio of huge arches supported on massive cylindrical columns with cushion capitals, almost neo-Norman in style (see Figure 4.45). At roof level, solidity gives way to flamboyance, with four seventeenth century pedimented half-dormers topped by high pediments and obelisks across the roofline. The ashlar façade and central heraldic panel, too, assert this as a building of high prestige, a town house for the powerful Earls of Glencairn, who were great Protestant landowners in the South–West.[205]

THE 'THRIE ESTATES' IN THE SCOTTISH BURGHS: THE NOBILITY

The burghs were not solely inhabited by merchants and craftsmen, although these groups dominated their power structure.[206] All the three Estates needed town houses, and it is interesting to observe how clearly their style was differentiated, as if to identify the patron's affiliation.

Edinburgh's best residences, known as 'ludgings', could be rented for special occasions such as sittings of Parliament or royal entries,[207] but most nobles would also have a family lodging in their local town. Such houses are often characterised by a rural appearance, like a miniature nobleman's castle transported to the town. A typical example is the Kellie Lodging in Pittenweem, built in about 1590 in the style of the Earl's nearby country seat, Kellie Castle, (see Figure 4.46). It shares with the castle the gabled tower with a lofted stair turret in the angle, although the finely chiselled corners of the parent tower are here chamfered to protect them from damage. With its costly masonry and baronial language, the tower would have been easily identifiable as the progeny of a lord's seat. Sir Robert Sibbald called it 'the Principall House' in Pittenweem.[208] Abertarff House in Inverness, dating from 1593, is a similarly diminutive version of a Highland castle, (see Figure 4.47). Some noble lodgings were even more modest. A remarkable survival, only recently demolished, was the Earl of Kinnoull's lodging in Perth, a small three-storey house with a simple stair turret at one corner, hiding behind projecting timber galleries (See Figure 4.48).[209] This was, however, merely an annexe to his grand, *hôtel*-style mansion, Gowrie House, demolished in 1805.[210]

At the opposite extreme, some lordly lodgings were effectively palaces. The magnificent Thunderton House in Elgin originally belonged to the Earls of Moray, but in the seventeeth century it was remodelled and updated by Alexander, Lord Duffus whose initials adorn the pediments (See Figure 4.49).[211] Its tall, square tower (now demolished) consciously emulated a nearby, newly built and prominent

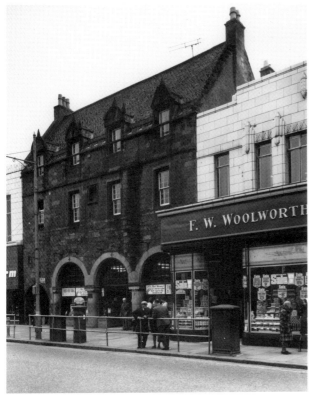

FIGURE 4.44 (*above*)   Dundee, Greenmarket, house of Provost Pierson, with its corner towers truncated, drawn just before its demolition in the nineteenth century. From MacGibbon and *Ross, Castellated and Domestic Architecture*, vol. IV.

FIGURE 4.45 (*left*)   Dumbarton, High Street, the 'Glencairn Great Tenement'.

FIGURE 4.46 (*left*)   Pittenweem, Fife, High
Street, Kellie Lodging, *c*.1590. Water-colour
sketch by W. F. Lyon, 1870.
FIGURE 4.47 (*below*)   Inverness, Church
Street, Abertarff House, 1593.

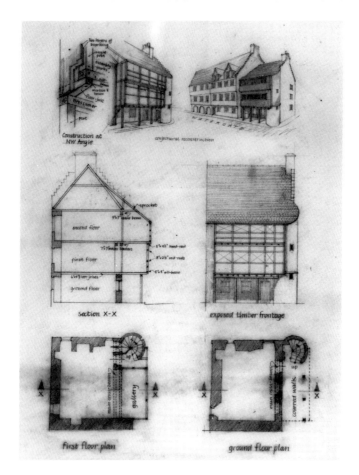

FIGURE 4.48   Perth, Watergate, the Earl of Kinnoul's Lodging, reconstruction drawings based
on the emergency survey made before its demolition in 1966.

country mansion, namely Innes House, designed by William Aytoun, the master
mason who succeeded Wallace at Heriot's Hospital. Even more conspicuous from
the outside, though apparently providing only limited accommodation inside, was
the structure known as Mar's Wark, the house of the Earl of Mar at the head of
Broad Street in Stirling. It was probably begun shortly before the Earl of Mar's
regency in 1571–2.[212] Dominating the market-place from its elevated, east-facing
site, the building functioned as stage scenery, providing a backdrop for ceremonial
arrivals at the castle (see Figure 4.50). With its huge heraldic panels painted and
gilded, it would have made a magnificent effect, especially when lit by the raking
sun of winter. The Earls of Mar were hereditary keepers of Stirling Castle. It is
therefore appropriate that the design borrows some of the most idiosyncratic
features of James V's palace block at Stirling Castle, such as the statues on corbelled
engaged columns, and the recessed panels between the windows (see Figure 2.5).
The view by Billings shows the exaggeratedly slim colonnettes which once adorned

the central gatehouse, outlining the polygonal towers with their finely drawn shadows.[213] The presence of gun-muzzle gargoyles just below the wall-head suggests that a flat or shallow roof was intended, perhaps a lead roof, a costly solution reserved for buildings of the highest prestige (such as Parliament House half a century later).[214] This was no military rampart, although its strategic position allowed it to adopt this function surprisingly effectively to ward off the Hamilton invasion in 1572, when the building was still unfinished.

THE 'THRIE ESTATES': THE CHURCH

Before the Reformation, Scottish bishops lived well, as the ruins of their splendid palaces reveal. Cardinal David Beaton had entertained on a lavish scale at St Andrews before his assassination in 1546.[215] His successor, Archbishop Hamilton, remodelled the forework of the castle to transform it into a Renaissance palace block, entered through a splendid heraldic triumphal entrance (see Figure 4.51). The portal was framed by tall, slender colonnettes like those on the Portcullis Gate of Edinburgh Castle (see Figure 2.13) and on the façade of Mar's Wark – unclassical in their proportions perhaps, but undeniably elegant and refined. Remains of corbelled platforms at the eavesline suggest that there were once four roof-level oriels. The system of pre-Reformation ecclesiastical patronage meant that bishops and archbishops were members of powerful families, and in consequence their architectural imagery tended to express their high rank.

When the German nobleman Lupold von Wedel visited Scotland in 1584–5, the Archbishop of St Andrews was still very much in evidence, officiating at a service which von Wedel attended in Perth: 'He is a gentleman and a rich bishop, for there are sixteen stately sees in Scotland. He had a long red taffety coat on.)[216] It was not until 1587 that the property was transferred to the crown.[217] By this time, however, the Archbishop of St Andrews had already acquired a more modest house in North Street, attached to the corner of St Salvator's college, where he erected a simple L-plan house, dignified only by its conical-roofed tower projecting into the street.[218]

After the Reformation, although the episcopal structure remained loosely in place, bishops and archbishops were not in a position to embark on ambitious building works. As Bishop of Orkney, Adam Bothwell inherited the fine palace in Kirkwall reconstructed by his equally scholarly predecessor, Bishop Robert Reid. In 1568, however, he was forced by Earl Robert Stewart to exchange the Orkney see for the lay commendatorship of Holyrood.[219] Back in Edinburgh, Bothwell occupied the house in Byre's Close that still bears his name, its wing at the rear terminating in bay-windows on every floor (see Figure 4.52). Two of the three surviving segmental pediments which surmount this apsed jamb have suitably learned Latin inscriptions from Horace and Ovid, while two of the five dormers facing east were inscribed 'LAVS VBIQVE DEO' (Praise be to God everywhere) and 'FELICITER INFELIX' (Happily unhappy).[220] It is tempting to imagine Bothwell unhappily enjoying the stunning views across the Forth to Fife, the expansive prospect reflecting the breadth of his scholarly horizons.

FIGURE 4.49 (*upper*)   Elgin, Thunderton House, remodelled in *c.*1640, anonymous engraving.
FIGURE 4.50 (*lower*)   Stirling, 'Mar's Wark', *c.*1570, from Billings, *Baronial and Ecclesiastical Antiquities*, vol. IV.

FIGURE 4.51   St Andrews Castle (Archbishop Hamilton's Palace), *c.*1555. Photo of *c.*1900.

After the Reformation, the church had little money for building, but ministers' houses could be of some dignity – those in Edinburgh in St Giles' kirkyard were so splendid that in 1597 they were made available to the King himself for his own use.[221] A wealthy minister could supplement the funds available for building his manse – at Anstruther Easter in 1590, for instance, the minister paid 3,500 merks out of his own pocket, while the parish supplied the 'stane and lime'.[222] The result was a stately L-plan house with crow-stepped gables and a view of the sea (see Figure 4.53).

THE 'THRIE ESTATES': THE BURGESSES

In this age of growing capitalism and commercial adventure, it was possible for some merchants to become extremely rich, but there was a wide economic spread among the burgess class, extending down to the humblest craftsmen. Unskilled towndwellers, if they had homes at all, lived in the meanest rooms in the urban tenements, or in hovels so temporary that they have long since disappeared.[223] As in any society, the houses of the richest, most successful citizens were, as a rule, the most inventive and influential architecturally.

The most remarkable survival of a Renaissance town house in Scotland must

FIGURE 4.52 (*left*) Edinburgh, Byre's Close, Adam Bothwell's House. Bothwell died in 1593, and the house later passed to Sir William Dick of Braid.

FIGURE 4.53 (*below*) Anstruther Easter, Fife, Kirk Manse, 1590.

FIGURE 4.54   New Aberdeen, Provost Skene's House, the north and south elevations.

surely be Provost Skene's House in Aberdeen, saved from demolition at the instigation of the Queen Mother (see Figure 4.54). The title deeds of the house date from 1545, but the house was altered and embellished twice in the seventeenth century, first by the Covenanter Andrew Lumsden who owned the house in 1622 to 1641, and later by Sir George Skene of Rubislaw, a merchant who had made a fortune through trade in the Baltic, and who was Lord Provost of Aberdeen in 1686.[224]

The house takes the form of a south-facing wing along a close off the Broadgate, with a square stairtower at the east end and a gabled cross-wing to the west. Two tall conical-roofed stairtowers rise from the re-entrant angles, one corbelled out at second-floor level, the other originally similar but now extended to ground level. Before the site to the south was cleared in the post-war years, only the tops of the towers would have been visible at a distance, apart from the end wall facing the Broadgate, the finest street in New Aberdeen at this time. The granite rubble walls, now elaborately pointed like crazy paving, must originally have been harled, drawing attention to the fine detail of the dressed stone. The roof of the main

FIGURE 4.55   New Aberdeen, Provost Skene's House, painted ceiling of Lumsden's gallery, 1626.

block is flat and lined with lead, a solution reserved for the buildings of highest prestige, as we have already seen. The arms of Andrew Lumsden and his wife adorn the half-dormers of the gabled cross wing, but the main entrance at the foot of the grand staircase, luxuriously embellished with fruity swags, seems to be from Provost Skene's time.

Although some of the rooms have Restoration plasterwork and chimneypieces inserted by Skene, early seventeenth-century rooms from Lumsden's time survive unaltered in the cross-wing and on the third floor. These rooms have roll-moulded fireplaces, deeply set windows, and solid studded doors with long hinges and original latches. The panelled walls may be of Baltic pine imported by Skene, but the effect is reminiscent of the earlier seventeenth-century panelling at nearby Craigievar. The most remarkable interior in the house is the painted gallery dated 1626, rediscovered in 1947 in the top floor of the Lumsden wing. The construction of the coved ceiling is simple, but the design is sophisticated and the execution accomplished.[225] Scenes from the Life of Christ are set in a geometrical framework of feigned coffering in the Italian style (see Figure 4.55). The compartments are framed with florid strapwork, and the setting of blue and gold gives a heavenly aura to the paintings. On the walls, illusionistic fluted Corinthian columns alternate with feigned tasselled hanging blinds.

Inevitably, the distinction between burger imagery and the idiom of the lairds was blurred, just their roles overlapped to some degree. Wealthy merchants often invested some of their profits in land, while nobles with surpluses from their estates or industrial enterprises such as mines or salt pans would engage in trade. Nevertheless, the merchants' houses tended to be less French in style, conveying instead a dour northern solidity, more akin to the ports of the Low Countries and the Baltic. This is clear even in houses such as Bailie McMorran's House in

Edinburgh and Lamb's House in Leith, already mentioned as houses with pulleys for lifting merchandise, both of which were so highly regarded that they were used for royal welcomes. Bailie McMorran, Edinburgh's wealthiest merchant, rebuilt the houses around Riddle's Court in about 1591, the year in which he appealed to the council to be allowed to buy part of the old port and town wall on the site, which, he claimed, were no longer 'proffitabill nor commodius for the guid toun.'[226] He himself was to live in the L-shaped house on the south-west corner, with dramatic views to the south from the main rooms.[227] The building's status is reflected in its costly ashlar construction, but the design is irregular and almost self-consciously random. Around the courtyard, corbelled string-courses meander erratically, and the roofline rises and drops between chimneys and gables. Not one entrance door greets the visitor, but three side-by-side, each one framed by slim pilasters and topped by stylised thistles (see Figure 4.56). The central doorway leads to the main spiral staircase, and thence to the main hall, while those on either side gave access to the cellar and the kitchen – as if storage and food were as important as formality. The house was used for a banquet at the council's expense to welcome the Queen's brother, the Duke of Holstein, in 1598.[228]

Lamb's House in Leith, where Mary Queen of Scots was received on her return to Scotland in 1561, seems to have been rebuilt in the early part of the seventeenth century, displaying some of the same wilful anarchy in its design (see Figure 4.57).[229] Although the plan is regular and symmetrical, with a central spiral staircase opening on to two main rooms on each floor, the exterior defies the symmetry in its expressive geometries and eventful skyline (see Figure 4.58). The windows on the two main living storeys are neatly arranged in pairs, but this gesture towards order is thwarted by the eccentric corbelling of the stairtower and the lopsided chimneys. As in Bailie McMorran's House, the half-shutters of the windows were elegantly carved (see Figure 4.59).[230] The white harl and red pantiles give the house a somewhat vernacular appearance, but the house was probably originally roofed with slates.[231]

On both sides of the Firth of Forth, burgesses' houses of this period reveal the same self-conscious enjoyment of plasticity and irregularity. The walls of the houses, blanketed in white harling as if wrapped in fleece, project and recede in unexpected places, with elaborate stone corbelling to draw attention to every movement. Billings, who loved such picturesque disorder, affectionately portrayed a fine example in Dysart (see Figure 4.60), and another virtuoso display of corbelling in Water Lane in Leith was recorded by MacGibbon and Ross.[232] Similar houses, both large and small, can still be seen in Burntisland, Pittenweem and Anstruther, amongst others.

It was easier for merchants to make a fortune than craftsmen. The Stirling merchant John Cowane not only built himself a fine house in St Mary's Wynd in Stirling – an updated and somewhat more sober version of Lamb's House in Leith – but also endowed Cowane's Hospital, a splendid almshouse built in 1639 by the royal master mason John Mylne (see Figure 4.61).[233] This is one of the finest buildings of the period, with its central tower topped by a pyramidal ogee dome,

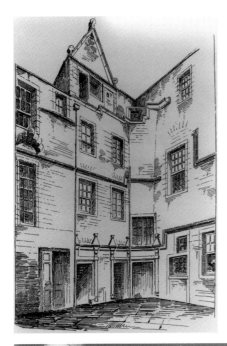

FIGURE 4.56 (*left*)   Edinburgh, Riddle's Court, Bailie
McMorran's House, *c.*1591. From MacGibbon and
Ross,
Castellated and Domestic Architecture of Scotland, vol. IV.
FIGURE 4.57 (*below*)   Leith, Water's Close, Lamb's
House, early seventeenth century, the south elevation.
Photo of 1963.

and a display of richly carved pediments on the side wing overlooking the town.[234]
Here there is no attempt to suppress symmetry, for order was appropriate for an
institution, even if many merchants sought to express conspicuous individuality in
their own houses.

It is not easy to identify craftsmen's houses at this period. A splendid castellated
town house in Aberdeen, drawn by Billings, was reputed to be the house of the
artist George Jameson, who was Scotland's foremost portrait painter in the first

FRONT   ELEVATION   CROSS-SECTION   ATTIC PLAN   EAST   ELEVATION

FIRST   FLOOR   PLAN   THIRD   FLOOR   PLAN

GROUND   PLAN   SECOND   FLOOR   PLAN

FIGURE 4.58 (*upper*)   Leith, Water's Close, Lamb's House, early seventeenth century. The
elevation, section and plans.
FIGURE 4.59 (*lower*)   Edinburgh, Canongate, Huntly House Museum, window from Bailie
McMorran's House.

FIGURE 4.60 (*left*) Dysart, Fife, town house, from Billings, *Baronial and Ecclesiastical Antiquities*, vol. II.

FIGURE 4.61 (*below*) Stirling, Cowane's Hospital, by John Mylne, 1639.

FIGURE 4.62 (*left*)   Aberdeen, house of the
painter George Jameson, from Billings,
Baronial and Ecclesiastical Antiquities, vol. I.
FIGURE 4.63 (*below*)   Pittenweem, Fife,
the Gyles (on the left) and Gyle House, 1626
(on the right).

half of the seventeenth century (see Figure 4.62).[235] Jameson had an impressive list of clients, but even so this house is unexpectedly grand. Its display of dentilled corbelling under the bartizans emulates the great castles of Deeside, and its smooth ashlar stonework would have made it a building of the highest prestige. Gordon of Rothiemay's description of Aberdeen in the mid-seventeenth century, despite its panegyric intentions, suggests that such gracious living was commonplace: 'The buildings of the toune are of stone and lyme, rigged above, covered with slaits, mostlie of thrie and four stories hight, some of them higher ... The dwelling houses are cleanlie and bewtifull and neat, both within and without ...'[236]

In the buildings that we have investigated, an interest in up-to-the-minute classical ornament is widespread — a house near the mercat cross in Culross even has a Greek inscription over the door. Some of the town houses are more erudite than others. When one remembers that of the twelve Crail ship-masters who signed a letter in favour of the Isle of May lighthouse in 1635, five could not write their own names,[237] it is hardly surprising that the magisterial sea captains' houses of this period that still surround the harbour of nearby Pittenweem have no classical ornament at all (see Figure 4.63). On the other hand, Heriot's Hospital and Glasgow University were richly adorned, like the Argyll Lodging, with motifs from architectural treatises (see Figures 4.25, 4.29 and 4.36). At the same time there is little notion of the concept of polite classical discipline that was to characterise much eighteenth-century building in Scotland. The five orders of architecture rarely articulate large-scale designs, though they may embellish door-ways or chimneypieces. Columns are used merely decoratively as modelling devices, regardless of the canons of proportion laid down in Renaissance treatises, as the façade of Mar's Wark demonstrates (see Figure 4.50). To judge by the buildings in which they lived and worked, the townsmen of Scotland did not want to conform, but rather to display their individuality and enterprise.

CHAPTER FIVE

The Church

'The greatest part of the Scotts', wrote an English visitor (Sir William Brereton) in 1636, 'are very honest and zealously religious.'[1] Perhaps he was responding to the mood of religious fervour that was soon to result in the Covenant. Nevertheless, his observation also reminds us that the Scottish Reformation's greatest success lay in bringing the ordinary citizen back into the church. Brereton described his experience of Sunday worship at the university church in Edinburgh: from eight or nine o'clock in the morning until about four in the afternoon, with only a short break for lunch, the congregation listened to sermons and readings and joined in prayers and the singing of psalms – and this was by no means exceptional in Scottish burghs of the time.

The revival of parochial worship was the most fundamental achievement of the Reformation in Scotland. Those who were tempted by rival attractions such as piping, taverns or golf were threatened with fines; and burgh council or kirk session orders tried to encourage people to attend the twice-weekly preaching days as well as the long Sunday services.[2] Less insistence was placed on the attendance of daily prayers, but in Elgin in 1599 it was declared that 'na man or woman be vagand on the streittis, idlie sittand under stairis, nor at pastyme on the calsaye [causeway]' during prayer times, and shoppers in the fish market were expected to follow suit.[3] Congregations grew, until at St Andrews in 1600, for example, 'Saboth day aftir nune, in this sumer seasoun, the peopill convenis sud frequentlie to the preaching that the kirk may nocht convenientlie contene thame.'[4]

Much popular mythology has grown up around the deep-rooted religious changes of the Scottish Reformation, and before we consider the effects on the churches themselves, we should try to set the myths in context.[5] The first myth is that before the Reformation, communities were drawn together by shared religious fervour to worship in beautiful churches, their craftsmen driven to excel by faith and devotion. In fact, the functions of medieval parish churches were secular as well as religious. They served as the centre of a wide range of activities, commercial, social, or educational, many of which were in no sense devotional.[6] Moreover, by 1560, churches at parish level were starved of funds. Almost 90 per cent of parish revenues were syphoned off to support collegiate churches, cathedrals, abbeys and universities to which they had become subordinate.[7] Parish priests were scarcely paid a living wage, forcing them to supplement their income with other jobs or additional livings. Their morality was lax, their education minimal; in 1562, the

Jesuit missionary de Gouda described them as 'laymen of low rank, ... quite unlearned, being tailors, shoemakers, tanners or the like'.[8] In rural areas, the parish church was often far away or even totally inaccessible. Many church buildings were derelict: the best-known evidence is the report made on the churches of Berwickshire in 1556, when twenty-two were said to be in ruins.[9] Anxiety was even felt in Rome, where in the same year it was reported that 'very many churches and monasteries had been established of old in stately buildings, but within the last ten years or thereabouts had been reduced to ruins by hostile inroads, or through the avarice and neglect of those placed in charge were crumbling to decay'.[10] The papal response was to order that all 'rulers, abbots and heads of churches' in Scotland should spend a quarter of their revenues on the repair of church buildings, but the measure came too late.

The belief that the Scottish Reformation marks a sudden breakaway from papal authority is similarly misleading, generated by analogy with the English situation. The break with the Papacy had begun long before, as James V began to assume rights previously assumed to be papal. It is startling to reflect that the annual income of the church in Scotland in 1560 has been estimated at £400,000, ten times as great as the total revenues of the crown, but the fact is that much of this income was now passing into lay hands. The secularisation of church property had begun in earnest in the time of James V who had himself appropriated an estimated £10,000 per year of revenues due to the church. This measure had been authorised by the Pope, ostensibly in return for the promise to establish a College of Justice in Scotland, but implicitly in return for a promise of loyalty to Rome.[11] James had also accelerated the tendency for important abbeys to be placed under lay commendators; when he was just 20 years old, the Pope allowed him to grant three abbeys to his illegitimate sons. Three further abbeys were to go to his bastard sons in due course. But James continued to demand greater independence from the Papacy, until in 1535 the Pope conceded him the right of the Scottish crown to fill ecclesiastical vacancies. In practice, therefore, the political significance of the events of 1560 was to free the country from French domination, and to adopt a more peaceful, Anglophile policy, rather than simply to break away from papal control.[12] Knox himself endorsed this shift of allegiance, praying that English raids would cease.

Another myth is that the Reformation was a sudden, cataclysmic event. Certainly, the political events of 1560 were of far-reaching consequence, but in reality Protestantism was well established in Scotland by the 1550s. There was already a well-organised network of 'Privy Kirks' in Lowland Scotland, with energetic preachers – as well as elders and deacons – using the English prayer book.[13] As early as 1525, the need for an Act of Parliament against the import of Lutheran books suggests that such books were already circulating. Nine years later, a royal letter complained of Lutheran books entering Scotland through the east coast ports.[14]

Within the Catholic church, too, there had been attempts at reform in the same years: for example, the reformed catechism of John Hamilton, Archbishop of St

Andrews, in 1552 anticipated the serious, sabbatarian mood of the Reformed church.[15] Significantly, too, Archbishop Hamilton's catechism made no mention of the Papacy. Even during the regency of Mary of Guise, laws had been passed against adultery, profanity and the failure to observe holy days. The three reforming General Councils of the Scottish Church in 1549, 1552 and 1559 proposed such remedies as the repair of churches, improvements in education, tackling improper behaviour in church and raising the standard of the priesthood.[16] The need for reform was widely recognised even within the Catholic church as well as outside.

It is also a fiction that the Scottish Reformation resulted in the large-scale destruction of churches. Aside from the rowdy events in Perth and other Lowland cities, there was little structural damage to buildings.[17] Much of Scotland, especially the Highlands and Islands and some parts of the North–East, remained staunchly Catholic. Besides, Knox's *First Book of Discipline* insisted on the retention of all buildings suitable for parish worship or educational use. The legend that churches were 'cast doun' is only plausible in the case of church furnishings and statues.[18] Rood screens were broken up, choir stalls torn out, wall-paintings whitewashed and images mutilated, but most of the churches were still needed, once the interiors had been rearranged. Pitscottie records that in St Giles in Edinburgh 'the ten commandementis and the lordis prayer … was painttit on the wallis'.[19] As we have seen, churches and even cathedrals were already in poor repair before 1560 – as early as the 1420s, the cathedrals of Dornoch and Dunblane were said to be derelict. After 1560, cathedrals needed for parochial use were maintained, a policy supported by the General Assembly of 1573. Thus, while St Andrews fell into decay because another more suitable burgh church was available, Glasgow was kept in good repair.

The new role of the cathedrals is made difficult to assess when we consider the reality behind another myth, that Scotland acquired an established Presbyterian church at the Reformation. In practice, several bishops supported the new Protestant faith and were accepted into it, and Knox is said to have wanted 'more bishops and better bishops'.[20] His policy of creating a network of regional superintendents was similar to – and easily compatible with – the existing episcopal structure, and indeed it was only put into practice in areas where the diocesan administration was deficient.[21] Just five of the projected ten superintendents were appointed. It was not until after Andrew Melville's return from Geneva in 1574 that episcopalianism was effectively challenged in Scotland.[22] From then until 1638, when the High Anglican policies of Charles I provoked the Covenant, Scotland's episcopal administration remained unobtrusively in place, although it seems likely that much of the rich ceremonial had been abandoned. To use Professor Donaldson's apt expression, the prevailing system was 'congregationalism with a dash of episcopacy'.[23]

The mythology surrounding the fate of Scotland's monasteries was created by extension from the earlier events in England. As early as 1559, the English Bishop Jewel remarked that 'all the [Scottish] monasteries are everywhere levelled to the ground'.[24] Yet in practice he can only have been referring to the combined effects of neglect and English invasions. In fact, the monasteries of Scotland were scarcely affected by the Reformation. The decline in the number of monks had begun long before (in 1555 the once huge monastic community at Melrose Abbey numbered only sixteen);[25] and the religious orders had become progressively less well endowed, as lay donors turned their support to burgh and collegiate churches.[26] Nevertheless, monks seem to have lived inconspicuously respectable lives, sustained by their steady 'portions' or stipends.[27] Whereas pre-Reformation parish clergy had numerous illegitimate children, few monks succumbed, and no record of any friar's offspring has survived in Scotland. (This does not apply to the nunneries, which were a source of scandal, the one notable exception being the house of St Catherine of Siena at Sciennes outside Edinburgh.)[28] Given the quietly acceptable lifestyle of the male religious orders, the Reformation tacitly accepted their existence, and monks were even allowed to retain their modest 'portions'. Only a few monks and friars became readers or ministers in the Reformed church.

The destruction of the monasteries was more the result of slow disintegration and secularisation than violent iconoclasm. Church lands had already begun to pass into lay ownership, both by feuing and by the introduction of lay commendators mentioned earlier.[29] The number of monks was becoming steadily smaller, and after the Reformation their buildings were used as quarries of good building stone. Where local communities existed, as in the case of Holyrood and Melrose Abbeys, the churches – usually only the nave or the choir was needed – were converted for parish use.[30] Less favoured by the Reformation were the burgh friaries, for the mendicant orders attracted popular resentment by their practice of begging for alms in the streets. Nevertheless, several friary churches, too, were converted to parish use, such as that of the Greyfriars in Edinburgh.[31]

As we have seen, most of the changes associated with the Reformation were gradual and far from rigid. Scotland did not legally become a Protestant country until 1567, after the departure of Mary Queen of Scots. The saying of the Catholic mass now became a capital crime, but in practice there were few martyrs. Indeed, several powerful noble families, such as the Gordons of Huntly, never abandoned the Catholic faith. A remarkable number of the priesthood became Protestant ministers: almost half in Galloway; as many as 60 per cent in Orkney, where Bishop Bothwell's reforming zeal was deeply felt; and about a quarter elsewhere.[32] Indeed, this element of continuity was one of the Reformation's greatest strengths, but it had to be backed up by very fundamental administrative reforms.

The most important change, already laid down in the *First Book of Discipline* in 1560, was to keep more of the church's revenues in the parishes, in order to finance the ministry, the upkeep of churches, poor-relief and education.[33] The income from cathedral lands was to be used to finance the universities, while monastic estates were assumed to have passed into lay ownership. Local parish administration was to become more democratic, with the ministers, readers and elders elected by the congregation, though in practice ecclesiastical patronage was not easily wrested from the crown and feudal superiors.[34] Clergy were allowed to marry, and their standard of living seems to have risen rapidly, since in 1574 a measure was already needed to forbid ministers and their wives from wearing rich clothing or jewellery.

The chief inducement to improve education was the congregation's active involvement in services. In 1579, an Act of Parliament declared that all house-holders, yeomen and burgesses were to have copies of the Bible and Service Book in their homes. The growing printing industry responded to the demand, although one privately printed psalm book was found to include 'ane baudie song callit Welcum Fortoun' at the end![35] The public, now expected to join in the responses and psalm singing, needed to be literate, and the new emphasis on the Word required ministers, readers and elders to be well educated.

LITURGICAL CHANGE AND CHURCH BUILDINGS

What were the changes in worship that were to affect the architectural arrangement and fittings of Reformed parish churches?[36] The mass was now condemned as idolatrous because of the elevation and veneration of the host and the doctrinal opposition to transubstantiation. As a result, the high altar became redundant, so that the former focal point in any Catholic church, large or small, became mean-ingless. Saints' days and feast days, with the sole exception of Easter, were also abolished, although it proved difficult to stamp out Yuletide celebrations.[37] Minor altars, reliquaries and effigies of saints were likewise removed.

The sacrament of communion itself was retained in the new form of worship. The aim of the reformers was to increase the frequency of communion from once to twice or four times a year, but the habit of annual Easter communion was deeply imbued in Scottish society.[38] The introduction of communal communion, with the whole congregation seated around a huge table, had important architectural consequences. Floor space for the great table had to be made available, either in front of the pulpit or in a special communion aisle. At first, the former choir was often used, as for example at Crail, Culross and Perth.[39] Silver chalices and communion plates were discarded, usually for sale – at St Giles in Edinburgh the proceeds were used for repairs to the building. Precious communion vessels were replaced by what one critic scathingly described as 'basins and cups furth of any profane taveroun'.[40] Indeed, so many had been discarded that an Act of Parliament in 1617 ordered all parishes to be supplied with 'Basines and Lavoris ... and couppes'. A simple but dignified early seventeenth-century silver chalice from Haddington Church, now in Glasgow, must reflect the impact of this ruling.[41] There was much practical good sense in the new arrangements – for example, in Anstruther in 1592 the communion service was held early in the day 'before the people go to the fishing', while in Edinburgh in 1574 different quarters took communion on different days to ease congestion.[42] The unleavened bread was often none other than shortbread, and such huge quantities of claret were consumed that some parishes resorted to watering down the wine. Knox's three communion services in 1560 used 23 gallons of good claret![43]

The form of service adopted closely resembled the Anglican ante-communion, consisting of prayers, readings, parish notices and, above all, the sermon. Just as the

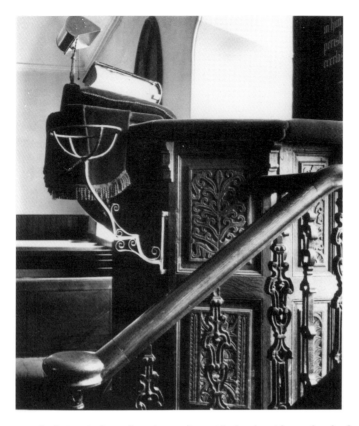

FIGURE 5.1   Pencaitland, East Lothian, the pulpit in the parish church, with woodwork of
c.1600, and wrought-iron bracket for baptismal font.

minister's sermon was the focal point in the service, so too the pulpit became the new
focus of the church's interior. No longer was the priest a remote figure dressed in rich
vestments, mumbling in Latin, and dimly glimpsed through a rood screen or pulpitum.
Now the minister stood among the people, an imposing presence dressed in a dark,
voluminous gown, raised authoritatively on his pulpit. Windows on either side of the
pulpit allowed the minister to ensure that his congregation paid attention. Above the
pulpit was a wooden sounding board to prevent distracting echoes from the roof. A
finely carved wooden pulpit, dated 1598, from the church at Parten in Kirk-
cudbrightshire can be seen in the National Museum of Antiquities in Edinburgh. A
sounding board from the pulpit at St Monance Church in Fife is now a table top in
nearby Balcaskie House! Baptism was a simple occasion, often held at the pulpit, with
the jug and basin supported on a metal bracket on the side (one is still preserved at
Pencaitland in East Lothian), rather than at a font (see Figure 5.1).[44] Attending a
baptism at Greyfriars' Church in Edinburgh, the English visitor Sir William Brereton
in 1636 was struck by the absence of ceremony, as well as by the large number of
witnesses or godparents, which could often be as many as twenty.[45]

     The practice of endowing masses to be said in perpetuity for the soul of the benefactor or one of his relatives was ended at the Reformation. Responsibility was now placed on the shoulders of the individual to seek his own salvation by leading a godly life. This ended the need for chantry chapels and altars for deceased souls; and, in theory at least, burial within the church was forbidden. In practice, however, as we shall see, important families could still erect a family aisle, with a 'laird's loft' over the burial vault.

The sacrament of confession was replaced by moral scrutiny of the parishioners by the elders. Communicants were often examined by the elders before the day of the service and given tokens or tickets if considered fit to attend.[46] Offenders were publicly denounced, especially for sexual crimes such as adultery and fornication. In practical terms this meant the removal of confession boxes from pre-Reformation kirks, and the provision of a stool of atonement on which sinners were to sit during services. In 1636, Sir William Brereton wrote of his recent visit to Greyfriars' Church in Edinburgh,

> This stool is a public and eminent seat, erected towards the lower end of the church about two yards from the ground, either about some pillar, or in some such conspicuous place, where the whole congregation may take notice of them; this seat is capable of about six or eight persons.[47]

On this occasion, he remarked, three women were standing on the stool, but were allowed to sit during the sermon. 'Those other fornicators,' he added, 'are enjoined three days penance on this stool; adulterers are censured to stand every Lord's Day upon this stool during twelve months in a sheet of hair.' Sinners had to make public repentance from the stool in front of their own congregations, which, as Brereton noted, some refused to do, thereby earning the full wrath of the preacher. During his Scottish travels in 1598, Fynes Moryson was entertained to learn that a visiting gentleman had recently mistaken the stool of atonement in St Giles for a pew: 'taking it for a place wherein Men of better quality used to sit, [he] boldy entred the same in Sermon time, till he was driven away with the profuse laughter of the common sort, to the disturbance of the whole Congregation'.[48]

There was no puritanical opposition to music in the early years of the Scottish Reformation. As early as 1542, John Wedderburne of Dundee compiled *The Gude and Godlie Ballattis*, transforming a number of Luther's 'dytements' into Scots verse and 'sundriye uther Ballatis changeit out of prophane sangis'. The anthology was published by Wedderburne and one of his brothers in 1576.[49] Whereas the borrowing of melodies from earthy secular ballads was outlawed by the Council of Trent when reforms to the Catholic church were formulated in the same period, in Scotland the familiarity of such tunes was seen as an asset. With psalm book in hand, the Scots worshipper soon became skilled in four-part congregational singing.[50] By the time of Pennant's visit in 1769, however, the legacy of the Covenant had made its impact:

> There is no music either in this or any other of the *Scotch* churches, for *Peg* still faints at the sound of an organ. This is the more surprising, as the *Dutch*,

who have the same established religion, are extremely fond of that solemn instrument; and even in the great church of *Geneva* the Psalmody is accompanied with an organ.[51]

If music was increasingly regarded with suspicion, church bells were required in every parish church, at least by 1642.[52] Dutch bells were imported to many parts of Scotland, those from the Burgerhuys foundry in Middelburg being the most highly prized.[53] Defoe even remarked on a *carillon* at St Giles, playing tunes from a keyboard in the Dutch manner (except, of course on Sundays!), but it is uncertain when this instrument was fitted.[54] It was certainly after Brereton's visit in 1636, for he had complained that 'few bells [are] rung in any of their churches in Edenborough, and, as I was informed, there are but few bells in any steeple, save in the Abbey Church'.[55]

THE CONVERSION OF CHURCHES FOR PRESBYTERIAN WORSHIP

According to the *First Book of Discipline*, the financial burden of building costs was to be shared by the ministry (from the teinds which paid the clergy's salaries) and the people. In practice, however, the responsibility for the erection and maintenance of churches after the Reformation remained with the feudal superiors in country parishes, but as we shall see, in the larger towns the burgh councils increasingly took over the initiative. One minister, though the son of a Fife laird, adamantly refused to contribute to the repair of his church.[56]

The religious architecture of the century following the Reformation must be seen against the background of widespread poverty, as wealth and property passed from the church to the laity, and a consequent scarcity of resources for church building. The fact that many churches in rural areas were still roofed with thatch aroused a pejorative response from English visitors. In 1629, as he rode through Eskdale, Lowther observed: 'All the churches we see were poor thatched and in some of them the doors sodded up with no windows.'[57] As late as 1769, Thomas Pennant was to remark that 'Many of the churches are thatched with heath, and in some places are in such bad repair as to be half open at the top.[58] Documents of the period must be treated with caution, however, for the work 'thaiking' is often used to mean roofing in general, rather than literally thatching with straw. When Sir John Shairp of Houston died in 1607, his sons and heirs built 'ane yle in the kirk of Strathbrok about and abone the buriall place', for which two Glasgow stonemasons received payment in 1609 'for thaiking, pamenting [paving] and compleiting of the Yle'.[59] The Houston aisle still survives at Uphall in West Lothian (then known as Strathbrock, or Valley of the Badgers). That such a costly building, with its tunnel vault and fine ashlar masonry, should have been roofed with thatch seems surprising, but the projection of the gable above the present ridge may suggest that this was, indeed, the case (see Figure 5.2).

High priority in the *First Book of Discipline* was given to the repair of churches:

The reparation must be according to the ability and number of Kirks. Every Kirk must have dores, close windowes of glasse, thack able to withold raine,

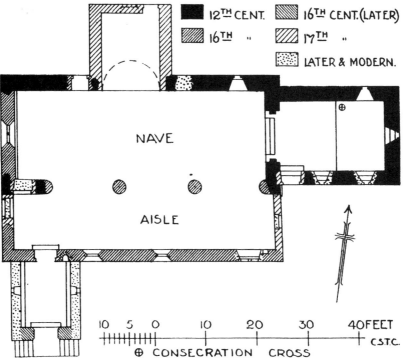

FIGURE 5.2 (*upper*)   Uphall, West Lothian, the parish church, showing Houston aisle on the left.

FIGURE 5.3 (*lower*)   Aberdour, Fife, St Fillan's Church, plan showing the post-Reformation enlargement on the south side.

a bell to convocate the people together, a pupet, a basen for baptizing and tables for ministration of the Lords Supper.[60]

This applied only to parish churches, whereas 'Abbeyes, Monkeries, Frieries, Nonries, Chappels, Chanteries, Cathedrall Churches, Chanonories, Colledges [i.e. collegiate churches], others then presently are Parish Churches or Schooles, [are] to be utterly suppressed.'[61]

The first task was the conversion of existing churches to reformed worship by removing rood screens and altars. Small, rectangular country churches required little alteration, for the pulpit could be moved to the centre of one of the side walls, and the door moved from the west end to a more central position at one side. One of the most effective conversions was that of the church of St Fillan's at Aberdour in Fife, where the south aisle was united with the nave under a single gabled roof to make the space broader and more centralised (see Figure 5.3).[62] A new entrance and three rectangular windows were opened up on the south side. The pyramidal belfry is dated 1588, presumably the date of the completion of the conversion. Other adaptations were less successful, the most ungainly being the improvised transformation of the nave of Melrose Abbey into a parish church in 1618 by erecting a lopsided barrel vault within the old nave.[63] St Giles in Edinburgh was hastily subdivided into four smaller churches in 1562–3, following the quartering of the burgh into four separated parishes.[64] As we have already seen, the courts, a school and the tolbooth were also squeezed into the shell of the old burgh church, and meetings of the General Assembly and the Parliament were held there during the later sixteenth century.[65]

Cathedrals proved most vulnerable, for their size and ceremonial character made them unsuitable for parish needs. Mercifully Kirkwall survived almost unscathed, under the watchful eye of Bishop Bothwell. Elgin Cathedral, on the other hand, lost its lead roof as early as 1567, and that of Fortrose rapidly fell into ruin when its lead roof, too, was removed in 1572 because it was 'na paroch kirk bot ane monasterie to sustene ydill belleis'.[66] After 1600, some attempt was made to restore the cathedrals that served parish needs – Dunkeld, Dunblane, Aberdeen and Dornoch, for example;[67] and the efforts of Charles I to revive the episcopalian functions of the cathedrals in the 1630s gave a further impetus for restoration, but the aftermath of the Covenant only renewed the threat to their survival. It will be more heartening here to dwell on the inventive solutions to new problems, than to lament the passing of the old order and the decay of its architectural legacy.

THE FIRST NEW POST-REFORMATION CHURCHES

The problem faced by the designers of new churches in the wake of the Reformation in Scotland was comparable to that later confronted by Wren when he designed some fifty new churches after the Great Fire of London. In other words, a new typology and an architectural idiom appropriate for Protestant worship had to be devised. In Scotland, of course, the task was in the hands of no single architect, and no funds on the scale of the Coal Tax and the London merchant community

were at hand. Nevertheless, the long-term implications of this architectural revolution were as great as in London, even if in Scotland it proceeded modestly and
slowly by comparison. This was one of those rare moments in architectural history
which called for a sudden rejection of long-established traditions. Moreover, since
the Presbyterian service was even more different from Catholicism than Anglican
worship, an even more radical rethinking had to occur.

The first new churches of Reformation Scotland show a vigorous zest for
experiment, given the financial limitations. Although the number of surviving
examples is small – fewer than a dozen new churches can be securely dated to the
period 1560 to 1620 – they are remarkably consistent in their architectural
expression. Almost all are to be found in the Central Lowlands, the heart of
Presbyterian influence; and all make a self-conscious break with the Catholic legacy
in both plan and architectural idiom.

The earliest surviving example seems to be the church of Kemback in Fife, dated
1582 over the door.[68] This church, now roofless, apparently replaced an even older
church about half a mile away. Its crow-stepped gables and simple, rectangular
doors and windows show a conscious rejection of Gothic forms, investing the
church with an almost secular character. The layout is a simple rectangle, opening
through a segmental arch into an aisle on the south side to form a T-plan. This was
the solution that was eventually to take root as one of the most appropriate and
successful for Scottish Presbyterian worship. Unusually, however, the church is lit
from the north, whereas later kirks were to prefer a south light, for the sake of
warmth and brightness. The large east window is a legacy from pre-Reformation
times, but the austerity shows the impact of Knox's condemnation of idolatry. Of
a similar date is the old parish church at Stenton in East Lothian, with its crow-
stepped tower evoking Dutch and Scandinavian medieval examples (see Figure
5.4).[69] Like Kemback, Stenton preserves one *horizontal* rectangular window, an
innovation symptomatic of the search for a new architectural language. Apart from
the roll-moulded, arched entrance, the church was economical and restrained, with
its rubble masonry and plain stone dressings in the warm red local sandstone. The
plan is a simple rectangle, with the tower straddling the corner at one end. At the
opposite end are the remains of two burial aisles, one free-standing, the other
abutting the church but not linked to it internally.

If Kemback and Stenton were radical in their simple, secular architectural detail,
they were less so in their layout and structure, retaining the gabled rectangular formula
that had characterised small country churches for centuries. Apart from the prominence
of the burial aisles, a subject to which we shall return, the main modification of plan
was the erasing of the pre-Reformation division between choir and chancel, to create
a single, unified space. The same solution was retained even in the highest-prestige
project of the later sixteenth century, the Chapel Royal at Stirling, rebuilt for the
baptism of the infant Prince Henry in 1594 (see Figure 2.10).[70] This project has already
been explored in Chapter Two. Seen in the context of post-Reformation church design,
its importance lies in the adoption of classical forms, making a break with the older
royal palace convention (seen most clearly at Linlithgow) that chapels, and even little

FIGURE 5.4   Stenton, East Lothian, the old parish church, the west tower, c.1580.

private oratories, should be marked out as devotional spaces by their Gothic windows. With its two-light, round arched windows of Florentine inspiration, and its triumphal-arched entrance centrally placed on the long side, this apparently simple and conservative chapel gave royal endorsement to the rejection of Gothic forms and the emphasis on the centre.

Significantly, it was not in the orbit of the court that the most imaginative church design of the period was invented, but in one of the rapidly expanding ports on the Firth of Forth, namely Burntisland (see Figure 5.5). This is the church that most vividly embodies the sense of initiative that blossomed in the burghs after the Reformation, as they grew in prosperity and gained political authority through their new alliance with the church. Within such a rapidly evolving society, there was little inducement to adhere cautiously to long-established cultural traditions.

The circumstances of the rebuilding of Burntisland Church reveal an astonishing level of self-confidence in the ranks of the burgess class. The previous church stood

FIGURE 5.5   Burntisland, St Columba's Church c.1589.

half a mile to the north, where the ruins of 'a Popish chapel' were still to be seen in the late eighteenth century.[71] In 1589 the citizens of the town, newly created a Royal Burgh by James VI, commissioned the Convention of Royal Burghs for support 'for the vpbigging of ane kirk within thair said burgh'.[72] The responsibility of the feudal superiors was boldly disregarded. As the *Statistical Account* recorded, the burgesses asked only for their consent, and 'at the same time, as an inducement, granted them proper seats, with certain privileges, taking the whole burden of building and repairing upon themselves'.[73] In 1592, the Convention of Royal Burghs granted to the citizens of Burntisland the right to finance their new church by taxing the timber passing through their harbour.[74]

   Thus the new church both celebrated and depended on the rapidly growing North Sea trade, especially the import of Baltic pine. Its raised coastal site, overlooking the fine harbour built in 1540–2, symbolised the new affinity between church and burgh. We do not know who designed this remarkable building –

perhaps it was the mason John Roche, who received his final payment in 1596 for 'ye warke wrought be him to the kirk'.[75] The timberwork of the central steeple was completed in 1600 by the Leith wright, John Scott.[76]

The structural principle behind the design of Burntisland Kirk is one that was widespread in centralised domed churches in Italy and the Byzantine world, except that the central space carries a tower rather than a dome. The plan is almost exactly square, with the tower carried on four free-standing piers linked by semicircular arches (see Figure 5.6). Its weight is buttressed by the subsidiary arches of the surrounding 'aisles'. The tower was completely reconstructed in stone in the mid-eighteenth century, but the gilded weathercock that surmounted the original wooden superstructure is still to be seen.[77] The ashlar buttresses at the corners were presumably added in 1822 when the outer walls were raised and the present sash windows inserted.[78]

The uninhibited originality of Burntisland Kirk has puzzled historians looking for neat progressions in artistic development. It had no precedent in Scotland, and inspired no imitations. This was the boldest attempt to create a radically new architectural formula for Protestant worship, expressing in eloquent visual terms the radical break with Catholicism. In the 1630s, Archbishop Laud likened the church to a large, square pigeon house, complaining that there was no place for the altar; but it was never intended to satisfy such High Anglican aspirations as Laud's. As Radford and Donaldson remarked, 'the building reflects the temporary triumph of the left-wing movement of the 1590s'.[79] Indeed, the year in which the church was probably begun, 1592, was the date of the Presbyterian 'Magna Charta', a significant victory for the anti-Episcopal faction in Scotland.[80]

Burntisland provided a truly centralised space focused on the pulpit, rather than simply a rectangular space entered in the centre, the solution adopted at Stirling Chapel Royal in the same years. We do not know how the space was originally lit, but the two-light rectangular windows around the lower aisles appear to be original. There must also have been windows in the wooden tower – the evidence of the Ely octagon shows how effectively a timber structure can admit light. It was presumably the effect on both statics and lighting of its later replacement in stone that led to the need for additional windows and buttressing in 1822.

Merchants' horizons were opening up as they traded with the Low Countries, the Baltic and the ports of south-west France and northern Spain, and it is worth considering where the burgesses of Burntisland could have found inspiration for this unique design. It has often been assumed that the source was Dutch but as Hay observed no comparable Protestant churches were erected in Holland before those of Jacob van Campen in the 1640s, such as the Nieuwe Kerk in Haarlem.[81] Timber-framed farmhouses in North Holland had pyramidal roofs supported on four posts, and this formula was later adopted for Calvinist churches in the same region, but again not before the seventeenth century.[82] The plan of Burntisland Kirk is almost identical to that of the little church of San Geminiano, begun in 1505, which stood at the opposite end of Piazza San Marco in Venice from St Mark's itself and was demolished under Napoleonic rule.[83] The articulation, however, is very different,

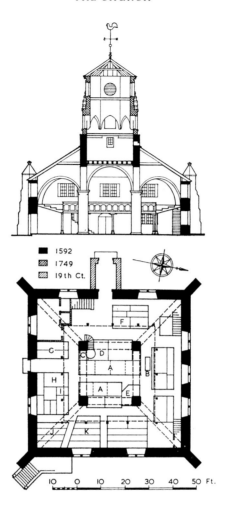

FIGURE 5.6   Burntisland, St Columba's Church, section and plan. From Hay, *Architecture of
Scottish Post-Reformation Churches*. The letters refer to the early nineteenth century arrangement
of pews: A. communion table pews with movable divisions; B. communion 'head table'; C.
baptismal space; D. elders' pew; E. castle (now magistrates') pew; F. manse pew; G. shoemakers'; H. town council's; I. strangers' seat; J. fleshers'; K. weavers'. The other pews on the
plan belonged to various individuals, estates and companies, and the remaining merchant and
craft guilds had their seats in the loft.

for San Geminiano had a central dome and five smaller domes in the corners,
and boasted an elaborate marble façade with paired pilasters designed by Jacopo
Sansovino.[84] This source, though conspicuous and well known, is highly unlikely
to have had any direct influence on Burntisland. Kuyper has pointed out, however,
that this Byzantinizing type spread through Hungary and Poland to Scandinavia,
where it could have inspired Scots merchants.[85] An even more intriguing prototype,
also suggested by Wouter Kuyper, is the former Huguenot church at La Rochelle,
a port often visited by Scots merchants.[86] This Huguenot church was a square, free-

standing structure with a pyramidal roof and appropriately Protestant associations. The fact that the mason at Burntisland was named John Roche is perhaps significant – could he have been a Frenchman from the Bordeaux region?

It was in the furnishing of the interior that Burntisland provided a relevant and enduring model. Gone was the pre-Reformation division between laity and clergy (see Figure 5.6). Every part of the church was now as sacred as any other; instead, the divisions were those of the community outside.[87] The pulpit stood at the foot of the south-west pier, with the 'Castle Pew', reserved for the heritors of the parish, on the opposite corner of the crossing. Communion tables originally occupied the central space beneath the tower, confirming the emphasis on the Eucharist sought by the early Reformers. All the other powerful groups in the burgh – chiefly the merchant and craft guilds, the elders of the kirk, the Town Council and the minister's family – had their appointed places, the pews embellished with carved and painted decoration and insignia. The surviving pews date from between 1603 and 1733. That of the Castle Pew (now the Magistrates' Pew) is one of the earliest, dating from 1606 and embellished with the arms of Sir Robert Melville and his wife Dame Joanna Hamilton.[88]

The precise social stratification within Burntisland Kirk was by no means unique in post-Reformation Scotland. Lowther wrote of his visit to Selkirk in 1629:

> They have a very pretty church where the hammermen and other tradesmen have several seats mounted above the rest, the gentlemen below the tradesmen in the ground seats; the women sit in the high end of the church, with us the choir, there is one neat vaulted porch in it, my Lord Bucplewgh's seat is the highest in the church and he hath a proper passage into it in at the outside of the vaulted porch.[89]

The church which Lowther visited was rebuilt in 1748, just a few years after James Gibbs replaced the west church of St Nicholas in New Aberdeen. There, too, an early traveller, Richard Franck in 1656, had recorded precise social delineations in the seating:

> where the magistrates sit under the sovereignty of the mace, and every merchant in his peculiar pew; where every society of mechanicks have their particular seats, distinguished by escutcheons, sutable to their profession; ... every one [is] entertained answerable to his quality.[90]

Every man might be equal before God, but the worshippers cannot have felt equality within the kirk, where the burgh hierarchy was so clearly demarcated – and even *celebrated* in the profusion of heraldic devices that adorned the pews.

On the opposite side of the Firth of Forth, facing Burntisland, another pioneering new church was soon to provide a less idiosyncratic and ultimately more enduring model for Protestant worship. The minister responsible was John Davidson, one of the most vigorous Calvinist churchmen of the Scottish Reformation, who took charge of Prestonpans in 1595, on the crest of the wave of Presbyterian confidence.[91]

The community of Prestonpans, situated on the coast of East Lothian north of

Preston, was growing rapidly in the late sixteenth century through its extensive salt-panning operations. Yet, when Davidson arrived to take up his ministry, there was no church in either Prestonpans or Preston. No burials were allowed in the parish because of the opposition of the two local landowners, Lord Seton to the east and Lord Newbattle to the west. Eventually, through the intervention of Lady Preston, a lesser laird, George Hamilton, was persuaded to grant a site for the new church and manse, as well as three acres for the glebe. 'This,' remarked Davidson with his usual eloquence, 'was a great ease provided of God in our straite, for ye people were beginning to cry out and tumultuously to rage.'[92]

Although Hamilton provided some financial assistance as well as the grant of land, Davidson raised most of the funding himself, some from friends in Edinburgh, the rest from his own pocket.[93] He regarded the church as a visible challenge to the uncooperative Lord Newbattle, once remarking as he passed the building site: 'With difficulty did we get that Church brot that length, but those walls shall stand to the coming of the Lord, as witnesses against the hinderers of it.'[94] Davidson must have been an uncomfortable adversary. His prophesy of Lord Newbattle's death in mysterious circumstances, and the alienation of the baron's land in the area, came uncannily true, thus apparently confirming the minister's capacity to call on the forces of divine wrath.[95]

It is important to see the design of Prestonpans Church in the context of Davidson's own religious views (see Figure 5.7). An outspoken critic of both Regent Morton and of James VI, who had twice been exiled to England, Davidson was a classical scholar able to turn his hand to Latin verse, but he also strongly regretted the decline in the vernacular that he believed was accompanying the Reformation in Scotland.[96] Latin, after all, was the language of international Protestantism, while the vernacular prayer book encouraged the Anglicisation of the Scots tongue. In an attempt to support a vernacular revival, Davidson himself wrote Scots poems. One of these was a panegyric poem in honour of John Knox, which included the lines:

> For weill I wait that Scotland never bure,
> In Scottish leid [language] ane man mair Eloquent.[97]

Knox (like himself) was able to hold his own in Greek and Latin with any scholar, but Davidson believed fervently in the potency of preaching in the vernacular in the fight against idolatry 'and chiefly that great Idoll of the Mes'.[98] Like Knox, Davidson had experienced life as an exile, and was aware of the European context of Scottish Calvinism. The Scottish Reformed Church was seen by both churchmen as a national faith, not through ignorant provincialism, nor in its dependence on centuries of past history, but rather, through the weaving of religion into the fabric of secular life by means of education, poor-relief and administrative reform.[99] Davidson himself founded a burgh school in Prestonpans for the teaching of Latin, Greek and Hebrew. He even constructed a house for the schoolmaster and endowed the school's future at his death in 1604.[100]

How far does the architectural character of the kirk of Prestonpans reflect

FIGURE 5.7   Prestonpans, East Lothian, the parish church, for John Davidson (minister 1595–1604), remodelled in 1774 and 1911, the south front.

Davidson's particular views (see Figure 5.7)? As it stands, the church is a T-plan church, with a tower at the west end and the Hamilton aisle projecting on the south. Like Burntisland, it occupies a raised site overlooking the Firth of Forth and, in this case, its salt pans. It was very substantially remodelled in 1774 – presumably the date of the Georgian Gothic glazing in the arched windows and the octagonal belfry. Further alterations were made in 1911 when the north jamb and the extensions at the east and west ends were added.[101] Nevertheless, we can still detect something of the character of the original church in the robust rubble masonry of the tower and the roll-moulded, round-arched south doorway with its big ashlar keystones. A round-arched window above this door, now blocked, suggests the scale and form of the original windows. The Hamilton aisle was reached by an outside stair and heated by a chimney, establishing the seclusion and dignification of the local laird's family who had granted the land. The architectural solution of the simple rectangle, transformed into a T-plan by the addition of a laird's aisle, could also be seen in recently converted pre-Reformation parish churches. This rooted the design within Scottish culture, reflecting Davidson's belief in the vernacular as the language of the eloquent preacher. At the same time, the simple classicism gave the building authority in the wider context of the sphere of European Protestantism. This was a 'modern' building reflecting the break with medieval tradition (in contrast to, say, a laird's house where references to historical roots resonated with meaning).

The T-plan appears again soon afterwards at Weem, in Perthshire, where the church was rebuilt in 1600, under the patronage of Sir Alexander Menzies of nearby Castle Menzies, and his wife Margaret Campbell (see Figure 5.8).[102] The south side is pierced by rectangular doors and windows, like Kemback in reverse, but the end gables are lit by large Gothic windows. Apparently original, these are the only pointed-arched windows in any surviving Scottish church built between 1560 and 1620. This example warns, however, of the difficulty of generalisation, for away from the centres of population in the Central Lowlands, Presbyterian zeal was less dogmatic. The little birdcage belfry – reminiscent of the belfries of the North-East which we shall consider later in this chapter – suggests a stronger episcopalian bent in this Perthshire rural setting than in, for example, the Lothians. The inscription on the Menzies tomb of 1616, proudly boasting of the patron's noble ancestry from Huntly, Edzell and Lawers (his mother being of 'the royal race of Ancient Britons) suggests that this family at least, like the Earls of Huntly, had remained Catholic.[103] As at Prestonpans, the Menzies aisle had a raised loft, heated by a fireplace. The galleries and furnishings have been lost, but on the exterior the jougs survive near the south-east door.

One further church from the period before the return of King James VI in 1617 should be mentioned, if only for the eloquent pleading which resulted in its rebuilding. In 1612, Sir Thomas Erskine, soon to be created the Earl of Kellie, was given permission by Parliament to rebuild the parish church of Dirleton in East Lothian on a new site further inland because the old kirk 'is sa incommodiouslie situat beside the sea sand that the same, with the kirk yard thereof, is continuallie overblawin with sand' (see Figure 5.9).[104] Here again we find a long gabled rectangle, its stately bell tower topped by a battlemented parapet bearing four obelisks. Simple round-arched windows affirm the restrained classicism that we have already seen at nearby Prestonpans. The Archerfield aisle on the south was added in 1664, but the minister's loft projecting from the north side, with its heated retiring room, seems to be original.

At Dirleton, the prime mover seems to have been Erskine himself, a personal friend of James VI who had been given the lands of Dirleton in 1600, and who was to buy the estate of Kellie on the opposite shore of the Firth of Forth in 1617. As with most of the churches of the period, we have no record of the identity of the designer, even when, as in the case of Burntisland the names of the mason and wright are preserved. The ultimate authority, of course, lay with the principal donor, whether the burgesses of Burntisland, the local lairds of Weem and Dirleton, or the charismatic minister of Prestonpans. This element of design control is clearly spelled out in the contract of 1620 for the new church at Falkland, erected by John Mylne, the master mason from Perth who had only recently completed the statue of James VI for the Netherbow Port in Edinburgh.[105] The contract gives ultimate authority over every detail of the design to the feudal superior, the Lord of Scone: the doors and windows were to be of the number and form devised by the patron; the design of the 'fair heiche belhous' on the gable was to be 'as the said Lord sall dewyis'; the outside wall was to have pillars of the form and number 'for decoring

FIGURE 5.8 (*above*)   Weem,
Perthshire, the old parish church,
1600, from the south-west.
FIGURE 5.9 (*left*)   Dirleton, East
Lothian, the parish church, 1612,
from the south, with Archerfield
aisle of 1664.

theirof as the said lord sall dewyis'; and so on. Drawings and templates, no doubt, were executed by Mylne himself, but the contract left him no room for artistic manoeuvre.

Mylne's parish church at Falkland no longer survives, for it was rebuilt in 1850, but we know from the contract that it stood on the site of an earlier church and that it consisted of a rectangle with a laird's aisle of the same width on the north side. In other words, it had a simple T-plan like Weem or Prestonpans. The building was built of the finest materials, slate-roofed, with broached ashlar masonry on the 'for wall'. The timber panelling of the laird's aisle was to be based on that of the Kirk of Scone. The church was remembered in 1876 as 'a low building of considerable antiquity with two porches' – presumably the 'pillars' mentioned in the contract adorned these entrances. Although most of the first post-Reformation churches, as we have seen, used classical rather than Gothic forms, columns (except for the piers supporting the roof at Burntisland) would have seemed too ostentatious and costly in earlier decades.

CHURCH BUILDING BETWEEN 1620 AND 1660

This later period shows a greater confidence, but also a much wider variety in architectural expression. This was the period of Charles I's attempt to enforce Episcopalianism, leading up to the National Covenant in 1638. There followed the disturbances of the Civil War and, from 1652, eight years of Cromwellian administration. There were many different factions and loyalties within ecclesiastical circles, as well as in the community at large, and this confusion is reflected in the overall picture, even if, in compensation, the designs of individual churches often display a bold assurance that makes their study a rewarding one. Meanwhile, the building of simple rectangular parish churches continued in examples such as Old Durness Church in Sutherland of 1619 and the parish church of Nigg in Easter Ross of 1626, the former now ruined, the latter a homely, cottage-like structure, since much altered.

One of the most idiosyncratic and memorable churches of these later decades is also one of the first, the parish church at Dairsie in Fife, dated 1621 over the west doorway (See Figure 5.10). It was rebuilt by John Spottiswoode, Archbishop of St Andrews, when he acquired the lands of Dairsie and took up residence in the nearby lordly house. The Archbishop conceived the church as a visual protest against Presbyterian austerity, himself writing that he 'publicly and upon his own charges built and adorned the church of *Darsy* after the *English* form.' He boasted that it was 'one of the beautifullest little pieces of church work that is left to that now unhappy country', which, he lamented, had been ravaged by 'the boisterous hand of a mad Reformation'.[106] The church had all the costly status symbols that Spottiswoode could muster: a flat lead roof (now replaced by a pitched one) drained by gargoyles below the parapet; an octagonal belfry flamboyantly corbelled out over the buttresses at the south-west corner; smooth ashlar masonry; and inside, daringly, a choir screen bearing the arms of Scotland and England. Following an order of the Assembly in 1647, however, the richly adorned interior was stripped

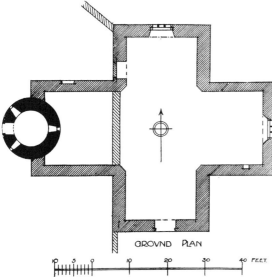

FIGURE 5.10 (*above*)　Dairsie, Fife, St Mary's (the old parish church), 1621, from the south, for Archbishop Spottiswoode.

FIGURE 5.11 (*left*)　Portpatrick, Galloway, the old parish church, 1622–9, plan.

of its 'monuments of idolatry and superstition'; and the offending screen 'dividing the bodie of the kirk fra there queir (as it is ordinarlie called in papistrie, and among them that follow papists)' was removed.[107]

Even in its stripped and altered state, Dairsie Church is an eclectic gem. Huge

Gothic windows with plate tracery (much restored) light the nave, separated by
buttresses and resting on a string-course which, unapologetically, steps up on the
west front to frame the round-arched door. The secular classicism of the west end,
with its obelisks and framed heraldic panel, is compromised only by the capitals in
the form of angels' heads above the spindly fluted pilasters.

Just as inventive, but liturgically at the opposite end of the spectrum, was the
church at Portpatrick in Galloway, dated 1622 and 1629 on the skewputs (see
Figure 5.11).[108] This church, long ruined, adopted a secular architectural idiom
throughout, with its roll-moulded rectangular two-mullioned windows topped by
heraldic panels, and a baronial-looking circular tower on the west 'quite riddled
with windows' as MacGibbon and Ross engagingly remarked.[109] Most innovative
of all was the Greek-cross plan, one of the first in post-Reformation Scotland. It is
anticipated only by Cawdor Church in Nairn, a church with a similarly secular-
looking tower (in this case a square parapeted version) erected in 1619, though
much restored in the nineteenth century. As at Cawdor, the west arm of Portpatrick
Kirk was partitioned off, although the dividing wall may not be – original Radford
and Donaldson suggest that it was a 'chancel' or communion aisle, but it may have
been a family vault.[110]

Two projects of the mid-1630s show the enormous range of aspirations, depend-
ing on the patronage and the character of the location. On a hillside at Grandtully
in Perthshire, overlooking the upper reaches of Strathtay, stands the church of St
Mary, a long, low, rectangular, gabled building, with no external features what-
soever to distinguish it as a church, apart from the gravestones in the grass outside
(see Figure 5.12).[111] This was the family chapel of the nearby castle of Grandtully,
erected a century earlier in 1533. The westernmost part, originally separated from
the rest by a partition, was probably the chaplain's house, to judge by its domestic
appearance. Originally, the chapel was lit by three plain rectangular openings on
the south side, now blocked. Inside, the visitor is amazed to find a glorious painted
ceiling – a profusion of festive ornament and bright colour that would have made
the decoration of the Chapel Royal at Stirling seem almost modest (see Figure
5.13). The ceiling is dated 1636 and resembles the painted galleries of great houses
of the period.[112] This is no Puritan scheme. Biblical scenes and heraldic panels are
set in feigned coffered panels adorned with strapwork and exuberant displays of
birds, fruit and flowers. The architectural richness and confidence of the painted
decoration could hardly contrast more strongly with the plainness of the church.
The scene of death and Resurrection in the centre, for example, is framed within
a pedimented aedicule of demure, erudite, cosmopolitan classicism.

Meanwhile, at Anstruther Easter in the East Neuk of Fife, the parish was erecting
a new church to reflect the separate identity of the community, formerly part of
the parish of Kilrenny further inland (see Figure 5.14). The central doorway on
the south side is dated 1634, and the top of the tower 1644.[113] There are three
identical roll-moulded doorways on the south side, facing the sea, set between big
three-light, round-headed windows. This is a large and dignified T-plan church,
ashlar faced on the entrance front as if to assert the prosperity of the community.

FIGURE 5.12 (*above*)   Grandtully,
Perthshire, St Mary's Church, 1533.
FIGURE 5.13 (*left*)   Grandtully,
Perthshire, St Mary's Church, detail of
the painted ceiling, 1626.

The burgh arms on the parapet of the tower suggest that the church was a municipal
project. This was a church of restrained classicism and Presbyterian conviction, as
if to challenge the High Anglican neo-medievalism of nearby Dairsie.

A similar anti-episcopalian stance was adopted in the Tron Church, erected in
Edinburgh between 1637 and 1647 under John Mylne (son of the mason of Falkland
Church) and John Scott (the wright who had built the church tower at Burntisland)
(see Figure 5.15). This was one of two new churches proposed to serve the parish

FIGURE 5.14   Anstruther Easter, Fife, the parish church, central door dated 1634, tower
1644. Photo of c.1890.

of Edinburgh after St Giles was made a cathedral in 1633 by Charles I. (The second
church on Castle Hill was never completed.) Ironically, by the time of the first
payments in 1640 the National Covenant had already been signed, and St Giles had
been repartitioned, but the role of the new church as a symbol of religious
independence sustained the impetus.[114] Although Mylne had newly succeeded his
father as royal master mason, the building shows none of the character of the 'court
style' of Heriot's Hospital or Parliament House. The Tron, instead, adopted the
main elements of its architectural ornament not from court circles, but from the
latest Dutch printed source, Hendrick de Keyser's *Architectura Moderna*, published
in 1631.[115] As the author of three of the four seventeenth-century churches that
ringed the city of Amsterdam, de Keyser was a fitting role model. Mylne's design
is a composite drawn from several of de Keyser's buildings – including not only
his churches but also Delft Town Hall, which inspired the Mannerist *aplomb* of the
Ionic pilasters, fluted above and rusticated below. The layout was a T-plan (later
truncated by late eighteenth-century road works to leave only a bald square), and

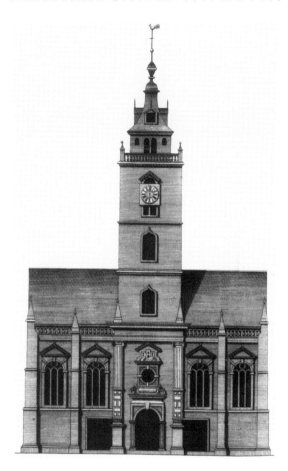

FIGURE 5.15 Edinburgh, High Street, Tron Kirk, by John Mylne, 1637–47, engraved by William Whitland, 1753.

the interior was embellished by John Scott's magnificent hammerbeam roof (similar to his ceiling for Parliament Hall), which still survives today. The original tower, destroyed by fire in 1824 and rebuilt to a different design, was also recognisably Dutch, asserting the burgh's emulation of Holland's prosperity and Calvinist values.

If Edinburgh was zealously Calvinist, the same cannot be said of Aberdeen and the North-East, where episcopalian traditions persisted even within the context of parish worship, and many areas remained almost wholly Catholic.[116] We must remember that the Church of Scotland's church retained its episcopalian structure until the reign of Charles I. In consequence, there was less need for radical adaptation of medieval churches, but the heritors asserted their pride in the maintenance or rebuilding of the churches by a series of remarkable birdcage belfries from about 1600 onwards. The typical belfry stood on the west gable, above the west door which, in deference to episcopalian practice, remained in use (whereas, as we have seen, in the more puritanical churches an entrance on the long side was preferred). These belfries were proudly inscribed with the date and the family arms or initials of the heritors, and surmounted by classical embellishments such as obelisks, finials, urns, and steep little pediments with scrolls clinging precariously to their slopes. Characteristic examples include Tullynessie (1604), Insch (1613), Longside (1620), Gartly (1621), Pitsligo, Turriff and Leslie (all of 1635), Clatt (1640), Kirkton of St Fergus (1644) and Fordyce (1661), each one different, but all conforming to the same general theme. The most distinctive is the double bell-cote at Turriff, although only one bell now hangs there (see Figure 5.16).

In the 1640s and 1650s, new churches in southern Scotland, in contrast to those of the episcopalian heartland of the North-East, were invariably Gothic, in direct opposition to the classicism of the English court style. Nevertheless, medieval types were modernised to mark the break with pre-Reformation values, adopting the favourite Presbyterian plans, the T-plan and the simple rectangle entered on the long side. Ingenious modifications of Gothic language were devised: at Lyne in Peeblesshire, each pointed-arched window contains two round-arched lights, (see Figure 5.17),[117] whereas at Fordell in Fife huge round-arched windows on the gable ends are filled with a profusion of rich Decorated Gothic tracery (see Figure 5.18).[118] (Fordell was the more flamboyant, being a family burial chapel rather than a parish church.)

No fewer than four new churches were built in Ayrshire in these two decades. The first of these, at Fenwick, dated 1643 over the entrance, is one of the most accomplished and satisfying of Scotland's early Presbyterian churches, built for a community of zealous Covenanters (see Figure 5.19).[119] Like Portpatrick and Cawdor, it has a Greek-cross plan, with a vestry and bell tower in the western arm. The pulpit, still equipped with its hour-glass (actually timing 40 minutes), stands against the west wall of the T-plan interior, which has galleries in each aisle (restored after a fire in 1929). The church is lit by large, plain Gothic windows in each of the crow-stepped gables. The east aisle contains the Rowallan loft, with its outside stair and ogee-pedimented doorway dated 1649. The jougs outside the south entrance serve as a reminder of the time when they were used to punish crimes such as 'cursing the day that ever the minister came to this countrie' or 'inhuman throwing of Elizabeth White over a brae'.[120]

The three other Ayrshire churches, Ayr, New Cumnock and Sorn, were all erected during the period of Cromwellian occupation. The new kirk at Ayr (now known as the 'Auld Kirk') was completed in 1666 (see Figure 5.20). In 1654, Cromwell had requisitioned the old church of St John the Baptist which stood on the site of his new citadel, and compensated the community with a gift of 1,000 merks towards the building of the new church.[121] In the event, this donation only amounted to a tenth of the total cost of rebuilding, but as at Burntisland the new kirk became a symbol of the prosperity and success of this thriving west coast port. Built on a T-plan, the new building is impressively urban in scale, lit by simple Gothic two-light windows. Big gabled dormers illuminate the three spacious lofts inside – these are not lairds' lofts but pews for the burgesses: the merchants, tradesmen and sailors. Over the Sailors' Loft still hangs a model ship, a tradition shared by the Dutch that was once more

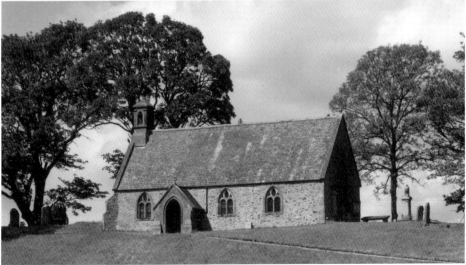

FIGURE 5.16 (*upper*)   Turriff, Aberdeenshire, the old parish church of St Congan's, from the
north-west, showing the double birdcage belfry, 1635.

FIGURE 5.17 (*lower*)   Lyne, Peebleshire, the parish church, from the south-east, *c.*1645.

FIGURE 5.18 (*upper*) Fordell Chapel, Fife, 1650, from the south-east.
FIGURE 5.19 (*lower*)   Fenwick, Ayrshire, the parish church, 1643, from the east, showing the
stair to Rowallan loft, 1649.

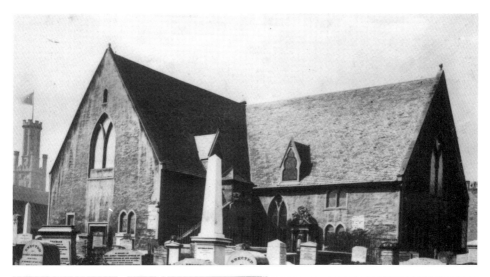

FIGURE 5.20 (*upper*)   Ayr, the Auld Kirk, 1654–66, from a photo of c.1900.
FIGURE 5.21 (*lower*)   Sorn, the parish church, 1658.

widespread in Scotland.[122] The neighbouring churches of New Cumnock and Sorn followed in quick succession in 1657 and 1658 respectively, both of them T-plan schemes. New Cumnock is now a roofless ruin, but the parish church at Sorn makes a fitting culmination to Scotland's church building in the century following the Reformation (see Figure 5.12). This modest country church in warm red sandstone, with its three lofts reached by outside stairs, satisfies all the principles of Presbyterian worship in its economical but intimate design, well lit by large Gothic windows. The authority of the church is expressed with a quiet dignity; here, too, the jougs still dangle poignantly outside the south door.

FAMILY AISLES AND MONUMENTS

The Reformation not only changed the worshipper's view of death and salvation –
it also brought fundamental changes in the way that the dead were remembered.
First with the elimination of the mass in the reformed Church of Scotland came
the end of the Catholic funeral rites and the practice of endowing regular masses
to commemorate the dead at family altars or in chantry chapels. Moreover, in 1581
the General Assembly of the Church of Scotland forbade burial within churches, a
stricture that was repeated four times between 1588 and 1643. This never became
law despite the support of James VI in 1593 for a proposed ruling 'that for the
avoyding of burialle in kirks, every nobleman s[h]ould bigg ane sepulture for himself
and his familie'.[123]

In this context, it is hardly surprising that the most flamboyant and inventive
religious architecture of the post-Reformation period in Scotland is to be found in
mausolea and funerary monuments. As we have seen in earlier chapters, initiative
and success were valued more highly than ever before within the society of the
time; and the passage of wealth from the church to the laity distributed power to
a wide range of private individuals, from small lairds to the most powerful courtiers.
With the Reformation, ecclesiastical patronage passed from the crown and the
church into the hands of this new, expanded class of landowners.[124]

Tomb monuments could still be erected inside churches that did not serve
reformed parishes. Where an erudite audience was expected, the most dignified
memorial consisted simply of a lengthy Latin inscription recording the achievements
and good deeds of the deceased. Carved in correct Roman lettering, the inscribed
panel would be framed with classical pilasters and topped by a heraldic panel
flanked by emphatic scrolls. This formula can be seen in the monument to the
architect William Schaw in Dunfermline Abbey, erected after his death in 1602 at
the request of Queen Anne (see Figure 5.22).[125] The monument to the university's
Rector Robert Wilkie in St Leonard's Chapel, St Andrews, was equally literary,
recording his bequest of 4,200 merks to the poor on his death in 1611.[126] It was
the epitaph that projected the fame of the deceased into the future, a carefully
edited 'Who's Who' entry that replaced the fading memory of the person himself.

The most obvious way to circumvent the restriction on burial within the body
of the church was to erect a monument in the graveyard. A monument built against
the boundary wall of the kirkyard allowed the design to be 'read' as one might
view a chimneypiece or the entrance portal of a house. Indeed, since the same
concerns for the display of heraldry and family status informed all such designs,
the architectural similarities present no surprise. Two monuments in Crail Kirkyard
show different approaches to this new open-air context.[127] In the monument to
James Lumsden of Airdie, who died in 1598, a classical language is improvised by
imitating thirteenth-century capitals (see Figure 5.23). A row of spindly columns
topped by corbelling daringly support the heavy, projecting upper tier, which
presumably contains the tomb itself. As well as the usual display of heraldry and
lettering on the central panels, a lifelike image of a balding, bearded head is to be
found on one return of the frieze, matched at the opposite end by a skull and

FIGURE 5.22   Dunfermline Abbey, Fife, the west tower, monument to William Schaw
(d. 1602).

crossbones. The monument of Sir William Bruce of Symbister, who died in 1630, expresses even more overtly the intimate connection between life and death, just as one might juxtapose images of the active and contemplative life (see Figure 5.24). The deceased man is represented by a lifesize standing figure in armour, flanked on the left side by a pilaster loaded with arms and trophies, and on the right by a similar one arrayed with funeral emblems.

At Greyfriars churchyard in Edinburgh, the walls are lined with monuments standing like book-frontispieces – indeed, in some cases adopting designs borrowed from books and treatises.[128] The graveyard had been presented to the burgh of Edinburgh as a burial ground by Mary Queen of Scots in 1562. In 1603, the burgh council decreed that 'na staynes aucht to be infixet or sett on ony graiffes in the buriall yard', but three years later they conceded the right to erect monuments against the walls.[129] This fine series of seventeenth-century monuments became a showground for the skills of Edinburgh stonemasons, who included William Wallace

FIGURE 5.23   Crail, Fife, monument to James Lumsden of Airdrie (d. 1598) in the kirkyard.

and William Aytoun, both of them master masons at Heriot's Hospital on the other side of the kirkyard wall.

In country parishes, local lairds preferred to build family burial vaults or aisles, adjoining the church itself. These fall into two rather distinct types. On the one hand, there were family aisles opening into the body of the church – 'semi-detached', as Howard Colvin engagingly put it – with a laird's loft or family pew overlooking the body of the church, above the burial vault.[130] In such cases the main vehicle for display was the loft itself, an elaborate timber gallery framing the real-life family members with elaborate signs of their importance, wealth and lineage. The finest surviving examples are the Findlater loft of 1602 at Cullen and the Forbes loft of 1634 from old Pitsligo Church, now re-erected in the present parish church at nearby Rosehearty (see Figure 5.25). Where a number of prominent families owned land in the parish, there could even be several lofts attached to a single church, as at Abercorn in East Lothian.

On the other hand, a family vault might be more specifically dedicated to burial,

FIGURE 5.24 (*left*)   Crail, Fife, monument to Sir William
Bruce of Symbister (d. 1630) in the kirkyard.
FIGURE 5.25 (*below*)   Rosehearty, Banff and Buchan, the
parish church, the Forbes loft, 1634 (formerly in the old
parish church at Pitsligo).

FIGURE 5.26   Kilmuir Easter, Ross and Cromarty, the parish church, Munro aisle, 1616.

either free-standing or adjoining a church without any internal connection. An aisle of this type would be, literally, a vault, with a stone tunnel vault, often roofed on the outside with flagstones laid on a shallow pitch. Early examples include the Ogilvy aisle at Banff of 1580 and the Hepburn aisle at Oldhamstocks, dated 1581 and now converted into a chancel, commemorating Thomas Hepburn, a minister of the parish, and his wife. Two family aisles in the Highlands, each added to the east end of the church, show how elements borrowed from secular architecture could express the worldly status of the founders. At Kilmuir Easter on the Cromarty Firth, the easterly chapel, dated 1616, built by George Munro of Milntown and his second wife, even boasts a sturdy, baronial-looking circular bell tower with a conical roof (see Figure 5.26). The mausoleum of the Frasers of Lovat at Kirkhill near Inverness, built by the mason William Ross in 1633–4, is trimmed with courtly buckle quoins (its tower is eighteenth-century).[131]

The appearance of mausolea or monuments built by private individuals in anticipation of their own death, rather than as executors of the will of a deceased ancestor, reveals the increasing preoccupation with self-glorification. The inscription at Kilmuir Easter records that George Munro 'beigit' (built) the chapel himself. Similarly, the flamboyant tomb to David, the Lord of Scone and later first Viscount Stormont, in the chapel at Scone Palace, was commissioned in 1618, almost a decade before his death.[132] (This was just two years before he engaged John Mylne to build the church at Falkland, already mentioned.)

The most curious – almost obsessional – relic of this concern for leaving a fitting memorial is the aisle at Largs, built by Sir Robert Montgomery of Skelmorlie (see Figure 5.27). The aisle is now a free-standing chapel, but originally opened on to the church, since demolished. The burial vault is in a crypt, below ground level, reached by a stair leading down to a wooden door. Above rises the family loft, an open stone gallery embellished with a glorious display of Mannerist strapwork, in the form of a triumphal arch reminiscent of schemes for festive scenery by de Vries.[133] As Adam White has shown, the design is based on the pair of monuments to Queen Elizabeth and Mary Queen of Scots, erected in Westminster Abbey at the behest of James VI between 1605 and 1613.[134] The tomb is dated 1639, and the outside door of the aisle 1637. Over the gallery soars a timber vault, decorated with one of the finest painted ceilings of the age, completed before the monument itself in 1636.[135] Apart from Grandtully, this is the only surviving painted ceiling to have been made for a religious setting. It is said that Montgomerie used to go down into the vault at night for private meditation, in preparation for his burial, emulating no less a figure than the Emperor Charles V, who had his funeral rites enacted before his death.[136] But Montgomery did not die until 1651![137] (His behaviour seems almost normal in comparison with the sixteenth-century laird of Cromarty who used to have his bed hoisted up from the courtyard of his palace to the parapet in order to rehearse his ascension.)[138] At Skelmorlie, more vividly than in any other family aisle of the period, the patron's resurrection was visually symbolised by the presence of live figures in the family aisle directly above the door to his tomb. Here there was no need for effigies of the children of the deceased, for they would be there in person every Sunday. In contrast to the more conventionally Catholic imagery of the Resurrection scene in the ceiling at Grandtully, this was not a mystical interpretation but a matter-of-fact and secular enactment.

It was the courtiers of James VI who were commemorated by the most splendid and architecturally coherent monuments of the age, especially after the transfer of the court to London. As John Weever remarked in his book *Ancient Funeral Monuments*, published in London in 1631, 'Sepulchres should be made according to the qualitie and degree of the person deceased, that by the Tombe every one might be discerned of what ranke hee was living.'[139] The tomb of George Home, first Earl of Dunbar, High Treasurer of Scotland and later Chancellor of the Exchequer in England, was erected in Dunbar Church after his death in London in 1611.[140] This lavish marble monument was carved in London by the Flemish sculptor Maximilian Colt, master sculptor to the crown.[141] Flanked by enigmatic caryatid knights, the effigy kneels in prayer before an open book, with the robes of the garter over his

FIGURE 5.27   Skelmorlie, Largs, Ayrshire, Montgomery aisle and monument, 1636–9.

suit of armour. Figures of virtues and heraldic displays adorn the upper tiers. The scheme of the Dunbar tomb was to be repeated with only minor changes in the tomb of David, Lord of Scone, which he commissioned in 1618, as we have seen. At Falkland Church he was to dictate the architectural formula very precisely, and it is likely that he specifically instructed Colt to produce a near replica of the dignified Dunbar monument.

It is significant that, in contrast to medieval tomb traditions, the effigy in each of the Colt tombs is shown alive and alert, rather than as a recumbent corpse. The dignitary's afterlife is expressed in the preservation of the memory of his *life* rather than his death. Both tombs follow the English Renaissance convention of placing the effigy in profile, like a donor figure in an altarpiece. The image unites body and soul, as if confident of salvation, but the figure is engaged in a private meditation, existing within a realm that is remote from the spectator.[142] More original and more challenging are the Scottish monuments of this period in which the effigies face the spectator, a design solution rarely seen in England.[143] In the Glencairn aisle at Kilmaurs in Ayrshire

FIGURE 5.28 Kilmaurs, Ayrshire, the parish church, Glencairn monument, 1600, from MacGibbon and Ross, *Ecclesiastical Architecture*, vol. III.

stands the monument to the eighth Earl of Glencairn and his wife, signed by the mason David Scougal of Crail and dated 1600 (see Figure 5.28). Half-length statues of the couple are arranged facing the spectator as if in a laird's loft, the Earl in prayer, his wife with demurely folded arms, while their mourning children are lined up, praying solemnly, in the tier below. The inscription over the figures reads: 'Nothing surer then [*sic*] death / Be terfor sobor and vatch in prayer'. On either side, two projecting Corinthian columns – their shafts licked by flames, and their capitals intriguingly different as if to recognise the individuality of the two figures – support a projecting entablature which bears the family's armorial panel.

Although tomb effigies that face the spectator are relatively rare in England at this time, in Scotland one can almost sense an echo of Calvin's words:

> We are afraid [of death] because we apprehend it not as it is in itself, but as grim, haggard and hideous … If we will but pause, stand our ground, and look death squarely in the eyes, we shall find it quite different from the way it has been depicted to us, and with a very different aspect from that of our miserable lives.[144]

Where better to 'look death squarely in the eyes' than in the monument to George Hay, Chancellor of Scotland, erected in 1635 in his family aisle at Kinnoull in Perthshire (see Figure 5.29). Hay died in 1634, just a year after he was created first Earl of Kinnoull. To MacGibbon and Ross, this tomb was 'of a pompous kind', failing to convey the feeling of reverence inspired by medieval tombs.[145] Yet the spectator senses vividly the presence of this enterprising and determined character: pioneer of glass manufacture, favourite of James VI, a cantankerous nuisance to Charles I.[146] This is not a body from whom the soul has been lifted, but a dynamic, theatrical tableau. The likeness of statue was evidently based on the fine full-length portrait by Daniel Mytens, now on loan to the Scottish National Portrait Gallery, which is reproduced in every detail – from the Lord Chancellor's purse on the table to the giant rosettes of the shoes on his gouty feet.[147] The monument was originally painted in full polychromy, not only to allow the heraldry to dazzle, but more importantly to make the effigy seem more real, as if the two-dimensional painted portrait had been given a corporeal afterlife. The hovering angels (their means of support mysterious even to the careful investigator) unveil the royal coat of arms on the table with a Baroque immediacy that must have stunned the spectator of the time. For Hay himself, brought up a Catholic, such Baroque splendour would doubtless have seemed entirely acceptable. The three columns that support the roof of the tabernacle bear Corinthian columns with their leaves barely unfurled, as if to imply life to come. The three shafts are all different: one entwined in leafy branches, one bearing Flemish-style strapwork ornament, and one 'Solomonic' like the twisted columns believed to come from the biblical Temple in Jerusalem. Here we see nature, manufacture and religion, lined up to frame the memory of this versatile individual who had risen to the top rank of his society through his own efforts.[148]

Whereas the Kinnoull monument is a native Scottish endeavour, uninhibited by the reins of courtly English taste, his fellow industrialist Sir George Bruce of Carnock, who died in 1625, was commemorated by a more English-style monument, erected by his eldest son in the family aisle at the abbey church at Culross (see Figure 5.30). Recumbent effigies of Bruce and his wife lie within in a shallow recess, surmounted by a tall superstructure (in itself a status symbol, as most family vaults were low).[149] Though the effigies themselves are lifeless, in front of the monument kneel life-size alabaster statues of his eight children, carved fully in the round, facing the audience and actively engaging their sympathy and respect. These statues were probably made in England, where similar figures can be seen, for instance, in the tomb of Sir Henry Lee (d. 1631) and his wife at Spelsbury in Oxfordshire, and in the monument to Sir John St John at Lydiard Tregoze in Wiltshire.[150]

The Lauderdale monument in Haddington Church presents an even more demure, Anglicising approach (see Figure 5.31). The tomb commemorates two generations of the Maitland family, Chancellor John Maitland Lord Thirlestane (who died in 1595) and his wife, and their son the first Earl of Lauderdale, who erected the monument (he died in 1638), with his wife.[151] In emulation of England, where recumbent effigies were still fashionable, these two couples are portrayed as sleeping figures, lifeless and emotionally detached from the spectator, who is obliged to read the expansive texts on funereal black panels to remember their achievements and virtues in life. These monuments assume a literary audience –

FIGURE 5.29   Kinnoull aisle, near Perth, monument to Chancellor George Hay, first Earl of
Kinnoull, 1635.

and one that would be impressed not by the exuberant polychromy of Kinnoull,
but by the translucent alabaster of the figures and the polished black columns
against the white surround. The architectural canopy consists of two arched bays
united beneath a single broken pediment, a deft abbreviation of the English double
tomb type seen in the monument to Sir Samuel and Sir Edwin Sandys (d. 1629,
1626) in Wickhamford, Worcestershire.[152]

CONCLUSION

In the immediate aftermath of the Reformation, as we have seen, the few new
churches that were built display an austere classicism that rejected the conventions
and idiom of the local, late medieval Gothic tradition. The shift from Gothic to

FIGURE 5.30   Culross Abbey Church, Fife, monument to Sir George Bruce of Carnock (d.
1625).

Renaissance forms was catalysed by the need to convey a clear expression of the
new religious ideology. Classicism could not be too Italianate, of course, for it was
the extravagance and decadence of High Renaissance Rome that had shocked Martin
Luther into the protest that had launched the Reformation. This early consistency
dissolved amid the religious confusions of the first half of the seventeenth century.
By the 1630s, Rome was entering another great period of creativity, the age that
we now call the High Baroque, but the emotional religious fervour of the churches
of Bernini and Borromini would have been even more repellant to the Protestant
Scotsman. Of the new churches of the first half of the seventeenth century,
Edinburgh's Tron Kirk was exceptionally exuberant, but its Dutch character seemed
acceptable because of the relevance of the Calvinist culture from which its elements
were borrowed. Meanwhile, architecture in London was being revolutionised by
the accomplished classicism of Inigo Jones, less flamboyant than that of Baroque
Rome, but obviously of Italian inspiration. In the North-East of Scotland,

FIGURE 5.31 Haddington, East Lothian, St Mary's parish church, Lauderdale monument, *c*.1638, from a nineteenth-century photograph.

episcopalian leanings removed any need to resist classicism, as we can see from the perky little birdcage belfries in that region. It was the Covenant that gave the designers of Scottish churches the impetus to return to the Gothic tradition, as if to protest overtly against the classical bent of the court and its English episcopalian associations. Ironically, Gothic elements were also revived, though in a much more decorative vein, in the ostentatiously Anglican church of Dairsie and in the chapel at Heriot's Hospital in Edinburgh. Extravagant displays of up-to-date classical finery were mainly confined to the monuments. Although Knox's condemnation of idolatry had banished saints and angels from the kirk, the lifelike, full-face effigies of deceased dignitaries must have excited almost as much reverence.

Most Scottish post-Reformation churches, whether classical or Gothic, were modest in scale and austere in expression, in comparison with the secular buildings of the age, but they were serious, inventive, thoughtful responses to the challenge of the new liturgy.

CHAPTER SIX

Conclusion

And howbeit it [the building] may be sumptuous and costlie mair
nor necessitie requyris, yit it is the maist tollerable kynd of prodi-
galitie and of sumptuous and immoderate cost; becaus the samyn
will be steidable to the posteritie, and decoir of the country.

Sir Richard Maitland[1]

This book has chronicled a remarkable period in the history of Scottish architecture – a time of widening horizons, religious upheaval, large-scale property
redistribution and increasing prosperity. The period saw the court removed to
London in 1603 and ended just before the Restoration of the Stewart monarchy
after eight years of Cromwellian occupation. Despite the intrigues that accompanied
the new social mobility, the long, peaceful reign of James VI had provided stable
conditions for building among all his 'Thrie Estates', each with its own aspirations
and proclivities. The architecture of the period is a rich and varied legacy, characterised by its inventiveness and its awareness of the whole European spectrum of
design. Individuality and novelty were valued commodities; yet there remains,
within the hundreds of surviving buildings, a unity that crossed these social barriers,
just as the class boundaries themselves were indistinct and constantly shifting. This
harmony of place and time is difficult to define, except in bald stylistic and
nationalistic categories that hardly do justice to the warmth and energy inherent in
the buildings themselves. There is a humanity in the scale of the architecture – in
the size of the doors and windows, in the spacious, well-lit staircases, in the
intimacy of the frugal parish churches. This was a delicately balanced transition
between the claustrophobic defensiveness of the Middle Ages and the more monumental, grander style of the Restoration.

In the nineteenth century, the Cromarty stonemason-turned-writer Hugh Millar
described the portal of Cromarty House (since rebuilt) as 'somewhat resembling
an old-fashioned picture-frame'.[2] This was a perceptive observation, for it was the
roll-moulded doorways surmounted by heraldic panels or worthy inscriptions that
framed the acts of entrance and exit by the house-owners of the time. The plasticity
of the mouldings – the doorframes, the chimney piece surrounds, the newel posts
and the secretive little aumbries – gave the stone-carving an approachable, cushiony
texture. Details could be hard and forbidding, of course – we need only remember
the robust ironwork of yetts, window grilles and jougs. But more often (except
within the kirk) the most prominent buildings resounded with a dazzling display of

colour and carved ornament. Heraldic panels were richly painted and gilded; and, as we have seen, the flamboyant painted ceilings were one of the glories of the age. The palette of the tapestries, furnishings and clothes was just as festive, but it was offset by the frosty whiteness of the plaster ceilings, by the polished glow of wood panelling or by the knobbly woodwork of the exuberantly carved furniture. Inside and outside, colour and texture played out a visual dialogue that brought the designs to life.

THE ARCHITECTURAL PROFESSION

The story has been one without authors, for we still know tantalisingly little about who designed these buildings. Datestones, patrons' initials and heraldry were proudly displayed on churches and public buildings as well as on private houses, but we rarely find the name of the designer. The mason John Bel carved his name on the great armorial panel on the entrance front of Castle Fraser in 1617, but such clues are rare (see Figure 3.5).[3] The Glencairn monument is signed by the mason David Scougal of Crail, and John Mercer inscribed the Bruce tomb at Culross (see Figure 5.28 and 5.30), but these were stonecarvers who probably hoped to be remembered for their tomb effigies rather than for the architectural settings. The medieval practice of incising masons' marks on carved stones continued unchecked, but it is rarely possible to identify names from these hieroglyphs, and in any case the mark refers to the hand that carved each piece of stone, rather than the mason who designed its form.

Even documents are elusive and contradictory, for the word 'architect' was still one that was rarely adopted and barely understood.[4] As in England, examples of its use before 1600 are few. Pitscottie had criticised James III for the fact that his friends included an architect named Cochrane.[5] The term 'architect' was applied to two royal masters of work in Scotland between 1560 and 1660. The first was William Schaw who, after his death in 1602, was described as 'most expert in architecture' on his monument in Dunfermline Abbey (see Figure 5.22);[6] this was twelve years before a similar compliment was paid to Robert Smythson in England, on his tomb in Wollaton Church[7]. And James Murray was described as 'architectus noster' when he was granted the lands of Kilbaberton by the King in 1612[8]

From the early sixteenth century, the crown buildings were controlled by a hierarchy, with one or more royal masters of works at the apex of the design pyramid. The two most prominent figures in the time of James V were Sir James Hamilton of Finnart and John Scrymgeour, who shared responsibility for the building works at the royal palaces.[9] They themselves employed and paid the master masons and acted as the clerks of works on site. These were educated men of the courtier class who probably had overall design control. It was the task of the master masons to design details and prepare templates for the stone-carving. This arrangement, known as the 'Direct Labour System', still prevailed in the period of this book, in the royal works and other schemes which involved building work and repairs over a long period.[10] Both the royal masters of works and the royal master masons were appointed by warrant and paid an annual salary, whereas the lesser

craftsmen were given a weekly wage, and casual manual labourers were paid by
the day.[11]

During the reign of James VI, the most prominent royal master of works was
William Schaw, appointed in 1583 as 'grit maister of all and sindrie his hines
palaceis, biggingis and reparationis, and grit oversear, directour and commandar'.[12]
Schaw was from a family of lairds at Sauchie near Stirling; like all the holders of
that office in the period of this book, he was not a master craftsman but a courtier,
well educated and well travelled, as his epitaph proudly declares (see Figure 5.22).
Nevertheless, he was active in Masonic circles and was responsible for laying down
the statutes of the Scottish lodges, whereby, according to David Stevenson's recent
study, 'he created freemasonry'.[13] The Masonic lodges were distinct from the
masons' craft incorporations or guilds; though they might share both members and
premises, they enjoyed rituals and secret doctrines that marked them out from the
more practical concerns of the incorporations. Schaw's involvement suggests that
at least from this time influential figures from higher social ranks were admitted to
the lodges along with the master craftsmen themselves. It is not unlikely that this
context gave added status to the stonemasons and assisted the rise in their social
status that helped to create the profession of architect.

The most important of Schaw's successors in the office of royal master of work,
in terms of his designing role, was James Murray, who was appointed in 1607,
'our Soverane lord understanding perfytlie ... [his] skilful experience, knawledge
and habilitie'.[14] Like his father before hime, Murray had been a master wright to
the crown, but his grant of the lands of Kilbaberton in 1612, already mentioned,
assured his entry into the laird class. He was knighted in 1633, the year before his
death. Murray administered all the repairs and construction work at the royal
palaces between 1607 and 1634. How closely he controlled the master masons,
for instance William Wallace at Edinburgh Castle and Linlithgow Palace, remains
uncertain. Stylistic links with Wallace's other documented work at Heriot's Hospital and Winton House suggested that the mason was allowed considerable liberty
by Murray. We know, however, that Murray himself designed the new Parliament
House in Edinburgh, for which he was paid the enormous sum of £1,000 for
services to the burgh's works and 'for drawing up of the modell of the workes of
the Parliament and Counsel hous presentlie intendit'.[15] He also designed his own
house at Baberton, erected in 1622–3. According to Aonghus MacKechnie he was
prominent in the creation of what may be called the Scottish 'court style', a bookish
classicism infused with Flemish-style Mannerist ornament.[16]

Except in such major initiatives as court buildings, by the seventeenth century
most building projects in Scotland were organised, instead, by the 'Contract
System', by which the patron employed a contractor – usually a master mason,
but occasionally a master wright – to carry out a particular work according to
written specifications laid down in the contract.[17] Contracts and documents of the
time usually make no reference to drawings – we have already mentioned the
contract to John Mylne the Elder for Falkland Church in 1620, in which all
the dimensions and design details were to be 'devyseit' by the patron, the Lord of

Scone.[18] Similarly, the contract drawn up in 1611 for the building of Partick Castle near Glasgow, published by MacGibbon and Ross, required the mason to follow exactly the form determined – verbally rather than graphically – by the patron, who had the last word on every aspect of the project.[19] In the contract of 1612 for the construction of Baldovan Mill, near Dundee, the mason 'Andro Wast' had to follow the design specifications supplied by the town council's master of works.[20] It is inconceivable, however, that sketches were not passed between the patron and the master craftsman, at least during the initial stages of such negotiations. In the absence of graphic material, contracts often made reference to other buildings as models: the West Port at St Andrews, for example, was to 'conform to the form and fassoun of the Naither-bow of Edinburghe', according to the contract of 1589.[21]

No Scottish architectural drawings appear to survive from the period before the Restoration, those made in 1663 by the youngest John Mylne for the remodelling of Holyrood Palace being the earliest known.[22] None the less, drawings are occasionally mentioned in documents. For example, Heriot's Hospital had to 'conforme to ye paterne and prescript maid be ye said Dean of Rochester' (George Heriot's executor).[23] This 'paterne', presumably the ground-plan based on a plate in Serlio's treatise, was sent from London before the final choice of the site had been made. Balanquhall was no more than an educated amateur, and it seems likely that many Scottish buildings of the time were designed in this way. Alexander Seton, first Earl of Dunfermline, the builder of Pinkie and Fyvie, was said to have 'great skill in architecture and herauldrie'.[24] We have already seen in an earlier chapter how church buildings could be closely controlled by the patron, whether the minister, the heritor or the burgh council. On the other hand, burgh records from the period indicate that, although each project had a master of works, this was usually a member of the town council whose responsibility was as a clerk of works rather than designer. In such cases, the principal mason or wright seems to have played the creative role.

Master masons certainly made drawings. William Wallace's 'haill muildis and drauchtis' for Heriot's Hospital were recovered from his widow after his death in 1631.[25] These must have been the templates and working drawings developed from Balanquhall's 'paterne', with ornamental details of Wallace's own invention. His successor at the Hospital, William Aytoun, was obliged in his contract 'to prosecute and follow forth the modell, frame, and building of the said wark, as the same is already begun; and to devyse, plott, ans sett down what he shall think meittest for the decorement of the said wark and pattern thereof'.[26] The difference in style between the ground floor, (largely complete at Wallace's death) and the first floor (executed under Aytoun), with its bolder broken pediments, shows that the master mason had considerable freedom, perhaps more than Wallace may have had in his work for the Crown. An anonymous double portrait of Aytoun and his wife – shown as a demure puritan couple who might have stepped out of a picture by Rembrandt – is still preserved at Heriot's Hospital. At Innes House, Aytoun was paid £26 13s. 4d. 'for drawing the form of the house on paper'.[27]

FIGURE 6.1   Craigston Castle, Aberdeenshire, entrance front, 1604–7 (the porch and wings are later additions).

Masonic secrets were not just the rituals of lodges but also the body of skill and technical experience passed down through the generations by the apprenticeship system. In Aberdeenshire, the remarkable Bel family of stonemasons seems to have been responsible for a group of castles which Harry Gordon Slade has called 'Scotland's finest and most distinctive contribution to western architecture'.[28] These castles include not only Castle Fraser (so proudly signed by John Bel in 1617), but also Craigievar, Midmar (where 'George Bel, Meason' was buried in the churchyard in 1575), Crathes and Fyvie (see Figures 3.5, 3.27 and 3.16). All share a delight in virtuoso corbelling and exotic skylines, but most strikingly they display an ability to design in three dimensions rather than two. Their complex arrangements of staircases, private apartments, turrets and unexpected angles cannot be graphically expressed, either in plans or in elevational drawings, in any easily understood way. The only one of the series with orthogonally imaginable façades and comprehensible plans is Craigston, with its four-square ground-plan and rectangular rooms, built in 1604–7 (see Figures 6.1 and 6.2). It seems that, exceptionally in this case, the patron John Urquhart may have supplied drawings on paper, perhaps by his own hand. Negotiations with patrons in the other examples must have been conducted by analogy with other castles in the group, or perhaps using three-dimensional models in wood or clay. The only one with a symmetrical façade, Fyvie, shows the impact of the taste and experience of the patron, Alexander Seton, but with his acknowledged skill in architecture he probably understood the mason's language.

The Bel family operated within the context of a region where Catholicism was still widespread, and where even within Protestant communities episcopalian

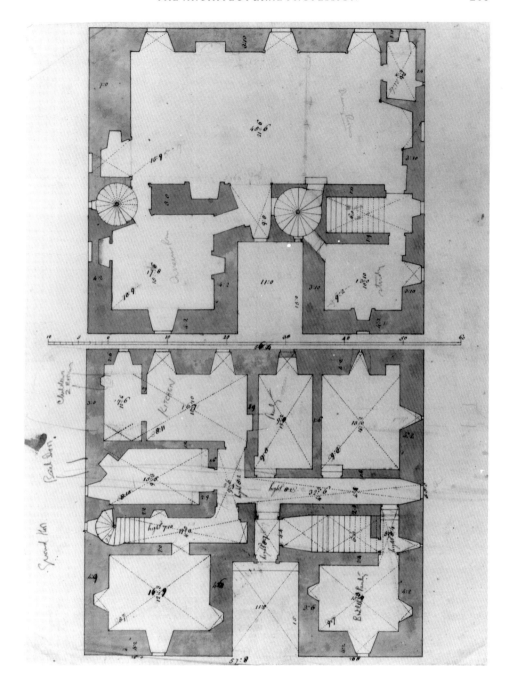

FIGURE 6.2   Craigston Castle, Aberdeenshire, plans of the first floor (above) and the ground floor.

leanings were prevalent. We do not know their own religious affiliation, but the Conn family of Auchry – Aberdeenshire lairds of and masons who probably designed such prominent nearby buildings as Towie Barclay, Gight and Delgaty – were presumably Catholics. One of their number was George Conn, the Catholic priest who tried to convert the court of Charles I, and retired to Rome where he is buried in San Lorenzo in Damaso.[29] Alexander Seton and William Schaw, too, were both Catholics, but this does not seem to have prejudiced their careers in either case.[30]

The Mylnes were Scotland's most famous masonic dynasty, descended from a family of masons active in Dundee in the sixteenth century – in 1537 Robert Mylne had supplied some of the stone and timber for Falkland Palace.[31] Three generations of the family were prominent during the period of this book. John Mylne (d. 1621), who rebuilt Lord Somerville's house at the Drum in 1584–5 was best known for building the new bridge over the River Tay in Perth, swept away by floods just four years after its completion in 1617.[32] We have already encountered his son John, who died in 1657, the mason who built the church at Falkland, since destroyed, and was the author of the famous sundial in the gardens at Holyrood Palace made for Charles I in 1633 (see Figure 2.21). His likeness is recorded in a pencil drawing in which he holds a pair of dividers, with three books on the shelf behind him – Archimedes, Euclid and Apollonius – asserting his intellectual status (see Figure 6.3). Like William Aytoun before him, he is shown as a sober burgess dressed in black, with a white puritan collar. Three years later, he resigned his post as royal master mason, to be succeeded by his son, also called John, who built the Tron Kirk in Edinburgh and the engaging Cowane's Hospital in Stirling (see Figures 5.15 and 4.61).[33] He succeeded Aytoun as master mason at Heriot's Hospital in 1643. The youngest John's brother, Alexander, was best known as the sculptor who carved the figures for Parliament House. All three John Mylnes were active Freemasons; but it was the youngest of the trio who rose most rapidly up through the social spectrum, becoming not only Dean of the Edinburgh Masons but also a town councillor and eventually, in 1662, a member of Parliament. The epitaph on his monument in Greyfriars' churchyard begins: 'Great Artisan grave Senator'.[34] A portrait of this youngest John Mylne survives in the Scottish National Portrait Gallery: in oil on copper, it shows him resting his hand on a classical bust, with an architectural plan on the table before him.[35] His remarkable social mobility was commemorated in the extract from his tomb epitaph which was inscribed over the entrance of St Mary's Chapel, the home of Edinburgh's Lodge and Incorporation of Masons in Niddry's Wynd (now demolished):

> Rare man he who could unite in one
> Highest and lowest Occupation
> To sit with Statesmen, Counsellor to Kings
> To work with Tradesmen in mechanick things.[36]

Mylne had risen through the ranks to the top of his profession, to be compared with Vitruvius after his death,[37] but unlike James Murray he became not a laird, but a respected burgess and public figure. Though his father had been strictly circumscribed in the design of Falkland Church, there can be no reason to doubt that Mylne himself designed Edinburgh's Tron Kirk (see Figure 5.15). This was

FIGURE 6.3   Portrait of John Mylne (d. 1657, the second of the three royal master masons of
that name), by an unknown artist.

perhaps the most accomplished piece of classicism that we have seen in this book,
with the classical orders used to articulate, rather than merely to decorate, the
structure. The use of architectural books would not have been unexpected in a
figure who was portrayed in such intellectual guises. It is not implausible, however,
that he was specifically directed to de Keyser's treatise by Nicholas Stone who had
married the Dutch architect's daughter. Stone was sent to Edinburgh before the
visit of James VI to undertake alterations to Holyrood Chapel,[38] and he may well
have met Mylne's father and grandfather at Holyrood on this visit.

We have seen how the profession of master mason gradually acquired increasing
design responsibilities during the century covered by this book, and how the
masons' educational level and social standing rose accordingly. From the French
masons at Falkland in the time of James V to the career of the last John Mylne,
one could chart the steady rise of the architectural profession as we know it, setting
the scene for the great gentleman architect of the Restoration, Sir William Bruce,

called by Defoe 'the Kit Wren of Scotland'.[39] However, the picture, in reality, is far less simple. There were always gentlemen architects in Renaissance Scotland – not only the royal masters of works such as Sir James Hamilton of Finnart and William Schaw, but also educated amateurs like Alexander Seton and John Urquhart. Any patron had some design input, whether a laird, a minister or a burgh council. And as we have seen, the wide social range within the Masonic lodges blurred such simple boundaries yet further.

THE CONCEPT OF NATIONAL STYLE

It was chiefly through patrons that ideas from abroad were assimilated, for few master craftsmen, unless imported from the Continent, had travelled widely. Inevitably, therefore, foreign elements were radically transformed in the process: metamorphosed by tricks of memory, only to be awkwardly expressed in unprofessional sketches or verbal descriptions. Only through two-dimensional, linear representations in treatises could other architectural cultures be grasped with any degree of accuracy – though divorced from their own cultural milieu, these too, acquired different nuances.

With the invention of printing, architectural ideas could cross national boundaries more easily than ever before, but as David Thomson has recently emphasised, 'The classical architectural culture of the Renaissance was not a pan-European acceptance and assimilation of the Roman past nor of the Italian present.'[40] Scotland did not produce any architectural treatises in this period, although the fine quality of the frontispieces of books such as Napier's *Logarithms* (see Figure 1.3) shows that they had the printing skills to do so. We know from other writings of the time, however, that architecture was regarded as an art of high prestige. In the *History of the House of Seytoun*, for example, particular attention is paid to the architectural enterprises of the family. These included not only the King's Chancellor Alexander Seton, the first Earl of Dunfermline, and his two kinsmen who built Barnes Castle and Winton House, but even Lady Jane Hepburn (whose husband, George the third Lord of Seytoun, had been killed at the battle of Flodden in 1513) who built the 'foirwerk of Seytoun aboue the yet' and transformed the collegiate church nearby.[41]

Architectural books were imported, however, and used freely in bookish projects such as Heriot's Hospital and the Tron Kirk. Classicism did not appeal as a system of articulation or as a source of proportional harmony. The only example of the orders superimposed in the 'orthodox' succession proposed by Serlio and Vignola is to be found in the courtyard turrets of Heriot's Hospital. The knowledge was to hand, for it was to be rapidly assimilated after the Restoration, most conspicuously in William Bruce's courtyard at Holyrood Palace, but such theoretical classicism found few resonances in a culture so preoccupied with outward display.[42] Foreign treatises were used chiefly as pattern books, offering designs for tombs, doorways and elaborate Mannerist ornament.

Nevertheless, the correspondence between verbal language and architecture did not pass unnoticed in this increasingly literate and erudite age. In 1651, while imprisoned in London, the scholarly eccentric Sir Thomas Urquart of Cromarty invented a new language, which he tried to promote by analogy with buildings:

> Thus it is that, as according to the largeness of the plat of a building and compactedness of its walls, the work-master contriveth his roofs, platforms, outjettings and other such like parts and portions of the whole; just so, conform to the extent and reach which a language in its flexions and compositions hath obtained at first, have the sprucest linguists hitherto bin pleased to make use of the words thereto belonging.[43]

This was a period in which national identities were a source of pride; and the recognition of distinctions between one culture and another allowed the choice of style to convey finely tuned messages about the aspirations of the patron and the intention of the building. Even Castiglione had remarked on the way that courtiers could express national affiliations in their dress.[44] This awareness of national style is evident in Sir Robert Ker's advice to his son William Earl of Lothian in 1632 to build either 'in the fashion of this country or France'.[45] These were regarded as definable and distinct modes of building, still the preferred styles in the ranks of the Scottish nobility.

This book has shown how the choice of elements borrowed from abroad could make statements about religious or political allegiances. Thus, for instance, Dutch models inspired a wide variety of urban buildings, for the prosperous Calvinist society of Holland embodied desirable virtues which Scottish burgesses hoped to emulate. More specifically, after 1603 the ostentatious decoration of a house with Tudor roses as well as thistles – often as finials on the steep little pediments of dormers – could express support for the union of the Crowns and loyalty to the King. Where Gothic elements were revived in churches after 1620, this could express either a Laudian High-Anglican bias or, in more sober versions, the leanings of devout Covenanters.

If the old nobility adhered to Scottish and French traditions, the burghs tended to reveal more affinity with their Northern European trading partners in Holland and Scandinavia.[46] The whole picture is, however, complicated by the impact of English culture north of the border during the period of this book. Even before 1603, a subtle Anglicisation was occurring with the modification of the language encouraged by the introduction of the English Bible.[47] After 1603, many of the highest courtiers spent periods in London where they were regarded by some of their English counterparts as boorish philistines, a reception which must have induced the more ambitious of them to emulate English characteristics in their buildings. A house such as the Binns, for example, is more symmetrical and lower than a typical Scots laird's castle. Moreover, it has an English-style 'laigh hall', and its rich plaster ceilings were a decorative feature imported from England. It was not artistic insensibility but a strong local cultural identity that allowed Scottish architecture to retain many of its native characteristics under the impact of this radical shift of focus.

As the poet Alasdair MacLean remarked in his elegiac book *Night falls on*

Ardnamurchan, 'A culture is the most natural thing in the world. It appears at the same time as its region and is both cause and effect; it cannot be adopted later or manufactured.'[48] The architecture of Scotland between 1560 and 1660 gained enormously in finesse, technical expertise and visual repertoire, without rejecting the skills and experience of earlier generations. As times became more secure, and capital was released into the laird and burgess classes to be invested in agriculture, industry, trade and eventually in building, there followed a building boom that abounded in inventiveness, erudition, and even wit. Buildings were so elaborately three-dimensional in conception that the ingenious multifaceted sundials that stood in their gardens seem merely an extension of this new outward vision of the world and of Scotland's place within it.

Notes

NOTES TO CHAPTER ONE

1   Boswell, *Journal to the Hebrides*, p. 308.

2   On this theme, see Brown, *Bloodfeud in Scotland*.

3   Summerson, *Architecture in Britain* p. 525.

4   Dunbar, *Architecture of Scotland*, p. 65.

5   Paterson, 'Scottish Architecture', p. 63.

6   Cruden, *The Scottish Castle*, p. 164.

7   MacGibbon and Ross, *Castellated and Domestic Architecture*, vol. II, p. 4.

8   See Porter and Teich, *The Renaissance*.

9   For a recent stimulating discussion of this theme, see Thomson, *Renaissance Architecture*, pp. 101–58.

10   See McQueen, *Humanism in Renaissance Scotland*.

11   See the preceding volume in this series: Fawcett, *Architectural History of Scotland*.

12   See Martin Kemp and Clare Farrow, 'Humanism in the Visual Arts, *circa* 1530–1630', in McQueen, *Humanism in Renaissance Scotland*, pp. 32–47. See also Denys Hay, 'Scotland and the Italian Renaissance'; and Glanmor Williams, 'The Renaissance', in Williams and Owen Jones, *Celts and the Renaissance*', pp. 1–15. The latter volume also contains articles by John McQueen on 'The Renaissance in Scotland' (on pp. 41–56) and by Peter Smith on 'Architecture in Wales during the Renaissance' (on pp. 101–45). For the literary context, see Jack, *Scottish Literature*, pp. 4–21. The most self-consciously Italianate Scottish building of the period is probably the Renaissance wing of Crichton Castle, erected by the Earl of Bothwell after his return from Italy in 1581.

13   See Braudel, *Out of Italy*; and Porter and Teich, *The Renaissance*. The British angle will be explored in Gent (ed.), *Albion's Classicism*.

14   Benesch, *The Art of the Renaissance* p. 61.

15   See the pertinent observations in Ackerman, *Distance Points*, pp. 3–22 (essay on style first published 1963, and postscript).

16   See Williams and Owen Jones, *Celts and the Renaissance*.

17   MacKechnie, 'Some French Influences', p. 7.

18   On the cultural dislocation in England, see Aston, 'English Ruins'.

19   See Trevor Roper, *Religion, the Reformation and Social Change*.

20   Burckhardt, *Civilisation of the Renaissance*, p. 107.

21   Williamson, *Scottish National Consciousness*, p. 24.

22   See Mason, 'Scotching the Brut'; and Williamson, *Scottish National Consciousness*.

23   Lowenthal, *The Past*, pp. 213–14.

24   See Sanderson, *Mary Stewart's People*, pp. 55–74; Macmillan, *Scottish Art*, pp. 44–5.

25   Dr Rosalind Marshall has suggested to me that the inclusion of Tantallon in the portrait may have been intended to affirm his nephew's victory in a former, long-running dispute over the ownership of the castle (personal communication, 29 Nov. 1993).

26   These restorations will be considered in the following chapter, but pertinent observations can be found in Cox, 'The Politics of Stuart Medievalism'.

27   See Corbett and Lightbown, *The Comely Frontispiece*, pp. 162 ff.

28   For a perceptive analysis of this topic in the context of the 15th century, see Stell, 'Architecture', pp. 153–83.

29   Donaldson, *Scotland: James V–James VII*, pp. 212 ff.

30   For a review of the region in this period, see Barrow et al., *The Seventeenth Century*.

31   See Billings, 'On Certain Features'; id., *Baronial and Ecclesiastical Antiquities*.

32   MacGibbon and Ross, *Castellated and Domestic Architecture*; id., *Ecclesiastical Architecture*. See also David Walker, 'The Architecture of MacGibbon and Ross: The Background to the Books', in Breeze, *Studies in Scottish Antiquity*.

33   Individual articles by all these authors will be cited later in the book, but in the general context, I mention especially Hay's 'Scottish Renaissance Architecture'.

34   These have included helping me to lay on the RIAS Edinburgh Festival exhibition *The Architecture of the Scottish Renaissance* in 1990, and supplying me with his numerous writings, both published and unpublished. See, for example, his 'The Recovery of Renaissance Scotland'.

35   See William James Anderson, 'Rome and Scotland 1513–1625', in McRoberts, *Essays*, pp. 415–62.

36   See, for example, Lythe, *Economy of Scotland*, pp. 139, 167–84; Antonia Fraser, *Mary Queen of Scots*, pp. 174 ff.; John Durkan, 'The French Connection in the Sixteenth and Early Seventeenth Centuries', *Scotland and Europe*, pp. 19–44.

37   Lythe, *Economy of Scotland*, p. 172.

38   Ibid., p. 139.

39   Macmillan, *Scottish Art*, p. 68.

40   Smout, *Scottish Trade*, p. 167.

41   Lythe, *Economy of Scotland*, p. 192.

42   Ibid., p. 192.

43   Ibid., pp. 41–2; Fleming, *Scottish and Jacobite Glass*, pp. 95–8.

44   Cherry, *Princes, Poets and Patrons*, p. 31.

45   See Thomas Riis, 'Scottish–Danish Relations in the Sixteenth Century', in Smout, *Scotland and Europe*, pp. 82–96.

46   Smout, *Scottish Trade*, p. 91.

47   Anna Bieganska, 'A Note on the Scots in Poland, 1550–1800', in Smout, *Scotland and Europe*, pp. 157–65; and Elsa-Britta Grage, 'Scottish Merchants in Gothenburg, 1621–1850', in ibid., pp. 112–27.

48   Smout, *Scottish Trade*, pp. 152 ff.; Lythe, *Economy of Scotland*, pp. 142 ff.; Arnvid Lillehammer, 'The Scottish Norwegian Timber Trade in the Stavanger Area in the Sixteenth and Seventeenth Centuries', in Smout, *Scotland and Europe*, pp. 97–111.

49   Comment by Charles McKean, letter to the author, 19 October 1993.

50   Anderson, 'The Shetland Germans'.

51   Smout, 'Scottish–Dutch Contact'.

52   Smout, *Scottish Trade*, p. 96.

53   Davison and Gray, *The Scottish Staple at Veere*; Rooseboom, *The Scottish Staple in the Netherlands*.

54   Smout, *Scottish Trade*, p. 95.

55   Grage, 'Scottish Merchants in Gothenburg', op. cit., pp. 112–14.

56   Smout, *Scottish Trade*, p. 98.

57   Lythe, *Economy of Scotland*, p. 135.

58   Ibid., pp. 125–6.

59   Mc Roberts, *Essays*; Wormald, *Court, Kirk and Community*, p. 71.

60   Hume Brown, *Scotland before 1700*, p. 299.

61   Ibid., p. 345.

62   Smout, *Scottish Trade*, pp. 77–8, 107–8, 184.

63   Lamb, *The Changing Climate*, pp. 163–5.

64   See the volume of essays by Barrow et al., *The Seventeenth Century*.

65   Smout, *Scottish Trade*, pp. 9–12.

66   Ibid., p. 10.

67   Lythe, *Economy of Scotland*, p. 97. Her mother, Mary of Guise, is said to have introduced the first coach to Scotland. See Breeze and Donaldson, *A Queen's Progress*, p. 51.

68   Chambers, *Domestic Annals*, vol. I, p. 378.

69   Carleton Williams, *Anne of Denmark*, p. 73.

70   Lynch, *Scotland*, p. 171.

71   Smout, *Scottish Trade*, p. 8.

72   Ibid., p. 20.

73   Hume Brown, *Early Travellers*, pp. 78–9.

74   Personal communcation of 19 Oct. 1993 from Charles McKean, who is preparing a biography of Finnart.

75   Smout, *Scottish Trade*, p. 4.

76   NACF, *Saved for Scotland*, p. 82.

77   Smout, *Scottish Trade*, p. 7.

78   Ibid., p. 237.

79   Lythe, *Economy of Scotland*, p. 34. James VI had visited Tycho Brahe's Observatory in 1590, and the Scots mathematician John Craig corresponded with Tycho. On the scientific ability of the Scots, see Donaldson, *Scotland: James V–James VII*, pp. 256–7.

80   On the effects of the printing revolution, see Eisenstein, *The Printing Press*.

81   See Duncan Shaw, 'Adam Bothwell: A Conserver of the Renaissance in Scotland', in Cowan and Shaw, *Renaissance and Reformation*, pp. 141–69.

82   Sanderson, *Scottish Rural Society*, p. 173.

83   RCAMS, *Inventory ... Edinburgh*, Edinburgh, 1951, p. xlviii.

84   Kemp and Farrow, 'Humanism in the Visual Arts', op. cit., p. 39 and plate 15.

85   See Simpson, *Scottish Handwriting*.

86   Quoted in Cherry, *Princes, Poets & Patrons*, p. 25.

87   Ibid., p. 68.

88   Lythe, *Economy of Scotland*, p. 122.

89   Alex Keller, 'The Physical Nature of Man', in McQueen, *Humanism in Renaiss-ance Scotland*, pp. 113–14.

90   Hay, *Architecture of Churches*, pp. 5–6.

91   Smout, *Scottish Trade*, p. 171.

92   Lythe, *Economy of Scotland*, p. 121.

93   The relationship between Calvinism and humanist learning is explored in Allan, *Virtue, Learning and the Scottish Enlightenment*, pp. 30–78.

94   Donaldson, *Scotland: James V–James VII*, p. 259.

95   Smout, *Scottish Trade*, pp. 15–16.

96   On the role of women in Scottish society of the time, see especially Marshall, *Virgins and Viragoes*; Sanderson, *Mary Stewart's People*; and R. A. Houston, 'Women in the Economy and Society of Scotland, 1500–1800', in Houston and Whyte, *Scottish Society*, pp. 118–84.

97   Lythe, *Economy of Scotland*, pp. 169–70, 173.

98   Ibid., p. 123. See also Chambers, *Domestic Annals*, vol. I, p. 477.

99   For pioneering observations on this theme, see Paterson, 'Scottish Archi-tecture', pp. 48–65.

100   Quoted in R. D. S. Jack, 'Scottish Literature: The English and European Dimensions', in Brink and Gentrup, *Renaissance Culture in Context*, p. 15.

101   See J. Bannerman, 'Literacy in the Highlands', in Cowan and Shaw, *Renaissance and Reformation*, pp. 183–99; Donald Withrington, 'Education in the 17th Century Highlands', in Barrow et al., *The Seventeenth Century* pp. 60–9

102   On the transformation of Scots courtiers in England, see Chambers, *Domestic Annals*, vol. I, pp. 429–30.

103   See, for example, Mennie Shire, *Song, Dance and Poetry*, pp. 228 ff.

104   Wormald, *Court, Kirk and Community*, p. 193.

NOTES TO CHAPTER TWO

1   See, for example, Strong, *Splendour at Court*.

2   On the élitism of court masques at the Stuart court, see Goldberg, *James I*, pp. 56–7.

3   Lindesay of Pitscottie, *History and Chronicles*, p. 336; quoted in McKean's article 'Finnart's Platt'.

4   See, for example, Dunbar, 'Some Aspects of the Planning'; Martin Kemp and Clare Farrow, 'Humanism in the Visual Arts, *circa* 1530–1630', in McQueen, *Humanism in Renaissance Scotland*, pp. 32–47; Howard, 'Scottish Master Masons'; and McKean, 'Finnart's Platt', pp. 8–14.

5   See Mitchell, 'The Influence of France'; Noad, 'The Influence of France' Bentley-Cranch, 'An Early Sixteenth-Century French Architectural Source'; Dunbar, 'French Influence'; 'Some Sixteenth–Century French Parallels'; and MacKechnie, 'Some French Influences'.

6   The Falkland gatelodge resembles the entrance to the Château de Langeais in the Loire region. John Dunbar has likened the palace to Francis I's Château de Villers–Cotterets, Aisne (Dunbar, 'Some Sixteenth–Century French Par-allels').

7   Reliefs of classical busts in circular medallions appear on the Renaissance wing of the château of Le Lude, as well as in the staircase of Azay-le-Rideau and the hall of Chenonceau.

8   See Marshall, *Mary of Guise*.

9   McKean, 'Finnart's Platt'. His biography of Finnart is in preparation.

10   Dunbar, 'The Palace of Holyrood'.

11   Howard, *The Early Tudor Country House*, pp. 51–3. Henry VIII's Nonsuch
     Palace, built between 1538 and 1547, is illustrated on p. 125.

12   Examples of waisted baluster columns include the doorways of the Lonja in
     Granada and of the Convento della Piedad in Guadalajara, the façade of the
     Hospital de la Sangre in Seville, a first-floor portal in the palace of La Calahorra
     near Granada, the Lucas Cranach Haus in Leipzig, and a Bishop's tomb of
     1535 in Merseburg Cathedral. It is not intended to suggest that these are
     specific sources, but merely to indicate that the motif was common in both
     Germany and Spain in the Renaissance period. Square-shouldered busts in
     roundels very similar in style to the wooden heads that decorated the ceiling
     of the King's Hall in James V's Palace block can be seen on the façade of the
     Ayuntamiento in Seville.

13   See Nieto, Morales and Checa, *Arquitectura del Renacimiento*, pp. 111–14.
     Charles V's interest in the Alcazar of Seville began about 1535. Other And-
     alusian examples include the portal of the royal monastery of Santa Clara in
     Ubeda and the Puerto della Luna in the Cathedral of Baeza. Charles McKean,
     following Mitchell, traces these cusped arches, instead, to the Louis XII wing
     at Blois (Mitchell, 'The Influence of France', pp. 78–9; McKean, 'Finnart's
     Platt,' pp. 11–12). It seems to this writer unlikely that a monarch so aware
     of his stature as a European monarch would have turned to such an outdated
     model. John Dunbar and Aonghus MacKechnie both agree that the building is
     primarily of French inspiration, but to this writer the link with France is much
     less convincing than its Imperial (Spanish–German) character. See Dunbar,
     'French Influence', pp. 5–6, and MacKechnie, 'Some French Influence', p. 3.

14   See Hay, *The Letters of James V*.

15   Furgol, 'The Scottish Itinerary'.

16   See Breeze and Donaldson, *A Queen's Progress*, pp. 31–5, 56.

17   Chambers, *Domestic Annals*, vol. 1, p. 255; RCAMS, *Inventory ... Edinburgh*,
     Edinburgh, 1951, pp. 21–2; and MacIvor, *Edinburgh Castle*, pp. 62 and 73.

18   See Wisch and Scott Munshower, *'All the world's a stage'*.

19   Lynch, 'Queen Mary's Triumph'.

20   Donaldson, *Scotland: James V–James VII*, p. 215.

21   Lynch, *Scotland* p. 237. Modern studies of the life and reign of James VI
     include Willson, *King James VI and I* Smith, *The Reign of James VI and I*; Lee Jr.,
     Government by the Pen; id., *Great Britain's Solomon*; Bergeron, *Royal Family, Royal
     Lovers*.

22   e.g., most recently, Timothy Clifford, in Pearson, *Virtue and Vision*, p. 10.

23   Chambers, *Domestic Annals*, vol. I, p. 194 and *passim*.

24   Cherry, *Princes, Poets & Patrons*, p. 71.

25   Lynch, 'Queen Mary's Triumph', p. 6; Goldberg, *James I*, p. 42.

26   Goldberg, *James I*, pp. 43, 45. See also Yates, *Astrea*, pp. 1–28;

27   Goldberg, *James I* pp. 33, 46, 47, 52.

28   Ibid., pp. 40–2.

29   Ibid., p. 25; Mennie Shire, *Song, Dance and Poetry*, pp. 97, 101, 209 (the poem
     is by Sir William Mure of Rowallan). On Mary Queen of Scots' identifications

with Astraea, Diana and Venus, see Lynch, 'Queen Mary's Triumph', pp. 11–20.

30   Mennie Shire, *Song, Dance and Poetry*, p. 98.

31   Ibid., pp. 98, 100–1.

32   Goldberg, *James I*, p. 18.

33   Mennie Shire, *Song, Dance and Poetry*, p. 58 and *passim*.

34   Donaldson, *Scotland: James V–James VII*, pp. 46–8. The papal concession was in return for the establishment of a College of Justice in Scotland.

35   Donaldson, *Scotland: James V–James VII*, pp. 301–2; Lynch, *Scotland*, p. 227.

36   Donaldson, *Scotland: James V–James VII*, p. 193; Lynch, *Scotland*, p. 226.

37   von Bülow, 'Journey', p. 245.

38   The letter is published, as an example of the King's Italic hand, in Simpson, *Scottish Handwriting*, letter no. 21.

39   e.g. Chambers, *Domestic Annals*, vol. I, pp. 193, 321.

40   Ibid., vol. I, p. 201.

41   On the financing of the royal works, see Imrie and Dunbar, *Accounts*, vol. II (1616–49), pp. xxxii ff. Of the Octavians, Sir Gilbert Murray of Elibank was most directly concerned with the funding of building works.

42   Donaldson, *Scotland: James V–James VII*, pp. 301–2.

43   See the pertinent observations of Braunfels's chapter 'Seats of a Princely Court', in his *Urban Design*, pp. 176 ff.

44   Wormald, *Court, Kirk and Community*, pp. 145 ff.

45   e.g. Imrie and Dunbar, *Accounts*, p. lxxxvi. See also the building of Stirling Chapel Royal, below.

46   Webster, *Dunfermline Abbey*, p. 228.

47   Paton, *Accounts*, vol. I (1529–1615), pp. 310–14.

48   Ibid., p. 311.

49   Aonghus MacKechnie, 'William Schaw', work in progress.

50   Stevenson, *Origins of Freemasonry*, pp. 26 ff. The development of the architectural profession in Scotland will be considered again in its wider context in the final chapter of this book.

51   Heiberg, *Christian IV*.

52   Gifford, McWilliam and Walker, *Edinburgh*, p. 126.

53   Chambers, *Domestic Annals*, vol. I, pp. 197–201; Donaldson, *Scotland: James V–James VII*, p. 30.

54   Aonghus MacKechnie has kindly made available to me the first draft of his research in progress on Holyrood Palace in the early 17th century.

55   Chambers, *Domestic Annals*, vol. I, p. 198.

56   Ibid., pp. 197–200; Carleton Williams, *Anne of Denmark*, pp. 28–32.

57   Mylne, *Master Masons*, p. 62.

58   MacKechnie, 'William Schaw', op. cit.

59   Paulsson, *Scandinavian Architecture*, pp. 108–10; and id., 'The Architecture of Christian IV', in Heiberg, *Christian IV*, pp. 463 ff.

60   Webster, *Dunfermline Abbey*, p. 228.

61   Mylne, *Master Masons*, p. 62.

62   Sinclair (ed.), *Statistical Account*, vol. X (*Fife*), p. 289.

63   Ibid.

64   Chambers, *Domestic Annals*, vol. I, p. 358.

65   Sinclair (ed.), *Statistical Account*, vol. X (*Fife*) pp. 289–90.

66   Hume Brown, *Early Travellers*, p. 115.

67   Stevenson, *Origins of Freemasonry*, pp. 31 and 93–4.

68   Webster, *Dumfermline Abbey*, p. 228.

69   Mylne, *Master Masons*, p. 62.

70   Stevenson, *Origins of Freemasonry*, pp. 26–7.

71   Gifford, *Fife*, p. 178.

72   Paton, *Accounts* p. 310; Dunbar, 'The Palace of Holyrood', p. 20; MacKechnie on Schaw, unpublished manuscript, p. 4.

73   Meikle, *Works of William Fowler*, vol. II, pp. 169–70. See also Stevenson, *Origins of Freemasowmy*, p. 94.

74   Jack, *Scottish Literature*, p. 9.

75   Elliott and Rimmer, *History of Scottish Music*, pp. 19–25.

76   Donaldson, *Scotland: James V–James VII*, p. 302, n. 16.

77   Meikle, *Works of William Fowler*, p. 171.

78   Richardson, *Stirling Castle*, p. 11. Traces of painted decoration are still visible: see Apted, *Painted Ceilings*, p. 10.

79   Lieberman, *Renaissance Architecture*, plate 70 and figure 1.

80   Strong, *Art and Power*, pp. 87–91. On Philip II's entry into Antwerp, see William Eisler, 'Celestial Harmonies and Hapsburgh Rule: Levels of Meaning in a Triumphal Arch for Philip II in Antwerp, 1549', in Wisch and Munshower, *'All the World's a Stage'*, pp. 332–57.

81   Serlio, *Tutte l'opere*, book III, p. 110. Serlio's third book was first published in Venice in 1540.

82   'William Adam's Library', p. 31, note 4 where the portal is compared to a frontispiece by Perret. See also Corbett and Lightbown, *The Comely Frontispiece*.

83   I am indebted to Christy Anderson for many stimulating discussions on the relationship between books and buildings.

84   MacKechnie, 'Stirling's Triumphal Arch'.

85   The royal arms over this arch were repainted 'in gold and oil colours' in 1628 (Apted, *Painted Ceilings*, p. 90).

86   Apted's conclusion that the English painter Valentine Jenkin must have executed the decorative scheme for the Chapel interior, since he was paid for other work at Stirling in 1628–9, seems tenuous (*Painted Ceilings*, pp. 89–90).

87   Meikle, *Works of William Fowler*, p. 180.

88   Ibid., p. 182.

89   On the awareness of the contemporary relevance of the texts of the Psalms, see Mennie Shire, *Song, Dance and Poetry*, p. 70.

90   Parry, *The Golden Age*, p. 231; Galloway, *Union of England and Scotland*, p. 33.

91   Meikle, *Works of William Fowler*, pp. 188–91.

92   Ibid., p. 174. See Young, *Tudor and Jacobean Tournaments*.

93   On the implications of the monarch as actor, see Goldberg, *James I*, p. 62; Lynch, 'Queen Mary's Triumph', pp. 9–10.

94   Meikle, *Works of William Fowler*, pp. 190–4. See Fergusson of Kilkerran, 'A Ship of State'.

95   Lynch, 'Queen Mary's Triumph', p. 12.

96   Hume Brown, *Early Travellers*, p. 236. See Fergusson, 'Ship of State', p. 95.

97   Stevenson, *Origins of Freemasonry*, p. 94.

98   Meikle, *Works of William Fowler*, p. 189.

99   RCAMS, *Inventory … Edinburgh*, op. cit., pp. 7 and 13; Gifford, McWilliam and Walker, *Edinburgh*, p. 91.

100   MacIvor, *Edinburgh Castle*, p. 71.

101   RCAMS, *Inventory … Edinburgh*, op. cit., p. 91; MacIvor, *Edinburgh Castle*, pp. 67–9.

102   Chambers, *Domestic Annals*, vol. I, p. 255.

103   Hume Brown, *Early Travellers*, p. 94.

104   Williams, *Anne of Denmark*, pp. 52 ff.

105   Paton, *Accounts*, p. 311.

106   Imrie and Dunbar, *Accounts*, p. xxi; Donaldson, *Scotland: James V–James VII*, p. 301.

107   Harris (with Savage), *British Architectural Books*, pp. 229–31; Parry, *The Golden Age*, ch. 1.

108   Strong, *Henry Prince of Wales*.

109   Parry, *The Golden Age*, p. 76. It is intriguing to notice that crowns of stars and columns rising to the clouds are symbols traditionally associated with the Immaculate Virgin, just as Queen Elizabeth had adopted the role of the Virgin Queen. Strong (*Art and Power*, p. 19) has suggested that Renaissance court display took the place of religious festivals in Protestant countries after the Reformation.

110   Imrie and Dunbar, *Accounts*, p. xxxviii.

111   Ibid., p. xxi.

112   Ibid., pp. li–liii, lviii–lix.

113   Research in progress. I am grateful to Aonghus MacKechnie for allowing me to read drafts of his work.

114   Imrie and Dunbar, *Accounts*, p. lix.

115   Ibid., p. xxvii.

116   Ibid., p. xli.

117   Mylne, *Master Masons*, p. 71.

118   MacIvor, *Edinburgh Castle*, pp. 72–4.

119   RCAMS, *Edinburgh*, e.g. figure 57 (Sandby, 1750); figure 63 (1689–1707); figure 67 (Rothiemay, 1647); and figure 71 (Elphinstone, c.1746).

120   MacIvor, *Edinburgh Castle*, p. 74.

121   Chambers, *Domestic Annals*, vol. I, p. 473; Imrie and Dunbar, *Accounts*, pp. lxxxvi–lxxxvii.

122   Chambers, *Domestic Annals*, vol. I, p. 478.

123   Mylne, *Master Masons*, p. 148; Dunbar, 'The Palace of Holyrood', p. vi.

124   Dunbar, 'Some Aspects of Planning', p. 18.

125   Imrie and Dunbar, *Accounts* p. xcvii; Hendrie, *Linlithgow*, p. 67.

126   Ibid., p. 67.

127   Ibid., pp. 66–7.

128   Imrie and Dunbar, *Accounts*, pp. xl, xcvii–c.

129   Apted, *Painted Ceilings*, p. 10.

130   Hume Brown, *Early Travellers*, p. 85.

131   See the discussions of oriel windows in the two following chapters of this book.

132   Apted, *Painted Ceilings*, *p. 10*.

133   *Imrie and Dunbar, Accounts*, pp. xxiv–xxv, xxxviii.

134   MacKechnie, research in progress.

135   Adam, *Vitruvius Scoticus*, Plate 3.

136   Imrie and Dunbar, *Accounts*, pp. lxxxviii–lxxxix.

137   Ibid., p. xcii.

138   Ibid., p. ci.

139   National Trust for Scotland, *Falkland Palace*, pp. 28–9.

140   RCAMS *Inventory … Edinburgh*, op. cit., pp. 151–2.

141   Hendrie, *Linlithgow*, p. 61.

142   RCAMS *Inventory … Edinburgh*, op. cit., pp. 152–3.

143   Somerville, 'Ancient Sundials'.

144   Imrie and Dunbar, *Accounts*, pp. xxxii–li.

145   Hume Brown, *Early Travellers*, p. 94.

146   Ibid., p. 236.

NOTES TO CHAPTER THREE

1   Hume Brown, *Scotland before 1700*, p. 143.

2   Descriptions of almost all the houses mentioned in this chapter can be found in MacGibbon and Ross, *Castellated and Domestic Architecture*. Most of the country houses of this period are in vol. II of 1897. A briefer outline is to be found in Cruden's *The Scottish Castle*. In the research for this chapter I have made extensive use of guidebooks, some published for Historic Scotland by HMSO, others produced by the National Trust and by private owners. For reasons of space these have not been listed individually in the footnotes.

3   Hume Brown, *Scotland before 1700*, p. 136.

4   Lynch, *Scotland*, p. 177.

5   Sanderson, *Scottish Rural Society*.

6   Lynch, *Scotland*, p. 248.

7   Donaldson, *Scotland: James V–James VII*, pp. 217–21; Sanderson, *Scottish Rural Society*, pp. 1988–90.

8   Lee, *Government by the Pen*.

9   Sanderson, *Mary Stewart's People*, p. 177.

10   Sanderson, *Scottish Rural Society* p. 77.

11   Smout, *Scottish Trade*, p. 78; Wormald, *Court, Kirk and Community*, p. 165.

12   Lynch, *Scotland*, p. 253.

13   Sanderson, *Scottish Rural Society*, pp. 147–9.

14   Lynch, *Scotland*, p. 249.

15   Hume Brown, *Scotland before 1700*, p. 299.

16   Marshall, *Virgins and Viragoes*, p. 139.

17   Ibid., pp. 127–30, and 137–8.

18   Sanderson, *Mary Stewart's People*, p. 45.

19   This point is made in Fawcett, *Architectural History of Scotland*, p. 237.

20   On the ideological background to this self-conscious medievalism in England, see, for instance, Aston, 'English Ruins', pp. 231 ff.; Cox, 'The Politics of Stuart Medievalism'. A general discussion of self-conscious or nostalgic attitudes to past epochs can be found in Lowenthal, *The Past*.

21   See Brown, *Bloodfeud in Scotland*.

22   Cruden, *The Scottish Castle*, p. 224.

23   Translation from McWilliam, *Lothian*, p. 338.

24   Mathews, *Scotland under Charles I*, p. 119, note 4.

25   Hume Brown, *Early Travellers*, p. 148.

26   Ibid., pp. 274–5.

27   Ibid., p. 259.

28   Dalyell and Beveridge, 'Inventory'. This extract is on p. 368.

29   Hume Brown, *Early Travellers*, pp. 259–60.

30   Ibid., p. 275.

31   Gordon Slade, 'Glamis Castle'.

32   Defoe, *A Tour through Great Britain*, p. 353. The plate from Slezer illustrated on p. 353, though labelled 'Glamms House', is not in fact Glamis, but probably represents Dalkeith Palace. See Cavers, *A Vision of Scotland*, pp. 85–6.

33   Fawcett, *Architectural History of Scotland*, p. 263.

34   Aonghus MacKechnie has observed that this motif is derived from Michelangelo's Porta Pia in Rome, in his article 'Aspects of Scots Renaissance Architecture'.

35   By James, 11th Lord Somerville (1679), quoted in Mylne, *Master Masons*, pp. 65–6.

36   MacGibbon and Ross, *Castellated and Domestic Architecture*, vol. II: 'Fourth Period 1542–1700'.

37   Summerson, *Architecture in Britain*, p. 525.

38   Serlio, *Tutte l'opere*, book III, pp. 121–3. Book III was first published in Venice in 1540.

39   See Hitchcock, *German Renaissance Architecture*, especially chap. 3–5.

40   MacGibbon and Ross, *Castellated and Domestic Architecture*, vol. II, pp. 333–6.

41   Maitland, *House of Seytoun*, p. 61.

42   Wilkinson–Zerner, *Zuan de Herrera*, p. 71.

43   Midhope, Muchalls and Barra represent each of these three types respectively.

44   See Davis, *Castles and Mansions*, pp. 14, 363–4.

45   See Girouard, *Robert Smythson*, pp. 144–57.

46   Gordon Slade, 'Glamis Castle'.

47   Davis, *Castles and Mansions*, pp. 151–2.

48   Others noted by Charles McKean are Auchterhouse, near Dundee, and Acheson House in Edinburgh (personal communication, 19 Oct. 1993).

49   Palladio, *I quattro libri*, book I, p. 60.

50   Anon., *Braemar Castle*, p. 1.

51   Billings, 'Certain Features', pp. 35–6.

52   Gordon Slade, 'Glamis Castle'.

53   MacGibbon and Ross, *Castellated and Domestic Architecture*, vol. II, pp. 350–5.

54   See McKean, 'The House of Pitsligo' especially pp. 376–7. McKean believes, however, that this staircase rose through a full four storeys (personal communication, 19 Oct. 1993).

55   Fawcett, *Architectural History of Scotland*, points out that straight stairs had long been preferred in the Highlands and Islands (p. 243).

56   McKean, 'The House of Pitsligo', p. 387.

57   Hume Brown, *Early Travellers*, p. 88.

58 Wormald, *Court, Kirk and Community*, p. 170. A rich source of information on
    the Glenorchy household is the chronicle known as *The Black Book of Taymouth*.

59 Chambers, *Domestic Annals*, vol. I, p. 314.

60 Hume Brown, *Early Travellers*, p. 128.

61 See Louw, 'The Origin of the Sash Window'; and id., 'Window-Glass
    Making'.

62 Fleming, *Scottish and Jacobite Glass*, pp. 79–81.

63 Serlio, *Tutte l'opere*, book IV, p. 157; book IV was first published in Venice in
    1537.

64 See Waddy, *Seventeenth-Century Roman Palaces*, pp. 3–13.

65 Simpson, *Huntly Castle*, pp. 7–9 and 28.

66 McKean, 'The House of Pitsligo', p. 378.

67 Kerr, 'Scottish Domestic Architecture', p. 89, asserts that the bartizans at
    Crathes are to serve as 'wardrobes for ladies' dresses'.

68 McKean, 'The House of Pitsligo', p. 390, note 22.

69 See Coope, 'The "Long Gallery"'.

70 The painted ceilings of this period will be discussed below.

71 RCAMS *Inventory … Fife, Kinross and Clackmannan*, Edinburgh, 1933, pp. 193–
    7.

72 See Apted, *Painted Ceilings*; Nic Allen, 'Artful Craft', in Mackay, *Scottish
    Interiors*, pp. 17–19.

73 Sinclair (ed.), *Statistical Account*, vol. XV, p. 205.

74 Sanderson, *Mary Stewart's People*, pp. 173–4.

75 Ibid., pp. 166 ff.

76 See Bath, 'Painted Ceilings'.

77 For documentary and bibliographical references, see Apted and Hannabuss,
    Painters in Scotland.

78 Marshall, The Days of Duchess Anne, pp. 39 and 58.

79 David Learmont, 'Exciting Find'.

80 See Barker, 'Scottish Plasterwork' pp. 80 ff.; Touche, *Worthies and the Regalia*.

81 See Galloway, *Union of England and Scotland*, pp. 33–4; Lynch, *Scotland* p.
    238.

82 Jourdain, *English Decorative Plasterwork*, p. 238.

83 Ibid., p. xiii.

84 Beard, *Decorative Plasterwork*, p. 81.

85 Savage, *Lorimer*, pp. 8–13.

86 John Gifford, 'Towie Barclay', in Mackay, *Scottish Interiors*, pp. 20–9.

87 MacKenzie, *A Scottish Renaissance Household*, p. 29.

88 McWilliam, *Lothian*, p. 54.

89 Marshall, 'The Plenishings', pp. 14, 16–17.

90 Robertson, *Inventaires*, p. 51.

91 Lowrey, 'Dutch Influence'.

92 Gordon Slade, 'Craigston Castle, Aberdeenshire', pp. 274–5.

93 Victor Chinnery, 'Chairs of the Trades', in Mackay, *Scottish Interiors*, pp. 69–
    71.

94 e.g. Marshall, 'The Plenishings', p. 16.

95 Hume Brown, *Early Travellers*, p. 89.

96 Marshall, 'The Plenishings', pp. 15, 17–18.

97 MacKenzie, *A Scottish Renaissance Household*, p. 18.
98 'Inventory of movables of the late Earl of Huntly 1562', in Robertson, *Inventaires*, pp. 49–51.
99 Marshall, 'The Plenishings', p. 15.
100 Margaret Swain, 'Embroidered Bed', in Mackay, *Scottish Interiors*, pp. 12–15.
101 John Maclean, 'Turkish Trove', in Mackay, *Scottish Interiors*, pp. 72–6.
102 NACF *Saved for Scotland*, p. 102, cat. no. 152.
103 Dalyell and Beveridge, 'Inventory', p. 358.
104 Hume Brown, *Early Travellers*, pp. 127–8.
105 NACF, *Saved for Scotland*, p. 82, cat. no. 108.
106 Marshall, 'The Plenishings', p. 17.
107 Dalyell and Beveridge, 'Inventory', p. 352 and *passim*.
108 Sanderson, *Scottish Rural Society*, p. 175.
109 MacKenzie, *A Scottish Renaissance Household*, p. 17.
110 Sanderson, *Scottish Rural Society*, p. 173.
111 Dalyell and Beveridge, 'Inventory', pp. 344–370.
112 Hume Brown, *Early Travellers*, pp. 135, 143, 231, 255. This process can be seen in action in Slezer's view of Dundee from the east.
113 Dean and Miers, *Scotland's Endangered Houses*, p. 133.
114 Sanderson, *Mary Stewart's People*, p. 45.
115 Hume Brown, *Early Travellers*, pp. 121–2.
116 Lowther, *Our Journall*, p.34.
117 On the concept of the 'banquet' – a dessert course based largely on imported delicacies – in the period, see Wilson, '*Banquetting Stuffe*'.
118 Hume Brown, *Early Travellers*, p. 231.
119 Ibid., p. 275.
120 Pennant, *First Tour*, p. 117.
121 Smout, *A History of the Scottish People*, p. 121.
122 RCAHMS, *North-East Perth: An Archaeological Landscape*, Edinburgh, 1990.
123 Ibid., pp. 9, 138.
124 Ibid., pp. 140–1.
125 Hume Brown, *Early Travellers*, p. 222.
126 Triggs, *Formal Gardens*, p. 49 and plate 85.
127 Geddes, *A Swing through Time*, p. 1.
128 Smout, 'Scottish–Dutch Contact', p. 31.
129 Geddes, *A Swing through Time*, pp. 10–11; Hendrie, *Linlithgow*, p. 56.
130 Geddes, *A Swing through Time*, p. 1.
131 Mair, *Mercat Cross*, p. 203.
132 Mathew, *Scotland under Charles I*, p. 178.
133 Hendrie, *Linlithgow*, p. 29.
134 Marshall, *Virgins and Viragoes*, p. 134.
135 See Triggs, *Formal Gardens*; Gillian Haggart, 'The Renaissance Garden', in Howard, *The Architecture of the Scottish Renaissance*, p. 23; and Howard, 'Chasse, sport et plaisir'.
136 Dr Rosalind Marshall informs me, however, that the 3rd Duke of Hamilton had a warrender in the 1690s (personal communication, 29 Nov. 1993).
137 See Triggs, *Formal Gardens*, p. 50.
138 Simpson, *Edzell Castel*, p. 12.

139 Ibid., p. 13.

140 Ibid., p. 30.

141 Grose, *Antiquities of Scotland*, vol. II, pp. 244–5.

142 On bathing in the Renaissance period, see Thornton, *Italian Renaissance Interior*, pp. 315–19.

143 Charles McKean has reminded me that several fountains can be seen in views by Slezer, including, for instance, Hatton House (personal communication, 19 Oct. 1993).

144 Sinclair(ed.), *Statistical Account*, vol. XV, pp. 204–5.

145 Reid, The *Scots Gard'ner*, pp. 26–31.

146 Serlio, *Tutte l'opere*, book IV, pp. 197 verso–199. Book IV was first published in Venice in 1537.

147 Reid, *The Scots Gard'ner*, p. 29.

148 Ibid., p. 22.

149 Ibid., pp. 69–70.

150 Annette Hope, introduction to facsimile edition of Reid's *The Scots Gard'ner*, pp. xv–xvi.

151 'Scottish Sundials' in MacGibbon and Ross, *Castellated and Domestic Architecture*, vol. V, pp. 357–514. See also Ross, 'The Ancient Sundials of Scotland'.

152 Somerville, 'Ancient Sundials'.

153 Hume Brown, *Early Travellers*, p. 206. An anonymous poet echoed the sentiment with the lines:

> Neptune doth kiss the foot of this great Fort;
> tolus environs it in powerful sort:
> Mars bellow(s) round upon its Walls in Thunder,
> It's marvellous above, more in the Cells that's under.
> (MacFarlane's *Geographical Collections*, vol. III, p. 232)

154 On the Wrychtishouses, see, for example, Grose, *Antiquities of Scotland*, vol. I, p. 39; Smith, *Historic South Edinburgh*, vol. I, pp. 67–9. Fragments of pediments from the Wrychtishouses, datable to the 1630s and 1640s, are now in the gardens at Woodhouselea (personal communication from Aonghus MacKechnie, 17 July 1991).

155 The view by Slezer labelled 'Glammis House' has been identified as a view of Dalkeith Palace (Cavers, *A Vision of Scotland*, p. 85).

156 *House of Seytoun*, p. 63. On Seton, see also Seton, *A History of the Family of Seton*, vol. II, pp. 634–58 (reference kindly supplied by Michael Bath); and Maurice J. Lee Jr., 'King James's Popish Chancellor', in Cowan and Shaw, *Renaissance and Reformation*, pp. 183–99.

157 Pennant, *First Tour*, p. 61.

NOTES TO CHAPTER FOUR

1 The first of these maps was commissioned by the burgh of Edinburgh (*Extracts ... Edinburgh 1641 to 1655*, p. 116). See Smout, *A History of the Scottish People*, p. 173; and Walter Makey, 'Edinburgh in Mid-Seventeenth Century', in Lynch, *The Early Modern Town*, pp. 192–218, especially pp. 198–201.

2   For a recent discussion of Ciceronian civic humanism in Reformation Scotland, see David Allan, *Virtue, Learning and the Scottish Enlightenment*, pp. 29–78.

3   Mackay Mackenzie, *The Scottish Burghs*; Houston, 'The Scottish Burgh'; McWilliam, *Scottish Townscape*; Adams, *The Making of Urban Scotland*; Dicks, 'The Scottish Medieval Town'; Fox, 'Urban Development'; Mair, *Mercat Crosses*; Naismith, *The Story of Scotland's Towns*.

4   See McKean, *Edinburgh: Portrait of a City*.

5   McKean and Walker, *Dundee*, p. 7.

6   Frank Arneil Walker, 'Origins and First Growths', in Reed, *Glasgow*, pp. 9–23.

7   Pennant, *First Tour*, p. 50.

8   Hume Brown, *Early Travellers*, pp. 83, 110, 139; Defoe, *A Tour through Great Britain*, p. 311.

9   Hume Brown, *Early Travellers*, p. 214.

10   The importance of skylines in towns has recently been explored by Kostoff, *The City Shaped*, pp. 279 ff.

11   See, for example, McMillan, *Building Stones*; The Falkland Society, *The Stones of Falkland*.

12   Hume Brown, *Early Travellers*, p. 190.

13   For a recent account of the building materials in different regions of Scotland, see Naismyth, *Buildings of the Scottish Countryside*.

14   Pantiles were certainly imported from Holland in the 17th century for roofing mills and salt-pans, but it is uncertain how extensively they were used domestically before 1700. See Howard, 'Dutch Influence', p. 37.

15   Gifford, McWilliam and Walker, *Edinburgh*, p. 81.

16   McKean, *Edinburgh: An Illustrated Architectural Guide*, p. 3. Many of these houses were demolished for fuel during the siege of 1572 (Lythe, *Economy of Scotland*, p. 119).

17   MacKenzie, *The Scottish Burghs*, p. 42.

18   See R. M. Spearman, 'The Medieval Townscape of Perth', in Lynch, Spearman and Stell, *The Scottish Medieval Town*, pp. 42–59.

19   Hume Brown, *Early Travellers*, p. 171.

20   Cullen, *The Walls of Edinburgh*.

21   McKean, *Stirling and the Trossachs*, p. 23; Mair, *Stirling*, p. 60.

22   Harris, 'The Fortifications and Siege of Leith'.

23   J. R. Hale, 'The End of Florentine Liberty: The Fortezza da Basso', in Hale, *Renaissance War Studies*, pp. 31–62. I am grateful to Caroline Elam for her help over the identity of Piero Strozzi.

24   *Extracts … Edinburgh 1557–1571*, pp. 69–70, 74, 97; Donaldson, *Scotland: James V–James VII*, p. 100; McKean, *Edinburgh: Portrait of a City*, p. 44.

25   Hume Brown, *Early Travellers*, p. 163.

26   RCAHMS, *An Inventory of Monuments in Fife*, Edinburgh, 1933, p. 259; Gifford, *Fife*, p. 389.

27   Gifford, McWilliam and Walker, *Edinburgh*, p. 66. See also Mylne, 'The Netherbow Port'.

28   *Extracts … Edinburgh 1604–1626*, pp. 18, 24, 26, 28–9, 39, 41–2, 56, 71, 73, 100.

29   Mair, *Stirling*, pp. 61, 99–100.

30   Hume Brown, *Early Travellers*, p. 191.

31   Gifford, *Fife* pp. 357–9, 389.

32   Macmillan, *Scottish Art*, p. 48.

33   *Extracts ... Edinburgh 1604–1626*, pp. 28, 131, 147. Lambert died while executing the work, which was completed by John Mylne (Ibid., pp. 369–71). The statue was solemnly removed in 1652 (see Drummond, 'Notice', pp. 110–11).

34   Mylne, *Master Masons*, pp. 105–6.

35   Macmillan, *Scottish Art*, pp. 62–3. On the sources for this fictive genealogy, see Mason, 'Scotching the Brut'.

36   For an illuminating study of this phenomenon in England, see Aston, 'English Ruins'.

37   Lynch, *The Early Modern Town*, p. 68.

38   Hume Brown, *Edinburgh before 1700*, p. 313.

39   See Williamson, *Scottish National Consciousness*.

40   Lynch, *The Early Modern Town*, p. 20.

41   Sinclair (ed.), *Statistical Account*, vol. XIV, pp. 279–82.

42   McWilliam, *Scottish Townscape*, pp. 35–6; Adams, *Making of Urban Scotland*, p. 45; R. G. Rodger, 'The Evolution of Scottish Town Planning', in Gordon and Dicks, *Scottish Urban History*, pp. 71–91.

43   MacKenzie, *The Scottish Burghs*, pp. 96–137; Lynch, *The Early Modern Town*, pp. 9–13.

44   Mary Verschuur, 'Merchants and Craftsmen in Sixteenth-Century Perth', in Lynch, *The Early Modern Town*, pp. 55–80; Lynch in ibid., p. 11.

45   Smout, *Scottish Trade*, p. 142.

46   Lythe, *Economy of Scotland*, p. 117.

47   Adams, *Making of Urban Scotland*, p. 57.

48   Mair, *Mercat Cross*, pp. 218–19.

49   Adams, *Making of Urban Scotland*, p. 51.

50   Ibid., pp. 55–6.

51   Smout, *Scottish Trade*, p. 5; Walter Makey, 'Edinburgh in Mid-Seventeenth Century', in Lynch, *The Early Modern Town*, pp. 192–218, especially pp. 205–6.

52   Lythe, *Economy of Scotland*, p. 117.

53   Smout, *Scottish Trade*, pp. 144–5.

54   Hume Brown, *Early Travellers*, p. 167.

55   Adams, *Making of Urban Scotland*, p. 51.

56   Smout, *Scottish Trade*, p. 138.

57   Stell, 'The Earliest Tolbooths'. On the architecture of town halls south of the border in the same period, see Tittler, *Architecture and Power*.

58   Sinclair (ed.), *Statistical Account*, vol. XV, p. 176.

59   Stell, 'The Earliest Tolbooths', p.453.

60   Sinclair (ed.), *Statistical Account of Scotland*, vol. XV, p. 420.

61   See the comments of Marguerite Wood, introduction to *Extracts ... Edinburgh 1604–1626*, p. xxxiii.

62   Stell, 'The Earliest Tolbooths', pp. 446–8.

63   Miller, 'The Origin of the Old Tolbuith', especially p. 363.

64   *Extracts ... Edinburgh 1557–1571*, p. 66.

65 Ibid., p. 131. The Master of Works was David Somers. On 11 April 1562, the Lords of Session were threatening to meet in St Andrews 'in defalt of ane hous heir' (Ibid., p. 133).

66 Ibid., p. 140. A loan was raised on 21 June 1563 on the security of the common mills for the completion of the tolbooth (Ibid., p. 163). The eventual aim seems to have been to rebuild a tolbooth outside St Giles, the burgh even acquiring additional land in 1562 'qhair the new tolbuth is bigand' (Ibid., p. 154). However, the burgh records indicate that the project did not proceed further, despite the assertion to the contrary by Miller, 'The Origin of the Old Tolbuith'. In 1575, the end gable of the old belhous, still awaiting its new extension, was rebuilt and made safe (*Extracts ... Edinburgh 1573–1589*, p. 38).

67 *Extracts ... Edinburgh 1557–1571*, pp. 169, 170, 172, 174–5.

68 Ibid., pp. 180–1.

69 Stell, 'The Earliest Tolbooths; p. 446.

70 *Extracts ... Edinburgh 1557–1571*, pp. 207–8. The transfer was delayed for two years (Ibid., p. 213, 224). Edinburgh finally took over the superiority of Leith on 2 July 1567 (Ibid., p. 233).

71 Repairs to the tolbooth and 'belhous' in 1605 confirm that a bell tower existed in Leith (*Extracts ... Edinburgh 1604 to 1626*, p. 11).

72 McWilliam, *Lothian except Edinburgh*, p. 335.

73 RCAMS, *Inventory ... Edinburgh*, Edinburgh, 1951, pp. 173–4. Bellenden was presumably a descendant of the Abbot of Holyrood who died in 1503 (Ibid., p. 136). The inventory gives an incorrect date for the restoration, which was in 1875, not 1879 (information kindly supplied by Neil Cameron).

74 See Howard, 'Dutch Influence'.

75 RCAMS, *Inventory ... Edinburgh*, op. cit., p. 174.

76 This has been exchanged with the town bell of 1618, now in the Kirk (Crail Preservation Society, *Historic Crail*, p.8).

77 The base of the tower seems to be 16th-century, although the top is 18th-century and the wing was rebuilt in 1814, probably replacing a wing of about 1607. See Gifford, *Fife*, p. 137.

78 Culross tolbooth is dated 1626 on a lintel, but the central tower was added in 1783. See Gifford, *Fife*, p. 152.

79 MacGibbon and Ross, *Castellated and Domestic Architecture*, vol. V, pp. 116–17.

80 Ibid., pp. 98–9.

81 MacFarlane's *Geographical Collections*, vol. III, p. 219; Gifford, *Fife*, p. 348.

82 *Extracts ... Edinburgh 1557–1571*, pp. 210–11.

83 *Extracts ... Edinburgh 1589–1603*, p. 197, (see also pp. 153, 159).

84 Ibid., p. 209.

85 Ibid., pp. 209, 264.

86 *Extract Edinburgh 1604–1626*, pp. 52, 55, 61. The fact that in 1610 Symsoun was commissioned to build another identical 'wairdhous', to be built 'under the samyn', suggests that on this occasion work was actually carried out (Ibid., p. 67).

87 *Extracts ... Edinburgh 1626–1641*, p. 109.

88 It is described as such by David Buchanan, writing in 1647–52 (Hume Brown, *Edinburgh before 1700*, p. 316).

89   See, for example, the view in Grant's *Old and New Edinburgh*, vol. 1, p. 133. Nasmyth designed the sets for the staged version of *The Heart of Midlothian* (see Campbell, *Drawings and Watercolours* p. 6). Walter Scott himself acquired a doorway from the demolished tolbooth, intended for making a back door to the wash-house at Abbotsford, although in the end it was placed at the west end of the house (Ibid., p. 12).

90   This is confirmed by the pedestrian drawing by the Reverend John Syme (published in Miller, 'The Origin of the Old Tolbuith'), and by the sketch published by MacGibbon and Ross, which was apparently made during the demolition in 1817 (MacGibbon and Ross, *Castellated and Domestic Architecture*, vol. V, p. 107). The watercolour by Henry Duguid also agrees with Sime's record of a symmetrical building (Campbell, *Drawings and Watercolours*, p. 31).

91   *Extracts ... Edinburgh 1626–1641*, p. 119. At this stage it was intended to erect the council chamber and exchequer on the site of some of the Luckenbooths 'above the new tolbuith'. These shops were hastily demolished and the site cleared in preparation for the visit of Charles I. There is no evidence over how this matter was concluded.

92   See note 31.

93   Instead, the burgh council approved a design by John Smith in 1668 (Colvin, *Biographical Dictionary*, pp. 570 and 759).

94   Mylne, *Master Masons* pp. 240–2. This evidence has, however, been interpreted differently by Colvin, who believes the 'old-fashioned' alternative to represent Mylne's own design (*Biographical Dictionary*, p. 570).

95   Howard, 'Dutch Influence', pp. 37, 40.

96   Thanks are due to Neil Cameron for suggesting these parallels to me.

97   *Extracts Glasgow 1573–1642*, p. 349.

98   Ibid., p. 352.

99   Ibid., p. 361.

100   Ibid., pp. 479, 366, 374.

101   Gomme and Walker, *Architecture of Glasgow*, pp. 43–4; Colvin, *Biographical Dictionary*, p. 381.

102   See MacKechnie, 'Evidence of a post-1603 Court Architecture in Scotland?' pp. 107–19.

103   Hume Brown, *Early Travellers*, p. 191.

104   Defoe, *A Tour through Great Britain*, pp. 331, 314.

105   On burgh trading privileges, see MacKenzie, *The Scottish Burghs*, pp. 62 ff.

106   See especially Mair, *Mercat Cross*, pp. 50–7.

107   See Drummond, 'Notice'.

108   The ceremonial of royal entries into Edinburgh is examined in McKean, *Edinburgh: Portrait of a City*, pp. 45 ff.

109   Miller, 'The Mercat Cross', especially p. 387. Bacchanalian scenes were enacted for the entry of Queen Anne of Denmark in 1590 (ibid.), and again for the coronation of Charles II in 1661 (Drummond, 'Notice', p. 111).

110   Drummond, 'Notice', p. 109.

111   Ibid., p. 111.

112   Ibid., p. 110.

113   Hume Brown, *Early Travellers*, p. 142.

114 *Extracts … Edinburgh, 1604–1626*, p. 152; Miller, 'The Origin of the Old Tolbuith', pp. 381–4.

115 *Extracts … Edinburgh 1626–1641*, pp. 82, 83.

116 Pennant, *First Tour*, p. 243.

117 *Extracts … Edinburgh 1626–1641*, pp. 103, 104, 109–10, 147–8, 163, 176, 187–90, 197–8, 203, 211, 215.

118 Hume Brown, *Edinburgh before 1700*, p. 315.

119 RCAMS, *Inventory … Edinburgh*, op. cit., pp. 90–2.

120 MacKechnie, 'Inventory', unpublished paper.

121 RCAMS, *Inventory … Edinburgh*, op. cit., p. 92. As well as the Fife timbers mentioned here, wood was purchased from a merchant in Denmark in 1636 (*Extracts … Edinburgh 1626–1641*, p. 184).

122 See Ross, 'Old Parliament Hall, Edinburgh'.

123 Illustrated in Girouard, *Robert Smythson*, p. 283.

124 For a brief account of Scottish education in the period, see, for example, Donaldson, *Scotland: James V–James VII*. pp. 262–70.

125 Wormald, *Court, Kirk and Community*, p. 181. According to Charles McKean, a large tower and lodgings were built for Fraserburgh University (personal communication, 26 Oct. 1993).

126 Brogden, *Aberdeen*, p. 87.

127 Hume Brown, *Early Travellers*, p. 66. The crown spire was rebuilt after a gale in 1633 (Brogden, *Aberdeen*, p. 86).

128 *Extracts … Edinburgh 1604–1626*, p. 99.

129 Gifford, *Fife*, pp. 373–4.

130 *Extracts … Edinburgh 1589 to 1603*, p. 281; *Extracts … Edinburgh 1604–1626*, introduction by Marguerite Wood, p. xxx.

131 Ibid., pp. 185, 164, 173; Fraser, *The Building of Old College*, pp. 27–37.

132 David Buchanan 'A Description of Edinburgh', in Hume Brown, *Edinburgh before 1700*, p. 316.

133 Fraser (*The Building of Old College*, p. 37) shows that Rothiemay's view showing three regular courtyards in his map of Edinburgh of 1647 is far from accurate.

134 *Extracts … Glasgow 1604–1626*, p. 375.

135 Gomme and Walker, *Architecture of Glasgow*, pp. 45–7, where the building is described as 'the most distinguished collection of seventeenth-century architecture in Scotland'.

136 Hume Brown, *Early Travellers*, pp. 152–3.

137 *Extracts … Glasgow 1630–1662*, pp. 316, 329, 454.

138 Hume Brown, *Early Travellers*, p. 237.

139 See Durkan, 'Education in the Century of the Reformation'.

140 *Extracts … Edinburgh 1642–1655*, pp. 74 f.

141 Ibid., p. 109.

142 Ibid., pp. 59–60, 104.

143 Ibid., p. 346.

144 *Extracts … Glasgow 1573–1642*, pp. 64, 465.

145 Ibid., pp. 210, 216–17.

146 *Extracts Glasgow 1630–1662*, pp. 329, 331, 339, 340.

147 See Scarisbrick, 'Anne of Denmark's Jewellery Inventory'.

148 The principal sources on the history of the Hospital are Anon., *Historical and*

Descriptive Account; Steven, *History of George Heriot's Hospital*; Gunn, *George Heriot's Hospital*.

149 Rowan, 'George Heriot's Hospital'.

150 Heriot's Hospital Archives, Records, p. 151 fo. 77).

151 Ibid., p. 228 (fo. 115 verso).

152 I have discussed this issue in my article 'Scottish Master Masons'.

153 Serlio, *Tutte l'opere*, book VII, pp. 78–9.

154 Rowan, 'George Heriot's Hospital', p. 556.

155 This allusion did not escape the French visitor Jorevin de Rochefors in 1661 (Hume Brown, *Early Travellers*, p. 222).

156 MacKechnie, 'Evidence of a post-1603 Court Architecture'.

157 See Girouard, *Robert Smythson*, pp. 210 ff.

158 Ibid., pp. 234 ff.

159 Pennant, *First Tour*, p. 56.

160 See Stell, 'Urban Buildings', especially pp. 62–3.

161 Donaldson, *Scotland: James V–James VII*, p. 258.

162 Lythe, *Economy of Scotland*, p. 133.

163 Ibid., pp. 47, 88.

164 *Extracts Edinburgh 1604–1626*, p. 90.

165 Mathew, *Scotland under Charles I*, pp. 95–6.

166 RCAMS, *An Inventory of Monuments: Fife, Kinross and Clackmannan*, Edinburgh, 1933, p. 27.

167 Sanderson, *Mary Stewart's People*, p. 45.

168 Grant, *Old and New Edinburgh*, vol. 1, pp. 267–9.

169 Chambers, *Ancient Domestic Architecture*, p. 2.

170 Hume Brown, *Early Travellers*, p. 141.

171 Defoe, *A Tour through Great Britain*, p. 358.

171 Gifford, *Fife*, p. 313 and plate 57.

173 Anderson, 'The Shetland Germans'.

174 MacFarlane's *Geographical Collections*, vol. II, pp. 60–5.

175 Ibid., p. 252.

176 Grant, *Old and New Edinburgh*, pp. 264–5.

177 McKean, Walker and Walker, *Central Glasgow*, p. 38; Gomme and Walker, *Architecture of Glasgow*, pp. 44–5.

178 Clear and comprehensive surveys are to be found in Stell, 'Urban Buildings', pp. 69–75; and in Stell, 'Scottish Burgh Houses'.

179 Stell, 'Scottish Burgh Houses', p. 15.

180 See Stell, 'Urban Buildings', p. 73.

181 The dormers have been completely rebuilt in a modern restoration, and their original form is uncertain. See the photographic archives in the National Monuments Record of Scotland, RCAHMS, Edinburgh.

182 Gifford, McWilliam and Walker, *Edinburgh*, p. 81.

183 See, for example, Antonia Fraser, *Mary Queen of Scots*, pp. 174 ff.; John Durkan, 'The French Connection in the Sixteenth and Early Seventeenth Centuries', in Smout, *Scotland and Europe*, pp. 19–44.

184 'Argyll's Lodging, Stirling', paper for blind readers by Charles McKean.

185 MacGibbon and Ross, *Castellated and Domestic Architecture*, vol. IV, pp. 449–51.

186   Ibid., vol. V, pp. 93–7; Burger, *Orkney*, p. 13.

187   MacGibbon and Ross, *Castellated and Domestic Architecture*, vol. IV, pp. 501–3.

188   Grant, *Old and New Edinburgh*, vol. I, pp. 257, 264.

189   MacGibbon and Ross, *Castellated and Domestic Architecture*, vol. II, p. 530.

190   RCAHMS, *An Inventory of Monuments in Fife*, Edinburgh, 1933, p. 257.

191   See Smout, 'Scottish – Dutch Contact'; and Howard, 'Dutch Influence'.

192   RCAMS, *Inventory ... Edinburgh*, op. cit., pp. 86–7; Gifford, McWilliam and Walker, *Edinburgh*, pp. 201–2.

193   Chambers, *Ancient Domestic Architecture*, pp. 15–17; Chambers, *Edinburgh Merchants*, pp. 15–17; Grant, *Old and New Edinburgh*, vol. I, p. 120.

194   Donaldson, *Scotland: James V–James VII*, p. 252.

195   Chambers, *Edinburgh Merchants*, pp. 5–6.

196   Lythe, *Economy of Scotland*, pp. 41–2.

197   *Extracts ... Edinburgh 1589 to 1603*, p. 91.

198   Frank Arneil Walker, 'Origins and First Growths', in Reed, *Glasgow*, pp. 21–2.

199   Gifford, McWilliam and Walker, *Edinburgh*, p. 81.

200   Chambers, *Ancient Domestic Architecture*, pp. 2–11.

201   Drummond, *Views of Old Edinburgh*, plate XIII.

202   RCAMS, *Inventory ... Edinburgh*, op. cit., pp. 74–8; Walter Makey, 'Edinburgh in Mid-Seventeenth Century', in Lynch, *The Early Modern Town*, pp. 192–218, especially pp. 202, 204. Old ships timbers were used by Glaidstanes, ingeniously adapting their curved from to the new structure, which contains a remarkable egg-shaped staircase.

203   Samuel Johnson, *A Journey to the Western Isles of Scotland*, ed. Peter Levi, Harmondsworth, 1984, p. 49.

204   MacGibbon and Ross, *Castellated and Domestic Architecture*, vol. V, pp. 68–72.

205   The country seat of the Earls of Glencairn was at Kilmaurs in Ayrshire. The T-plan mansion known as Kilmaurs Place was built about 1620 by William Cunningham, 9th Earl of Glencairn and Lord Chancellor of Scotland, replacing their 'ancient stronge building' which no longer survives. See Davis, *Castles and Mansions*, p. 301.

206   On the role of the nobility in burgh politics, see Michael Lynch, 'The Crown and the Burghs', in id., *The Early Modern Town*, pp. 55–80, especially pp. 55–9.

207   In 1616, Sir Robert Gordon's brother warned him that, in anticipation of the King's visit to Edinburgh, 'all the best ludgeingis are taikin alreaddy'. See Sanderson, *Mary Stewart's People*, p. 48.

208   MacFarlane's *Geographical Collections*, vol. III, p. 219.

209   Stell, 'Scottish Burgh Houses', pp. 17–18.

210   Gowrie House is described in Grose, *Antiquities of Scotland*, vol. II, pp. 244, and in Penny, *Traditions of Perth*, pp. 3–4.

211   McKean, *The District of Moray*, pp. 29–30.

212   McKean, *Stirling and the Trossachs*, pp. 17–19.

213   The slimness of these columns is seen also in the gateways to St Andrews and Edinburgh Castles. See Dunbar, 'French Influence', p. 7; MacKechnie, 'Some French Influences', p. 6.

214 The gargoyles make unconvincing the reconstruction with a pitched roof and dormers suggested by Noad, in 'The Influence of France', p. 110.

215 MacGibbon and Ross, *Castellated and Domestic Architecture*, vol. III, p. 334.

216 von Bülow, 'Journey', p. 245.

217 MacGibbon and Ross, *Castellated and Domestic Architecture*, vol. III, p. 336.

218 The house was bought by Archbishop Patrick Adamson in 1572 (Gifford, *Fife*, p. 395).

219 Simpson, *Bishop's Palace*, p. 9.

220 RCAMS, *Inventory ... Edinburgh*, op. cit., pp. 85–6. However, Gifford, McWilliam and Walker, *Edinburgh*, p. 202, suggest that the house was rebuilt when it passed to Sir William Dick of Braid in about 1630.

221 *Extracts ... Edinburgh 1589 to 1603*, pp. 180, 184.

222 Pride, *The Kingdom of Fife*, p. 153.

223 Smout, *A History of the Scottish People*, pp. 160–70.

224 Historical information displayed in the house.

225 Apted, *Painted Ceilings*, plates 31, 49.

226 *Extracts Edinburgh 1589 to 1603*, pp. 33–4. On McMorran's trading activities, see Chambers, *Edinburgh Merchants*, pp. 5–6.

227 See MacGibbon and Ross, *Castellated and Domestic Architecture*, vol. IV, pp. 439–49; Grant, *Old and New Edinburgh*, vol. I, pp. 110–13; RCAMS, *Inventory ... Edinburgh*, op. cit., pp. 81–3.

228 *Extracts Edinburgh 1589 to 1603*, pp. 218–19.

229 RCAMS, *Inventory ... Edinburgh*, op. cit., p. 257.

230 A window from Bailie McMorran's house with elaborately carved shutters is preserved in Huntly House, while a similar window from the French Ambassador's house in the Cowgate can be seen in the 'Dynasty' display in the Musuem of Antiquities in Queen Street, Edinburgh.

231 On the question of the introduction of pantiles to Scotland, see Howard, 'Dutch Influence' p. 37.

232 MacGibbon and Ross, *Castellated and Domestic Architecture*, vol. IV, pp. 506–7.

233 See Mair, *Stirling*, pp. 103, 107–11.

234 McKean, *Stirling and the Trossachs*, p. 22.

235 See Macmillan, *Scottish Art*, pp. 60–7. Jameson's early life and his property transactions are recounted in detail in Thomson, *The Life and Art of George Jameson*, pp. 15–25 and documents 1–24.

236 Quoted in Ibid., p. 17.

237 Mathew, *Scotland under Charles I*, p. 96.

NOTES TO CHAPTER FIVE

1 Hume Brown, *Early Travellers*, p. 147.

2 Cowan, *The Scottish Reformation*, p. 143.

3 Ibid., p. 140.

4 Ibid., p. 144.

5 See Wormald, *Court, Kirk and Community*, pp. 75 ff.

6 See Denis McKay, 'Parish Life in Scotland 1500–1560', in McRoberts, *Essays*, pp. 85–115.

7 Donaldson, *Scottish Reformation*, pp. 13–16; id., *Scotland: Chruch and Nation*, pp. 36–49.

8   Donaldson, *Scottish Reformation*, p. 85.

9   Ibid., p. 23; Donaldson, *Scotland: Church and Nation*, p. 45.

10   Donaldson, *Scottish Reformation*, p. 36.

11   Ibid., p. 41.

12   Donaldson, *Scotland: Church and Nation*, p. 54.

13   Kirk, *Patterns of Reform*, pp. 1–15.

14   Donaldson, *Scottish Reformation*, pp. 29–30; id., *Scotland: Church and Nation*, p. 50.

15   Donaldson, *Scottish Reformation*, p. 33; id., *Scotland: Church and Nation*, p. 65.

16   Smout, *A History of the Scottish People*, p. 54.

17   See David McRoberts, 'Material Destruction caused by the Scottish Reformation', in McRoberts, *Essays*, pp. 415–62.

18   Donaldson, *Scottish Reformation*, pp. 97–9.

19   Lindesay of Pitscottie, *History and Chronicles*, vol. II, p. 163.

20   Donaldson, *Scotland: Church and Nation*, p. 59.

21   Kirk, *Patterns of Reform*, pp. 154–231.

22   Donaldson, *Scotland: Church and Nation*, p. 76.

23   Ibid., p. 63.

24   Donaldson, *Scottish Reformation*, p. 76.

25   Richardson, Wood and Tabraham, *Melrose Abbey*, p. 40.

26   See Anthony Ross, 'Some Notes on the Religious Orders in Pre-Reformation Scotland', in McRoberts, *Essays*, pp. 184–244.

27   Ibid., pp. 4–8.

28   Donaldson, *Scotland: Church and Nation*, p. 37.

29   See above, Chap. 3, pp. 48–9. Margaret H. B. Sanderson's account of the life of Mark Ker of Newbattle serves well to illustrate this phenomenon (*Mary Stewart's People*, pp. 166–78).

30   Donaldson, *Scottish Reformation*, p. 98.

31   Gifford, McWilliam and Walker, *Edinburgh*, pp. 152–3.

32   Gordon Donaldson, 'The Parish Clergy and the Reformation', in McRoberts, *Essays*, pp. 129–44. See also Craven, *History of the Church in Orkney*.

33   Knox, *First Book of Discipline*.

34   Kirk, *Patterns of Reform*, pp. 368–425.

35   Cowan, *Scottish Reformation*, pp. 142–3.

36   Ibid., pp. 139–58

37   Ibid., pp. 156–7.

38   Ibid., pp. 144–5.

39   Hay, *Post-Reformation Churches*, p. 26.

40   Cowan, *Scottish Reformation*, pp. 148.

41   NACF, *Saved for Scotland*, p. 83, no. 110.

42   Cowan, *Scottish Reformation*, pp. 144–5.

43   Ibid., pp. 146–7.

44   Lindsay, *The Scottish Parish Kirk*, pp. 38–41.

45   Hume Brown, *Early Travellers*, pp. 146–7.

46   Cowan, *Scottish Reformation*, pp. 148.

47   Ibid., pp. 144–5.

48   Hume Brown, *Early Travellers*, pp. 83–4.

49   Donaldson, *Faith of the Scots*, pp. 66–9; Elliott and Rimmer, *A History of Scottish Music*, p. 25.

50   Ibid., pp. 25–32.

51   Pennant, *First Tour*, pp. 52–3.

52   Gifford, *Highlands and Islands*, p. 36.

53   Howard, 'Dutch Influence', pp. 42–3.

54   Defoe, *A Tour through Great Britain*, p. 313.

55   Hume Brown, *Early Travellers*, p. 147.

56   Cowan, *Blast and Counterblast*, p. 31.

57   Lowther, *Our Journall*, p. 13.

58   Pennant, *First Tour*, p. 234.

59   Sanderson, *Mary Stewart's People*, p. 32.

60   Knox, *First Book of Discipline*, p. 202.

61   Ibid., p. 94.

62   RCAHMS, *Inventory of Monuments: Fife, Kinross and Clackmannan*, Edinburgh, 1933, pp. 15–17.

63   Richardson, Wood and Tabraham, *Melrose Abbey*, p. 12.

64   Lynch, *Edinburgh and the Reformation*, p. 13.

65   See above, Chap. 4, p. 117.

66   Donaldson, *Scottish Reformation*, p. 98.

67   Hay, *Post-Reformation Churches*, pp. 26–7.

68   RCAHMS, *Inventory of Monuments: Fife*, Edinburgh, 1933, p. 160.

69   See, for example, Kavli, *Norwegian Architecture*, p. 51; Thomas Paulsson, *Scandinavian Architecture*, plates 3b, 14, 23b; van den Berg, *Noordelijk Oostergo*, p. 72.

70   See above, Chap. 2, pp. 30–35.

71   Sinclair (ed.), *Statistical Account*, vol. X (*Fife*), p. 97.

72   Gifford, *Fife*, p. 110.

73   Sinclair (ed.), *Statistical Account*, vol. X (*Fife*), p. 98.

74   Gifford, *Fife*, p. 110.

75   Ibid., p. 110.

76   Ibid., p. 110.

77   Ibid., p. 111.

78   Ibid., p. 110.

79   Radford and Donaldson, 'The Post-Reformation Church at Whithorn', p. 127.

80   Moffat Gillon, *John Davidson*, pp. 17–18.

81   Hay, *Post-Reformation Churches*, p. 32. See also Kuyper, *Dutch Classicist Architecture*, pp. 6–27.

82   See van Agt, *Nederlandse Monumenten*. I am grateful to Wouter Kuyper for providing this reference.

83   See McAndrew, *Venetian Architecture*, pp. 535–41.

84   See Howard, *Jacopo Sansovino*, pp. 81–4.

85   Personal communication, Dec. 1991.

86   See Hamberg, *Tempelbygge*, p. 43.

87   Hay, *Post-Reformation Churches*, p. 33.

88   RCAHMS, *Inventory of Monuments: Fife*, op. cit., pp. 38–9.

89   Lowther, *Our Journall*, p. 15.

90 Hume Brown, *Early Travellers*, p. 205.

91 Gillon, *John Davidson*, p. 130.

92 Ibid., pp. 137–8.

93 Ibid., pp. 138–9.

94 Ibid., p. 139.

95 Ibid., p. 267.

96 Ibid., p. 35.

97 Ibid., p. 38.

98 Ibid., p. 39.

99 See Storrar, *Scottish Identity*, pp. 28–33.

100 Gillon, *John Davidson*, p. 140.

101 McWilliam, *Lothian*, pp. 398–9.

102 See McGibbon and Ross, *Ecclesiastical Architecture*, vol. III, pp. 619–20.

103 The monument incorporates fragments of older carving, as if to assert respect for pre-Reformation tradition. The dedication is unusual in its feminine emphasis, for it honours his two wives, his mother, grandmother and great-grandmother! See Graham–Campbell, *Scotland's Story*, pp. 114–15.

104 Information panel in the church.

105 Mylne, *Master Masons*, pp. 110–11.

106 MacGibbon and Ross, *Castellated and Domestic Architecture*, vol. V, p. 155.

107 Ibid., p. 156.

108 RCAHMS, *Inventory of Monuments and Constructions in Galloway*, vol. I (*County of Wigan*), London, 1912, pp. 136–7.

109 MacGibbon and Ross, *Castellated and Domestic Architecture*, vol. V, p. 193.

110 Radford and Donaldson, 'The Post-Reformation Church', p. 128.

111 MacGibbon and Ross, *Ecclesiastical Architecture*, vol. V, pp. 571–4.

112 Apted, *Painted Ceilings*, pp. 21, 24–5.

113 See Gifford, *Fife*, pp. 67, 69.

114 *Extracts … Edinburgh 1626–1641*, p. xlviii.

115 Howard, 'Dutch Influence', pp. 40–2.

116 For an account of the complex picture in the Highlands, see James Kirk, 'The Jacobean Church in the Highlands', in Inverness Field Club, *The Seventeenth Century in the Highlands*, Inverness, 1986, pp. 24–51; reprinted in Kirk, *Patterns of Reform*, pp. 449–88.

117 RCAHMS, *Inventory of the Ancient Monuments of Peeblesshire*, vol. II, Edinburgh, 1967, pp. 199–201.

118 MacGibbon and Ross, *Ecclesiastical Architecture*, vol. III, pp. 565–7.

119 Gibson and McKellar, *A Guide to Fenwick*.

120 Ibid., p. 6.

121 Sinclair (ed.), *Statistical Account*, vol. VI (*Ayrshire*), pp. 24, 39.

122 A model ship can still be seen suspended in the church at St Monance in Fife. Pennant was shocked by the idolatry of the model ship hanging in a church in Aberdeen (Pennant, *First Tour*, p. 112). See Howard, 'Dutch Influence', p. 42.

123 Colvin, *Architecture and the Afterlife*, p. 296.

124 See James Kirk, 'The Survival of Ecclesiastical Patronage after the Reformation', in his *Patterns of Reform*, pp. 368–425.

125 RCAHMS, *Inventory of Monuments: Fife*, op. cit., p. 112. See also Webster, *Dunfermline Abbey*, pp. 229–32.

126 This monument is illustrated in Donaldson, *Faith of the Scots*, plate 14.

127 RCAHMS, *Inventory of Monuments: Fife*, op. cit., pp. 60, 61.

128 Gifford, McWilliam and Walker, *Edinburgh*, pp. 155–63.

129 Ibid., p. 156.

130 Colvin, *Architecture and the Afterlife*, p. 297.

131 On the two last chapels, see Gifford, *Highlands and Islands*, pp. 210–11, 430–1, and plates 25 and 51.

132 David Howarth, 'Sculpture and Scotland 1540–1700', in Pearson, *Virtue and Vision*, p. 28 and plates 2 and 19.

133 See Vriedeman de Vries, *Variae Architecturae Formae*, especially plate 12.

134 White, 'Westminster Abbey', pp. 19–29.

135 Apted, *Painted Ceilings*, pp. 21–3.

136 Sinclair (ed.), *Statistical Account*, vol. VI (*Ayrshire*), pp. 427–8. On Charles V's habitual rehearsing of his funeral, see Vriedeman de Vries, *Variae Architecturae Formae*, pp. 13–14.

137 Colvin, *Architecture and the Afterlife*, p. 298.

138 Gordon Slade, *Old Cromarty Castle*, pp. 13–14.

139 Quoted in Mercer, *English Art*, p. 218.

140 Howarth, 'Sculpture and Scotland', op. cit., p. 28, where, however, both Colt's Scottish tombs are dismissed as old-fashioned. See also Donaldson, 'The Dunbar Monument'.

141 On Colt's English career, see Esdaile, *English Church Monuments* (many refs); Mercer, *English Art*, pp. 242 ff; Whinney, *Sculpture in Britain*, pp. 19–21.

142 For theoretical reflections on Protestant tomb design, see Llewellyn, *The Art of Death*, pp. 101–30.

143 The few examples are discussed in Mercer, *English Art*, p. 240. See also Mann, 'English Church Monuments'.

144 Quoted in Ariès, *The Hour of Death*, p. 300.

145 MacGibbon and Ross, *Ecclesiastical Architecture*, vol. III, p. 580.

146 Graham–Campbell, *Scotland's Story*, p. 124. See also Deborah Howard, *The Kinnoull Aisle and Monument*, unpublished report, Cambridge, 1994.

147 Tindall et al., *Kinnoull Aisle*.

148 In my report mentioned in note 146 I have suggested a Ciceronian symbolism for these three contrasting columns.

149 Increasing height was also of concern in England at the time. See Llewellyn, *The Art of Death*, p. 106.

150 Dr Jean Wilson kindly pointed out these connections to me. See her article 'The Noble Imp'.

151 Graham–Campbell, *Scotland's Story*, pp. 122–4.

152 This monument is illustrated in Esdaile, *English Church Monuments*, plate 14, but disparagingly dismissed in Sacheverell Sitwell's introduction as resembling 'nothing else than a couple of grand old bedsteads dragged, without their curtains, into a corner' (Ibid., p. 22)!

NOTES TO CHAPTER SIX

1 *House of Seytoun*, p. 45.

2　　Quoted by Gordon Slade in *Old Cromarty Castle*, p. 5.

3　　Ash, *Castle Fraser*, p. 7.

4　　For a review of the parallel situation in England at this time, see Girouard, *Robert Smythson*, pp. 6–17.

5　　Lindesay of Pitscottie, *Historie and Chronicles*, vol. I, pp. 163–70.

6　　The Latin phrase is 'ARCHITECTVRAE PERETISSIMVS'. For a translation of the whole inscription, see Stevenson, *Origins of Freemasonry*, pp. 26–7.

7　　Girouard, *Robert Smythson*, p. 168 and plate 171.

8　　MacGibbon and Ross, *Castellated and Domestic Architecture*, vol. V, p. 547.

9　　See McKean, 'Finnart's Platt'.

10　　Dunbar, 'The Organisation of the Building Industry'.

11　　See Paton, *Accounts*.

12　　Stevenson, *Origins of Freemasonry*, p. 26.

13　　Ibid., p. 32.

14　　MacGibbon and Ross, *Castellated and Domestic Architecture*, vol. V, p. 48.

15　　Colvin, *Biographical Dictionary*, p. 567.

16　　MacKechnie, 'Evidence of a post-1603 Court Architecture'.

17　　Dunbar, 'The Organisation of the Building Industry', pp. 9–10.

18　　See above, Chap. 5, pp. The contract is published by Mylne in *Master Masons*, pp. 110–11.

19　　MacGibbon and Ross, *Castellated and Domestic Architecture*, vol. V, p. 5–8.

20　　McKean and Walker, *Dundee*, p. 121.

21　　RCAHMS, *Inventory of Monuments: Fife*, Edinburgh, 1933, p. 259.

22　　Published in Mylne, *Master Masons*, pp. 148–9. The drawings are now in the Bodleian (Colvin, *Biographical Dictionary*, p. 570).

23　　Quoted from the Hospital's archives by Howard, 'Scottish Master Masons', p. 282.

24　　Maitland, *House of Seytoun*, p. 63.

25　　Howard, 'Scottish Master Masons', p. 283.

26　　MacGibbon and Ross, *Castellated and Domestic Architecture*, vol. V, p. 560.

27　　Ibid., p. 561.

28　　Gordon Slade, 'Craigston Castle', p. 264.

29　　Timothy Clifford, 'Introduction' to Pearson, *Virtue and Vision*, p. 12.

30　　Stevenson, *Origins of Freemasonry*, p. 29.

31　　Mylne, *Master Masons*, pp. 48–9.

32　　Ibid., pp. 80–100.

33　　For a concise summary of the activities of these three John Mylnes, see Colvin, *Biographical Dictionary*, pp. 567–70.

34　　Stevenson, *Origins of Freemasonry*, pp. 115–6.

35　　The oil painting is reg. no. 1536 in the SNPG.

36　　Stevenson, *Origins of Freemasonry*, pp. 115–6.

37　　His epitaph records that he 'in his life Vitruvius' art had shown' (ibid.).

38　　Clifford, 'Introduction' to Pearson, *Virtue and Vision*, pp. 10–11.

39　　See Howard, 'Scottish Master Masons'; Colvin, 'Beginnings of the Architectural Profession in Scotland'.

40　　Thomson, *Renaissance Architecture*, p. 102.

41　　Maitland, *House of Seytoun*, p. 39.

42　　See the perceptive and wide-ranging account of Scotland's Renaissance visual culture by Martin Kemp and Clare Farrow, 'Humanism in the Visual Arts, *circa* 1530–1630', in McQueen, *Humanism in Renaissance Scotland*, pp. 32–47.

43 Urquhart of Cromarty, *The Jewel*, p. 66.

44 Castiglione, *The Courtier*, pp. 135–6.

45 Imrie and Dunbar, *Accounts* p. xx, n. 2.

46 For pertinent observations on culture in Protestant societies of the period, see Trevor Roper, *Religion, the Reformation and Social Change*, pp. 1–45.

47 On Knox's attitude to English culture, see Storrar, *Scottish Identity*, pp. 28–33.

48 MacLean, *Night falls on Ardnamurchan*, p. 192.

Bibliography

In the research for this book I have made extensive use of guidebooks, some published for Historic Scotland by HMSO, others produced by the National Trust and by private owners. For reasons of space, only a limited selection of these has been included in the footnotes and bibliography.

J. S. Ackerman, *Distance Points*, Cambridge (Mass.) and London, 1991.

William Adam, *Vitruvius Scoticus*, first published c. 1812, ed. James Simpson, Edinburgh, 1980.

I. H. Adams, *The Making of Urban Scotland*, London and Montreal, 1978.

David Allan, *Virtue, Learning and the Scottish Enlightenment*, Edinburgh, 1993.

James A. Anderson, 'The Shetland Germans', *Scots Magazine*, July 1987, pp. 366–71.

Anon., *Historical and Descriptive Account of George Heriot's Hospital, including a Memoir of the Founder*, Edinburgh, 1827.

M. R. Apted, *The Painted Ceilings of Scotland*, Edinburgh, 1966.

—— and S. Hannabuss, *Painters in Scotland 1301–1700: A Biographical Dictionary*, Edinburgh, 1978.

Philippe Ariès, *The Hour of Death*, trans. Helen Weaver, New York, 1982 edn.

Marinell Ash, *Castle Fraser*, National Trust for Scotland, Edinburgh, 1988.

Margaret Aston, 'English Ruins and English History: The Dissolution and the Sense of the Past', *Journal of the Warburg and Courtauld Institutes*, 36, 1973, pp. 231–55.

George P. Barker, 'Scottish Plasterwork', in his *The Art of the Plasterer . . . in England from the XVIth to the XVIIIth Century*, London, 1908, pp. 170–210.

G. W. S. Barrow et al., *The Seventeenth Century in the Highlands*, Inverness Field Club, 1986.

Michael Bath, 'Painted Ceilings, 1550–1650: Applied Emblematics in Scotland', *Emblematica: An Interdisciplinary Journal of Emblem Studies*, 7, 1993 (in press).

Geoffrey Beard, *Decorative Plasterwork in Great Britain*, London, 1975.

Otto Benesch, *The Art of the Renaissance in Northern Europe*, 1945, London, 1965 edn.

Dana Bentley-Cranch, 'An Early Sixteenth-Century French Architectural Source for the Palace of Falkland', *Review of Scottish Culture*, 2, 1986, pp. 85–95.

David M. Bergeron, *Royal Family, Royal Lovers: King James of England and Scotland*, Missouri, 1991.

R. W. Billings, *The Baronial and Ecclesiastical Antiquities of Scotland*, 4 vols, Edinburgh, 1847–52.

—— 'On Certain Features of the Ancient Architecture of Scotland', *Transactions of the Architectural Institute of Scotland*, Vol. III, 1852–3, pp. 27–39.

The Black Book of Taymouth, with Other Papers from the Breadalbane Charter Room, Edinburgh, 1855.

James Boswell, *The Journal to the Hebrides, 1775*, Harmondsworth, 1984.

Fernand Braudel, *Out of Italy*, trans. Siân Reynolds, Paris, 1991 (first published in Italian in 1974).

Wolfgang Braunfels, *Urban Design in Western Europe: Régime and Architecture 900–1900*, 1976, trans. K. J. Northcott, Chicago and London, 1988.

David J. Breeze (ed.), *Studies in Scottish Antiquity presented to Stewart Cruden*, Edinburgh, 1984.

—— and Gordon Donaldson, *A Queen's Progress*, Edinburgh, 1987.

Jean R. Brink and William F. Gentrup, *Renaissance Culture in Context: Theory and Practice*, Aldershot, 1993.

W. A. Brogden, *Aberdeen: An Illustrated Architectural Guide*, Edinburgh, 1986.

Keith M. Brown, *Bloodfeud in Scotland 1573–1625: Violence, Justice and Politics in an Early Modern Society*, Edinburgh, 1986.

Jacob Burckhardt, *The Civilisation of the Renaissance in Italy*, first published 1860, London, 1965 edn.

Leslie Burger, *Orkney: An Illustrated Architectural Guide*, Edinburgh, 1991.

Mungo Campbell, *Drawings and Watercolours of Edinburgh in the National Gallery of Scotland*, Edinburgh, 1990.

Ethel Carleton Williams, *Anne of Denmark: Wife of James VI of Scotland: James I of England*, London, 1970.

Baldesar Castiglione, *The Courtier*, first published Venice, 1528, trans. George Bull, Hardmondsworth, 1967.

Keith Cavers, *A Vision of Scotland: The Nation observed by John Slezer 1671 to 1717*, Edinburgh, 1993.

Robert Chambers, *Domestic Annals of Scotland from the Reformation to the Revolution*, 2 vols, Edinburgh, 1858.

—— *Edinburgh Merchants and Merchandise in Old Times*, lecture to Edinburgh Merchant Company, Edinburgh, 1859.

—— *The Ancient Domestic Architecture of Edinburgh*, lecture to the Archaeological Institute, Edinburgh, 1860.

Alastair Cherry, *Princes, Poets & Patrons: The Stuarts and Scotland*, Edinburgh, 1987.

Howard Colvin, *Biographical Dictionary of British Architects*, London, 1978.

—— 'The Beginnings of the Architectural Profession in Scotland', *Architectural History*, 29, 1986, pp. 168–82.

—— *Architecture and the Afterlife*, New Haven (Conn.) and London, 1991.

Rosalys Coope, 'The "Long Gallery": Its Origins, Use and Decoration', *Architectural History*, 29, 1986, pp. 43–94.

Margery Corbett and Ronald Lightbown, *The Comely Frontispiece: The Emblematic Title-Page in England 1550–1669*, London, Henley and Boston, 1979.

I. B. Cowan, *Blast and Counterblast: Contemporary Writings on the Scottish Reformation*, Edinburgh, 1960.

—— *The Scottish Reformation: Church and Society in Sixteenth Century Scotland*, London, 1982.

—— and Duncan Shaw (eds), *The Renaissance and Reformation in Scotland: Studies in Honour of Gordon Donaldson*, Edinburgh, 1983.

John D. Cox, 'The Politics of Stuart Medievalism', in Andrew Gurr (ed.), *Politics, Patronage and Literature in England 1558–1658: The Yearbook of English Studies (Special Number)*, vol. 21, 1991, pp. 187–96.

Crail Preservation Society, *Historic Crail: An Illustrated Survey*, St Andrews, 1987.

The Rev. J. B. Craven, *History of the Church in Orkney 1558–1662: Bishops Bothwell, Law and Grahame*, Kirkwall, 1897.

Stewart Cruden, *The Scottish Castle*, Edinburgh, 1981.

The Hon. Lord Cullen, *The Walls of Edinburgh,* Edinburgh, 1988.

James Dalyell and James Beveridge (eds), 'Inventory of the Plenishings of the House of the Binns at the Death of General Thomas Dalyell, 21st August 1685', *Proceedings of the Society of Antiquaries of Scotland*, 12 May, 1924, pp. 344–67.

Michael C. Davis, *The Castles and Mansions of Ayrshire*, Ardrishaig (Argyll), 1991.

J. Davison and A. Gray, *The Scottish Staple at Veere*, London, 1909.

Marcus Dean and Mary Miers, *Scotland's Endangered Houses*, London, 1990.

Daniel Defoe, *A Tour through the Whole Island of Great Britain (1724–6)*, ed. P. N. Furbank and W. R. Owers, New Haven (Conn.) and London, 1991 edn.

B. Dicks, 'The Scottish Medieval Town: A Search for Origins', in George Gordon and Brian Dicks (eds), *Scottish Urban History*, Aberdeen, 1983, pp. 23–51.

Gordon Donaldson, *Scotland: Church and Nation through Sixteen Centuries*, Edinburgh and London, 1960.

—— *The Scottish Reformation*, Cambridge, 1960.

—— 'The Dunbar Monument in its Historical Setting', *East Lothian Field and Naturalists' Society*, 1987, pp. 1–16.

—— *Scotland: James V–James VII*, Edinburgh, 1987.

—— *The Faith of the Scots*, London, 1990.

James Drummond, 'Notice of Some Stone Crosses, with Especial Reference to the Market Crosses of Scotland', *Proceedings of the Society of Antiquaries of Scotland*, 4, 1861–2, pp. 86–115.

—— *Views of Old Edinburgh*, Edinburgh and London, 1879.

J. G. Dunbar, 'The Palace of Holyrood House during the First Half of the Sixteenth Century', *Archaeological Journal*, CXX, 1963, pp. 242–54.

—— 'The Organisation of the Building Industry in Scotland during the 17th Century', in Alexander Fenton, Bruce Walker and Geoffrey Stell (eds), *Building Construction in Scotland: Some Historical and Regional Aspects*, Scottish Vernacular Buildings Working Group, Dundee and Edinburgh, 1976, pp. 7–15.

—— *The Architecture of Scotland*, London, 1978 edn.

—— 'Some Aspects of the Planning of Scottish Royal Palaces in the 16th Century', in Peter Draper (ed.), *Design and Practice in British Architecture: Studies in Architectural History presented to Howard Colvin, Architectural History*, XXVII, 1984, pp. 15–24.

—— 'French Influence in Scottish Architecture during the Sixteenth Century', *Scottish Records Association Conference Report*, no. 12, 1989, pp. 3–8.

—— 'Some Sixteenth-Century French Parallels for the Palace of Falkland', *Review of Scottish Culture*, 7, 1991, pp. 3–8.

John Durkan, 'Education in the Century of the Reformation', in David McRoberts (ed.), *Essays on the Scottish Reformation 1513–1625*, Glasgow, 1962, pp. 145–68.

Elizabeth L. Eisenstein, *The Printing Press as an Agent of Change: Communications and Cultural Transformations in Early-Modern Europe*, 2 vols, Cambridge, 1979.

Kenneth Elliott and Frederick Rimmer, *A History of Scottish Music*, London, 1973.

Katherine A. Esdaile, *English Church Monuments 1510 to 1840*, London, 1946.

Extracts from the Records of the Burgh of Edinburgh AD1557–1571, Edinburgh, 1875.

Extracts from the Records of the Burgh of Edinburgh AD 1573–1589, Edinburgh, 1882.

Extracts from the Records of the Burgh of Edinburgh AD 1589–1603, Edinburgh, 1927.

Extracts from the Records of the Burgh of Edinburgh AD 1604–1626, Edinburgh, 1931.

Extracts from the Records of the Burgh of Edinburgh AD 1626–1641, Edinburgh, 1936.

Extracts from the Records of the Burgh of Edinburgh AD 1641–1655, Edinburgh, 1983.

Extracts from the Records of the Burgh of Glasgow AD 1573–1642, Glasgow, 1876.

Extracts from the Records of the Burgh of Glasgow AD 1604–1626, Glasgow, 1881.

Extracts from the Records of the Burgh of Glasgow AD 1630–1662, Glasgow, 1881.

The Falkland Society, *The Stones of Falkland*, Falkland, 1993.

Richard Fawcett, *The Architectural History of Scotland from the Accession of the Stewarts to the Reformation 1371–1560*, Edinburgh, 1994.

Sir James Fergusson of Kilkerran, 'A Ship of State', in id., *The White Hind and Other Discoveries*, London, 1963, pp. 97–113.

J. A. Fleming, *Scottish and Jacobite Glass*, Glasgow, 1938.

R. Fox, 'Urban Development, 1100–1700', in G. Whittington and I. D. Whyte, *An Historical Geography of Scotland*, London and New York, 1983, pp. 73–92.

Andrew G. Fraser, *The Building of Old College: Adam, Playfair and the University of Edinburgh*, Edinburgh, 1989.

Antonia Fraser, *Mary Queen of Scots*, London, 1970.

Edward M. Furgol, 'The Scottish Itinerary of Mary Queen of Scots, 1542–8 and 1561–8', *Proceedings of the Society of Antiquaries of Scotland*, 117, 1987, pp. 219–31.

Bruce Galloway, *The Union of England and Scotland 1603–1608*, Edinburgh, 1986.

Olive M. Geddes, *A Swing through Time: Golf in Scotland 1457–1743*, Edinburgh, 1992.

Lucy Gent (ed.), *Albion's Classicism: The Visual Arts in Britain 1550–1660* (proceedings of conference held at the Warburg Institute, London, on 19–20 Nov. 1993), Yale University Press for the Paul Mellon Centre (forthcoming).

Rev. A. Cameron Gibson and Duncan McKellar, *A Guide to the Parish and Kirk of Fenwick*, rev. Sara Cockburn, Fenwick, 1985.

John Gifford, Colin McWilliam and David Walker, *Buildings of Scotland: Edinburgh*, Harmondsworth, 1984.

—— *Buildings of Scotland: Fife*, London, 1988.

—— *Buildings of Scotland: Highlands and Islands*, London, 1992.

Mark Girouard, *Robert Smythson*, New Haven (Conn.) and London, 1983 edn.

J. Goldberg, *James I and the Politics of Literature*, Baltimore and London, 1983.

Andor Gomme and David Walker, *Architecture of Glasgow*, London, 1987 edn.

George Gordon and Brian Dicks (eds), *Scottish Urban History*, Aberdeen, 1983.

Harry Gordon Slade, 'Craigston Castle, Aberdeenshire', *Proceedings of the Society of Antiquaries of Scotland*, 108, 1976–7, pp. 262–99.

—— 'Glamis Castle', lecture given to the Society of Antiquaries of London, 1st November, 1990.

—— *Old Cromarty Castle*, Cromarty, 1993.

David Graham-Campbell, *Scotland's Story in her Monuments*, London, 1982.

J. Grant, *Old and New Edinburgh*, 3 vols, London 1880–3.

Francis Grose, *The Antiquities of Scotland*, 2 vols, London, 1789–91.

C. B. Gunn, *George Heriot's Hospital: Memoirs of a Modern Monk*, Edinburgh, 1906.

J. R. Hale, *Renaissance War Studies*, London, 1983.

—— *The Civilisation of the Renaissance in Europe*, London, 1993.

Per Gustaf Hamberg, *Tempelbygge foer Protestanter*, Stockholm, 1955.

Eileen Harris (with Nicholas Savage), *British Architectural Books and Writers 1556–1785*, Cambridge, 1990.

Stuart Harris, 'The Fortifications and Siege of Leith: A Further Study of the Map of the Siege in 1560', *Proceedings of the Society of Antiquaries of Scotland*, 121, 1991, pp. 359–68.

Denys Hay (ed.), *The Letters of James V*, Edinburgh, 1954.

—— 'Scotland and the Italian Renaissance', in I. B. Cowan and Duncan Shaw (eds), *The Renaissance and Reformation in Scotland: Studies in Honour of Gordon Donaldson*, Edinburgh, 1983, pp. 114–24.

George Hay, 'Scottish Renaissance Architecture', in David J. Breeze (ed.), *Studies in Scottish Antiquity presented to Stewart Cruden*, Edinburgh, 1984, pp. 196–231.

—— *Architecture of Scottish post-Reformation Churches 1560–1843*, Oxford, 1957.

Steffen Heiberg (ed.), *Christian IV and Europe*, Council of Europe exhibition catalogue, Denmark, 1988.

W. F. Hendrie, *Linlithgow: 600 Years: a Royal Burgh*, Edinburgh, 1989.

Heriot's Hospital Archives, *Records*, vol., I; 1624–62.

Henry-Russell Hitchcock, *German Renaissance Architecture*, Princeton (NJ), 1981.

J. M. Houston, 'The Scottish Burgh', *Town Planning Review*, 25, 1954, pp. 114–27.

R. A. Houston and I. D. Whyte, *Scottish Society 1500–1800*, Cambridge, 1989.

Deborah Howard, *Jacopo Sansovino: Architecture and Patronage in Renaissance Venice*, New Haven (Conn.) and London, (1975), 1987 edn.

—— (ed.), *The Architecture of the Scottish Renaissance*, Royal Incorporation of Architects of Scotland, Edinburgh Festival exhibition catalogue, Edinburgh, 1990.

—— 'Scottish Master Masons of the Renaissance' (conference paper given in 1983), in Jean Guillaume (ed.), *Les Chantiers de la Renaissance*, Paris, 1991, pp. 279–85.

—— 'Dutch Influence on Scottish Architecture', in Julia Lloyd Williams, *Dutch Art and Scotland: A Reflection of Taste*, National Gallery of Scotland, Edinburgh, 1992, pp. 33–48.

—— 'Chasse, sport et plaisir autour des châteaux de la Renaissance en Écosse', in Jean Guillaume (ed.), *L'environnement du château et de la villa*, Paris (in press).

Maurice Howard, *The early Tudor Country House: Architecture and Politics 1490–1550*, London, 1987.

P. Hume Brown, *Early Travellers in Scotland*, Edinburgh, 1891.

—— (ed.), *Scotland before 1700*, Edinburgh, 1893.

John Imrie and John G. Dunbar, *Accounts of the Masters of Works for Building and Repairing Royal Palaces and Castles*, vol. II (1616–49), Edinburgh, 1982.

R. S. Jack, *Scottish Literature's Debt to Italy*, Edinburgh, 1986.

Margaret Jourdain, *English Decorative Plasterwork of the Renaissance*, London, 1926.

G. Kavli, *Norwegian Architecture: Past and Present*, Oslo, 1958.

Henry F. Kerr, 'Scottish Domestic Architecture from the Sixteenth to the Eighteenth Century', *Transactions of the Edinburgh Architectural Association*, X, 1933, pp. 86–112.

James Kirk, *Patterns of Reform: Continuity and change in the Reformation Kirk*, Edinburgh, 1989.

John Knox, *The First Book of Discipline*, ed. James K. Cameron, Edinburgh, 1972.

Spiro Kostoff, *The City Shaped: Urban Patterns and Meanings through History*, London, 1991.

Wouter Kuyper, *Dutch Classicist Architecture*, Delft, 1980.

H. H. Lamb, *The Changing Climate: Selected Papers*, London, 1966.

David Learmont, 'Exciting Find at House of The Binns', *Heritage Scotland*, 8 no. 2, Summer 1991, p. 23.

Maurice Lee Jr., *Government by the Pen*, Chicago and London, 1980.

―――― *Great Britain's Solomon: James VI and I*, Urbana (Ill.), *c*1990.

Ralph Lieberman, *Renaissance Architecture in Venice*, London, 1982.

Robert Lindesay of Pitscottie, *The History and Chronicles of Scotland*, ed. A. J. G. Mackay, 3 vols, Edinburgh, 1899–1911.

Ian G. Lindsay, *The Scottish Parish Kirk*, Edinburgh, 1960.

Nigel Llewellyn, *The Art of Death: Visual Culture in the English Death Ritual c.1500– c.1800*, London, 1991.

H. J. Louw, 'The Origin of the Sash Window', *Architectural History*, 26, 1983, pp. 49–72.

―――― 'Window-Glass Making in Britain c.1660–c.1860 and its Architectural Impact', *Construction History*, 7, 1991, pp. 47–68.

David Lowenthal, *The Past is a Foreign Country*, Cambridge, 1985.

John Lowrey, 'Dutch Influence on Seventeenth-Century Scottish Architectural and Garden Design', in *Scotland and the Low Countries: Sixth Conference of the Scottish Society for Art History*, Edinburgh, 26 Oct. 1992 (proceedings in press).

C. Lowther, *Our Journall into Scotland*, Edinburgh, 1894.

Michael Lynch, *Edinburgh and the Reformation*, Edinburgh, 1981.

―――― (ed.), *The Early Modern Town in Scotland*, London and Sydney, 1987.

―――― 'Queen Mary's Triumph: The Baptismal Celebrations at Stirling in December 1566', *Scottish Historical Review*, LXIX, 1990, pp. 1–21.

―――― *Scotland: A New History*, London, 1991.

―――― Michael Spearman and Geoffrey Stell (eds), *The Scottish Medieval Town*, Edinburgh, 1988.

S. G. E. Lythe, *The Economy of Scotland in its European Setting 1550–1625*, Edinburgh, 1960.

John McAndrew, *Venetian Architecture of the Early Renaissance*, Cambridge (Mass.), 1980.

Walter MacFarlane, *Geographical Collections relating to Scotland*, ed. Sir Arthur Mitchell and James Tosach Clark, 3 vols, Edinburgh, 1906–8.

David MacGibbon and Thomas Ross, *The Castellated and Domestic Architecture of Scotland*, 5 vols, Edinburgh, 1887–92.

―――― and ―――― *The Ecclesiastical Architecture of Scotland*, 3 vols, Edinburgh, 1896–7.

Iain MacIvor, *Edinburgh Castle*, London, 1993.

Sheila Macklay (ed.), *Scottish Interiors: Renaissance*, Edinburgh, 1987.

William Mackay Mackenzie, *The Scottish Burghs*, Edinburgh, 1949.

Charles McKean, 'Argyll's Lodging, Stirling', paper for blind readers, copy at RIAS, Edinburgh

―――― *Stirling and the Trossachs*, Edinburgh, 1985.

―――― *The District of Moray: An Illustrated Architectural Guide*, Edinburgh, 1987.

―――― *Edinburgh: Portrait of a City*, London, 1991.

―――― 'Finnart's Platt', in Deborah Howard (ed.), *Scottish Architects Abroad: Architectural Heritage II*, Edinburgh, 1991, pp. 3–17.

―――― 'The House of Pitsligo', *Proceedings of the Society of Antiquaries of Scotland*, 121, 1991, pp. 369–90.

—— 'The Recovery of Renaissance Scotland', in *Welcome: News for Friends of Historic Scotland*, Dec. 1991.

—— *Edinburgh: An Illustrated Architectural Guide*, rev. edn, Edinburgh, 1992.

—— and David Walker, *Dundee: An Illustrated Introduction*, Edinburgh, 1984.

——, —— and Frank Walker, *Central Glasgow: An Illustrated Guide*, Edinburgh, 1985.

Aonghus MacKechnie, 'William Schaw', unpublished paper.

—— 'Inventory of Stone Fragments from the Old Parliament Hall, now at Arniston, Midlothian', unpublished paper, n. d. (Historic Scotland).

—— 'Evidence of a post-1603 Court Architecture in Scotland?', *Architectural History*, 31, 1988, pp. 107–19.

—— 'Stirling's Triumphal Arch', *Welcome* (Historic Scotland News-sheet), Sept. 1991.

—— 'Some French Influences on the Development of 16th Century Court Architecture', *In House: Historic Scotland Research Papers*, July 1992.

—— 'Aspects of Scots Renaissance Architecture', in Ian Gow and Alistair Rowan, (eds), *Views on Scottish Country Houses*, Edinburgh (in press).

Ross MacKenzie, *A Scottish Renaissance Household: Sir William Hamilton and Newton Castle in 1559*, Ayrshire Archaeological and Natural History Society Monographs, Sept. 1990.

Alasdair MacLean, *Night falls on Ardnamurchan: The Twilight of a Crofting Family*, London, 1986.

A. A. McMillan (ed)., *Building Stones of Edinburgh*, Edinburgh Geological Society, 1987.

Duncan Macmillan, *Scottish Art 1460–1990*, Edinburgh, 1990.

John McQueen (ed.), *Humanism in Renaissance Scotland*, Edinburgh, 1990.

David McRoberts (ed.), *Essays on the Scottish Reformation*, Glasgow, 1962.

Colin McWilliam, *Scottish Townscape*, London, 1975.

—— *Buildings of Scotland: Lothian except Edinburgh*, Edinburgh, 1980, edn.

Craig Mair, *Mercat Cross and Tolbooth: Understanding Scotland's old Burghs*, Edinburgh, 1988.

—— *Stirling: The Royal Burgh*, Edinburgh, 1990.

Sir Richard Maitland, *The History of the House of Seytoun to the Year* MDLIX, with the continuation by Alexander Viscount Kingston to MDCLXXXVII, Glasgow, 1829.

J. G. Mann, 'English Church Monuments 1536–1625', *Walpole Society*, XXI, 1932–3, pp. 1–22.

Rosalind K. Marshall, *The Days of Duchess Anne*, London, 1973.

—— *Mary of Guise*, London, 1977.

—— *Virgins and Viragoes: A History of Women in Scotland from 1080–1980*, London, 1983.

—— 'The Plenishings of Hamilton Palace in the Seventeenth Century', *Review of Scottish Culture*, no. 3, 1987, pp. 13–22.

Roger A. Mason, 'Scotching the Brut: Politics, History and the National Myth in Sixteenth-Century Britain', in id. (ed.), *Scotland and England 1286–1815*, Edinburgh, 1987, pp. 60–84.

David Mathews, *Scotland under Charles I*, London, 1955.

Henry W. Meikle (ed.), *The Works of William Fowler*, Edinburgh and London, 1936, vol. II.

Helena Mennie Shire, *Song, Dance and Poetry of the Court of Scotland under King James VI*, Cambridge, 1969.

Eric Mercer, *English Art 1553–1625*, Oxford, 1962.

Peter Miller, 'The Origin and Early History of the old Tolbuith of Edinburgh – the Heart of Midlothian, and the Luckenbooths', *Proceedings of the Society of Antiquaries of Scotland*, 20, 1885–6. pp. 360–76.

—— 'The Mercat Cross of Edinburgh from 1365 to 1617 – its Site and Form', *Proceedings of the Society of Antiquaries of Scotland*, 20, 1885–6, pp. 377–89.

Thomas Mitchell, 'The Influence of France on the Architecture of Scotland during the Sixteenth Century', *Quarterly of the Incorporation of Architects in Scotland*, 23, Autumn 1927, pp. 69–94.

R. Moffat Gillon, *John Davidson of Prestonpans*, London, 1936.

The Rev. R. S. Mylne, 'The Netherbow Port', *Proceedings of the Society of Antiquaries of Scotland*, XLVI, 1892, pp. 379–88.

—— *Master Masons to the Crown of Scotland*, Edinburgh, 1893.

Robert J. Naismith, *Buildings of the Scottish Countryside*, London, 1985.

—— *The Story of Scotland's Towns*, Edinburgh, 1989.

John Napier, *Mirifici Logarithmorum*, Edinburgh, 1619.

National Art Collections Fund, (NACF), *Saved for Scotland*, Edinburgh, 1991.

National Trust for Scotland, *Falkland Palace and Royal Burgh*, Edinburgh, 1989.

Victor Nieto, Alfredo J. Morales and Fernando Checa, *Arquitectura del Renacimiento en España*, Madrid, 1989.

Richard M. Noad, 'The Influence of France on the Architecture of Scotland during the Sixteenth Century', *Quarterly of the Incorporation of Architects in Scotland*, no. 24, Winter 1927, pp. 101–12.

Andrea Palladio, *I quattro libri dell'architettura*, Venice, 1570.

Graham Parry, *The Golden Age restored: The Culture of the Stuart Court 1603–43*, Manchester, 1989.

A. N. Paterson, 'Scottish Architecture from the Fifteenth to the Seventeenth Century', *Transactions of the Edinburgh Architectural Association*, viii, 1914, pp. 48–65.

Henry M. Paton (ed.), *Accounts of the Masters of Works for Building and Repairing Royal Palaces and Castles, vol. I (1529–1615)*, Edinburgh, 1957.

T. Paulsson, *Scandinavian Architecture: Buildings and Society in Denmark, Finland, Norway and Sweden*, London, 1958.

Henry Peacham, *The Compleat Gentleman*, London, 1634.

Fiona Pearson (ed.), *Virtue and Vision: Sculpture and Scotland 1540–1990*, National Gallery of Scotland exhibition catalogue, Edinburgh, 1990.

Thomas Pennant, *First Tour of Scotland in 1769*, reprint of 3rd edn. (1774), Perth, 1979.

George Penny, *Traditions of Perth . . . during the Last Century*, Perth, 1836; facsimile reprint, Coupar Angus, 1986.

Roy Porter and Mikulás Teich, *The Renaissance in National Context*, Cambridge, 1992.

Glen L. Pride, *The Kingdom of Fife: An Illustrated Architectural Guide*, Edinburgh, 1990.

Ralegh Radford and Gordon Donaldson, 'The Post-Reformation Church at Whithorn', *Proceedings of the Society of Antiquaries of Scotland*, LXXXV, 1950–1, pt II, pp. 125–33.

Peter Reed (ed.), *Glasgow: The Forming of the City*, Edinburgh, 1993.

John Reid, *The Scots Gardner*, Edinburgh, 1683, facsimile edn. ed. Annette Hope, Edinburgh, 1988.

J. S. Richardson, *Stirling Castle*, HMSO, Edinburgh, 1978 edn.

—— Marguerite Wood and C. J. Tabraham, *Melrose Abbey*, Edinburgh, 1981.

J. Robertson (ed.), *Inventaires de la Royne Descosse Douarière de France*, Bannatyne Club, Edinburgh, 1863.

M. P. Rooseboom, *The Scottish Staple in the Netherlands*, The Hague, 1910.

Earl Rosenthal, ''Plus ultra, non plus ultra'' and the columnar device of the Emperor Charles V', *Journal of the Warburg and Courtauld Institutes,* XXXIV, 1971, pp. 204–28.

Thomas Ross, 'The Ancient Sundials of Scotland', *Proceedings of the Society of Antiquaries of Scotland*, 24, 1890, pp. 161–273.

—— 'Old Parliament Hall, Edinburgh: Statues of Justice and Mercy', *Proceedings of the Society of Antiquaries of Scotland*, LIII, 1918–19, pp. 30–3.

Alistair Rowan, 'George Heriot's Hospital, Edinburgh', *Country Life*, CLVII, 1975, pp. 554–7 and 634–7.

—— 'William Adam's Library', in Deborah Howard (ed.), *William Adam: Architectural Heritage I*, Edinburgh, 1990, pp. 8–33.

Royal Commission on the Ancient and Historical Monuments of Scotland (RCAHMS), *Inventories of Monuments in Scotland*, 33 vols, 1909–92.

Margaret H. B. Sanderson, *Scottish Rural Society in the 16th Century*, Edinburgh, 1982.

—— *Mary Stewart's People: Life in Mary Stewart's Scotland*, Edinburgh, 1987.

Peter Savage, *Lorimer and the Edinburgh Craft Designers*, Edinburgh, 1980.

Diana Scarisbrick, 'Anne of Denmark's Jewellery Inventory', *Archaeologia*, CIX, 1991, pp. 193–238.

Sebastiano Serlio, *Tutte l'opere d'architettura et prospetiva*, Venice, 1619 edn.

George Seton, *A History of the Family of Seton*, Edinburgh, 1896, vol. II.

W. Douglas Simpson, *Bishop's Palace and Earl's Palace, Kirkwall, Orkney*, HMSO guide-book, Edinburgh, 1965 edn.

—— *Huntly Castle*, HMSO guidebook, rev. C. J. Tabraham, Edinburgh, 1985 edn.

—— *Edzell Castle*, rev. Richard Fawcett, HMSO guidebook, Edinburgh, 1989 edn.

Grant G. Simpson, *Scottish Handwriting 1150–1650*, Aberdeen, 1973.

Sir John Sinclair (ed.), *The Statistical Account of Scotland 1791–1799*, modern repr., 20 vols, Wakefield, 1983.

John Slezer, *Theatrum Scotiae*, London, 1693.

Alan G. R. Smith (ed.), *The Reign of James VI and I*, New York, 1973.

Charles J. Smith, *Historic South Edinburgh*, 4 vols, Edinburgh and London (vols 1 and 2), Haddington (vols 3 and 4), 1978–88.

T. C. Smout, *Scottish Trade on the Eve of the Union 1660–1707*, Edinburgh and London, 1963.

—— *A History of the Scottish People 1560–1830*, London, 1972.

—— (ed.), *Scotland and Europe 1200–1850*, Edinburgh, 1986.

—— 'Scottish–Dutch Contact 1600–1800', in Julia Lloyd Williams (ed.), *Dutch Art and Scotland*, National Gallery of Scotland exhibition catalogue, Edinburgh, 1992, pp. 21–32.

Andrew R. Somerville, 'The Ancient Sundials of Scotland', *Proceedings of the Society of Antiquaries of Scotland*, 117, 1987, pp. 233–64.

Geoffrey Stell, 'Architecture and the Changing Needs of Society', in Jennifer M. Brown, *Scottish Society in the Fifteenth Century*, London, 1977, pp. 165–9.

—— 'Scottish Burgh Houses 1560–1707: A Conspectus and Some Recent Surveys', in Anne Turner Simpson and Sylvia Stevenson (eds), *Town Houses and Structures in Medieval Scotland: A Seminar*, Scottish Burgh Survey, University of Glasgow Department of Archaeology, Glasgow, 1980, pp. 1–31.

—— 'The Earliest Tolbooths: A Preliminary Account', *Proceedings of the Society of Antiquaries of Scotland*, 111, 1981, pp. 445–53.

—— 'Urban Buildings', in Michael Lynch, Michael Spearman and Geoffrey Stell (eds), *The Scottish Medieval Town*, Edinburgh, 1988, pp. 60–80.

W. Steven, *History of George Heriot's Hospital with a Memoir of the Founder*, rev. F. W. Bedford, Edinburgh, 1872.

David Stevenson, *The Origins of Freemasonry: Scotland's Century 1590–1710*, Cambridge, (1988) 1990 edn.

Jeannie C. Stewart (ed.), *Ancient Castles of Scotland: A Collection of Books and Papers of the Late Dr. W. Douglas Simpson*, Edinburgh, 1990.

William Storrar, *Scottish Identity: A Christian Vision*, Edinburgh, 1990.

Roy Strong, *Splendour at Court: Renaissance Spectacle and the Theatre of Power*, London, 1974; rev. version *Art and Power: Renaissance Festivals 1450–1650*, Woodbridge (Suffolk), 1984.

—— *Henry Prince of Wales and England's Lost Renaissance*, London, 1986.

Sir John Summerson, *Architecture in Britain 1530–1830*, Hardmondsworth, 1969 edn.

David Thomson, *Renaissance Architecture: Critics, Patrons, Luxury*, Manchester, 1993.

Duncan Thomson, *The Life and Art of George Jameson*, Oxford, 1974.

Peter Thornton, *The Italian Renaissance Interior 1400–1600*, London, 1991.

Benjamin Tindall et al., *Kinnoull Aisle and Monument*, unpublished restoration feasibility study, Edinburgh, 1992.

Robert Tittler, *Architecture and Power: The Town Hall and the English Urban Community c. 1500–1640*, Oxford, 1992.

John E. D. Touche, *The Worthies and the Regalia: Notes on a Linked Series of Plaster Ceilings 1599–1665*, unpublished dissertation (typescript in National Monuments Record of Scotland), 1973.

H. R. Trevor Roper, *Religion, the Reformation and Social Change*, London, 1967.

H. Inigo Triggs, *Formal Gardens in England and Scotland*, London, 1902.

Sir Thomas Urquhart of Cromarty, *The Jewel*, ed. R. D. S. Jack and R. J. Lyall, Edinburgh, 1983.

J. J. F. W. van Agt, *De Nederlandse Monumenten: De Provincie Noordholland . . . Waterland*, The Hague, 1953.

Herma van den Berg, *Noordelijk Oostergo: De Dongeradelen*, The Hague, 1983.

Gottfried von Bülow, 'Journey through England and Scotland made by Lupold von Wedel in the years 1584 and 1585'. *Transactions of the Royal Historical Society*, ser. II, IX, 1895, pp. 223–70.

Johannes Vriedeman de Vries, *Variae Architecturae Formae*, Antwerp, 1601.

Patricia Waddy, *Seventeenth-Century Roman Palaces: Use and the Art of the Plan*, New York, 1990.

The Rev. J. M. Webster, *Dunfermline Abbey*, Dunfermline, 1948.

Margaret Whinney, *Sculpture in Britain 1530 to 1830*, Harmondsworth, 1964.

Adam White, 'Westminster Abbey in the Early Seventeenth Century: a Powerhouse of Ideas', *Church Monuments*, IV, 1989, pp. 16–53.

Catherine Wilkinson-Zerner, *Zuan de Herrera: Architect to Philip II of Spain*, New Haven (Conn.) and London, 1993.

G. Williams and Robert Owen Jones (eds), *The Celts and the Renaissance: Tradition and Innovation*, Cardiff, 1990.

Arthur H. Williamson, *Scottish National Consciousness in the Age of James VI: The Apocalypse, the Union and the Shaping of Scotland's Public Culture*, Edinburgh, 1979.

D. H. Willson, *King James VI and I*, New York, 1956.

C. Anne Wilson (ed.), *'Banquetting Stuffe': The fare and Social Background of the Tudor and Stuart Banquet*, Edinburgh, 1991.

Jean Wilson, 'The Noble Imp: The Upper-Class Child in English Renaissance Art and Literature', *The Antiquaries' Journal*, LXX, 1990, II, pp. 360–79.

Barbara Wisch and Susan Scott Munshower (eds), *'All the world's a stage . . .': Art and Pageantry in the Renaissance and Baroque*, Part I *(Triumphal Celebrations and the Rituals of Statecraft)*, University Park, Pennsylvania, 1990.

Jenny Wormald, *Court, Kirk and Community: Scotland 1470–1625*, Edinburgh, 1981.

Frances Yates, *Astraea: The Imperial Theme in the Sixteenth Century*, London and Boston, 1975, pp. 1–28.

Alan Young, *Tudor and Jacobean Tournaments*, London, 1987.

Index